POSTCARD HISTORY SERIES

Grand Rapids

COMMUNITY AND INDUSTRY

On the front cover: Seen here is a view looking west down Monroe Avenue, from the intersection of Division Avenue, from 1910. At the right is the Peck Drug Store, and at the middle right, the old Morton House Hotel. In the distance is the old Pantlind Hotel at Campau Square, replaced with the present structure just a few years after this image was recorded.

On the back cover: Here is a real photo view of the motormen of the Grand Rapids Street Railway Company, outside the company's west side car barn, from around 1905. The streetcar in the picture is bound for the West Bridge Street/Grandville Avenue line, and carries a placard on its front fender advertising the current attraction at the Ramona Theater, at the railway line's eastern terminus.

POSTCARD HISTORY SERIES

Grand Rapids

COMMUNITY AND INDUSTRY

Thomas R. Dilley

ARCADIA PUBLISHING

ISBN 978-0-7385-4054-2

Published by Arcadia Publishing
Charleston, South Carolina

Printed in the United States of America

Library of Congress Catalog Card Number: 2006922338

For all general information contact Arcadia Publishing at:
Telephone 843-853-2070
Fax 843-853-0044
E-mail sales@arcadiapublishing.com
For customer service and orders:
Toll-Free 1-888-313-2665

Visit us on the Internet at www.arcadiapublishing.com

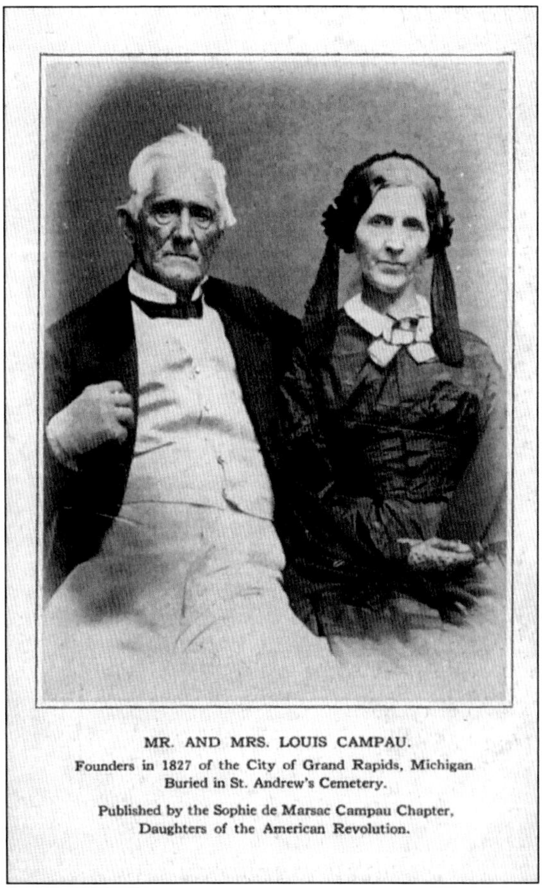

This commemorative portrait of the founders of the city of Grand Rapids, Louis Campau and Sophie de Marsac Campau, was originally taken about 1860. This card was published by the local chapter of the Daughters of the American Revolution in about 1910, probably in conjunction with the 60th anniversary celebration of the city in that year.

Contents

Acknowledgments		6
Introduction		7
1.	The Life of the Postcard	9
2.	Early Postcards in Business	25
3.	The City's Neighborhoods	55
4.	East Grand Rapids and Ramona	67
5.	The Mr. Rover Cards	93
6.	The 1910 Homecoming	107
7.	The Flood of 1907	125

ACKNOWLEDGMENTS

The completion of this book has benefited from, and indeed has been made possible by the assistance, cooperation, and encouragement of many people. I have benefited tremendously from the comments and reminiscences of those who have reviewed my previous book, *Grand Rapids in Vintage Postcards: 1890–1940*, and I am grateful for their assistance. As was the case before, my friends Ron Carowitz and Milt Ehlert have strongly encouraged this effort and have provided me with useful counsel and advice. Ron Carowitz, himself a recognized authority on Grand Rapids postcard history, generously arranged for my use of the excellent and probably most complete assemblage of the Mr. Rover cards in existence in the collection of the late Justin Tiery. I am grateful to Justin's widow, Ruth Tiery, for her generous permission to publish this part of her late husband's fabulous and important collection.

The staff and resources of the Grand Rapids Public Library, Special Collections Section, and especially my friend, Christine Byron, have again, as always, been most helpful. Charles and Patricia Bloom generously provided me with several of the cards that appear in the book, as well as their own reminiscences.

Once again, my work on this project has benefited greatly from the counsel and advice of my brother-in-law, Paul J. LaPorte. The staff of my publisher, and particularly Anna Wilson, have been most helpful and pleasant to work with.

All of these generous contributions, however, pale in comparison to the encouragement and support that has been ceaselessly provided to me by my wife, Debra, and daughter, Sarah. Without their kindness and support, this never would have happened.

INTRODUCTION

In the nearly 180 years that have passed since its founding by French fur trader Louis Campau on the banks of the Grand River in 1826, the village, town, and now city of Grand Rapids has undergone many changes. Some of these have been obvious and some more subtle, and all of them have seen the city grow from a rough and tumble outpost in the Old Northwest to a major manufacturing and cultural center of considerable sophistication. While trends and markets in goods and services have risen and fallen, Grand Rapids has, like countless other cities founded in the same era and under similar circumstances, faced and weathered financial panic and depression, two world wars, and repeated waves of change in its economic fortunes and ethnic populations. From each and all of these challenges, the city has emerged as a stronger, more diverse, and vastly interesting place to work and to live. While certainly these changes, some of them daunting, have come from political and economic forces from well outside the area, there can be no doubt that the most vibrant and constant force in the continuing history of this city has been the ever changing mix of people who have, from its beginning, worked and lived here.

The postcards that are presented in this book cover a variety of subjects in the history of the city, between 1900 and 1960. In continuation and supplement to the themes developed in *Grand Rapids in Vintage Postcards: 1890–1940*, here the images focus on particular aspects of the life in the city, and specific parts of the city that grew up and changed during this time. While many of the places depicted in the cards have changed considerably, or have disappeared altogether, in most instances sufficient evidence of the original surroundings remains to allow a careful observer to match an image 50 or 100 years old with the surroundings of today. The majority of the early postcards of Grand Rapids were actually produced in the East or in Europe, but many of the cards in this book were printed and distributed locally by a solid group of photographer-entrepreneurs who busily attended local events and developments and, in the process, earned a profit recording and selling these postcard images. Some of the cards were clearly published by local businessmen in an aggressive "boostering" of their products or of the city to extol its virtues as a manufacturing and cultural center. Still others were created to record disasters that befell the city and its river over the years and, by implication, the ability of the local citizens to survive and prosper in the face of adversity. A few others represent rare, probably unique "snapshot" real-photo images taken by individuals only to record events in their own lives, but which now provide a valuable historical insight into the life and times in which they lived.

Every effort has been made to accurately date and identify the location of the images presented, making use of postal cancellations and messages that appear on the reverse side of the cards or by consultation with a multitude of independent published sources and materials. Nearly all of the cards that appear in this book are from the author's own collection of Grand Rapids postcards or, where noted, have been generously lent from other local collections. It is hoped that this group of historical images, along with those appearing in the previous volume, will provide the reader with an interesting view of life in Grand Rapids in the first half of the 20th century.

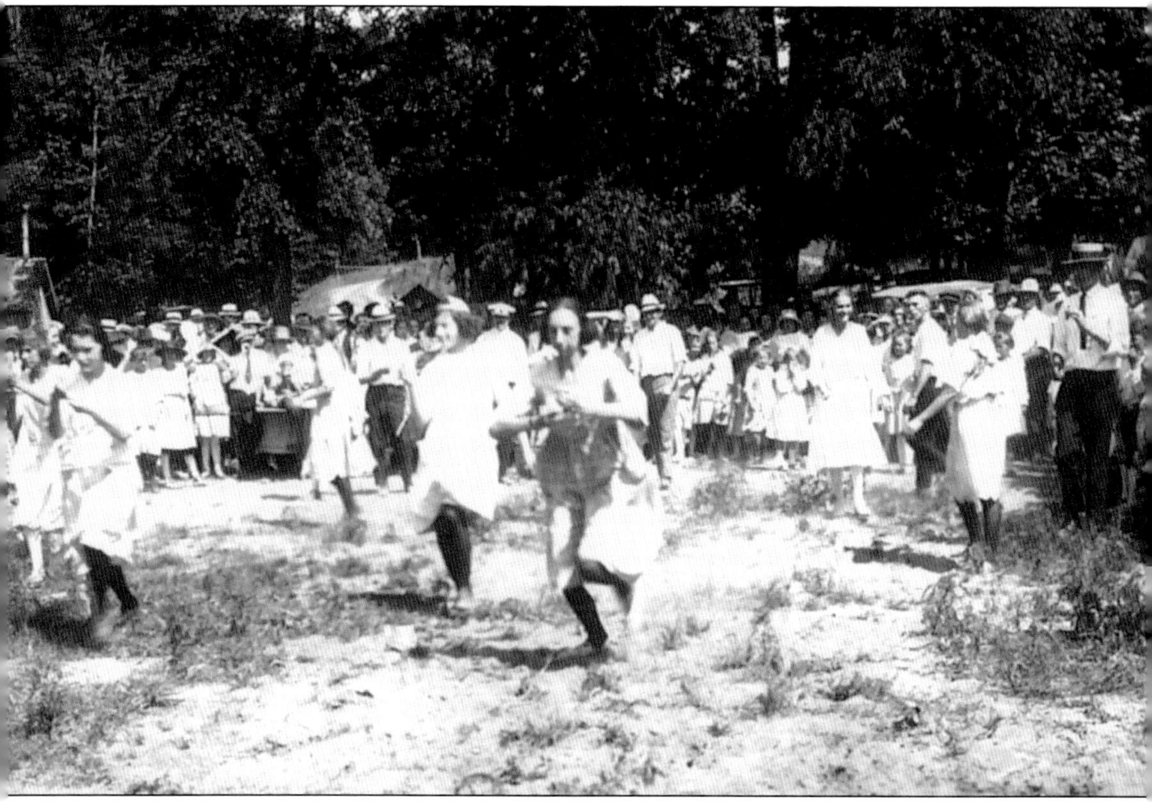

This is a souvenir real photo view of the Burton Heights Neighborhood Picnic, held at Green Lake, south of Grand Rapids, on July 21, 1921. The scene is obviously unposed, and illustrates the nature of many of the real photo postcards which appear elsewhere in this volume. This format allowed a photographer with modest, highly portable equipment, to take pictures of an event, and then process his snapshots into a postcard format quickly and cheaply, for immediate sale or distribution, before the interest of the event participants, and his market, faded away. It is in many of these very candid, and often quite rare real photo postcard images, that the lifestyles of a community like Grand Rapids were most effectively recorded.

One

The Life of the Postcard

The picture postcard, so much a part of American life, has its roots in Europe around 1869, when "postal mailing cards," bearing no printed image, were introduced in Austria. Though lacking the privacy of an envelope, these cards, easier to write and cheaper to mail, were an immediate success. Postcards spread to other European countries, including Great Britain, where they where widely used in the latter part of the 19th century at a time when telephones were expensive, unreliable . . . or nonexistent. The cards quickly jumped the Atlantic and were adopted in 1871 by the Canadian postal system. The first American postcards appeared in the early 1890s, and became wildly popular thereafter. The early cards were, like their European and Canadian cousins, issued by the postal service with printed postage, and unlike the postcards known today, they carried no picture or printed message, with the user's message written on one side and the address and postage on the other.

By the late 1890s, postal regulators relaxed certain restrictions and began allowing privately printed postcards, to which a 1¢ postage stamp was affixed for mailing and carrying a printed photographic image on one side. Until 1907, these cards allowed nothing but the mailing address and postage on one side. Because messages were not allowed on the postal side of the card, they were often written on a small blank next to the image or simply across the image itself. After 1907, postal regulations were changed again, allowing the "divided back" format with which people are familiar today, with the user's message on the left side and the address and postage on the right.

After 1895, the postcard printing business exploded along with postal use and collection of the cards. In the first two decades of the 20th century, hundreds of millions of postcards depicting every imaginable scene and greeting were sold in the United States. Nearly every region of the country, including some surprisingly rural areas, appeared in postcard images, many of which provide the only reliable views of the regions today. As the postcard business prospered, innovations, both local and national, began to appear. Postcard publishers explored variations in the postcard form to attract postal users, collectors, and souvenir-buyers.

The postcards in this chapter illustrate variations in the original form of the postcard, created to draw wider and, presumably, more profitable use of the postcard in the opening decades of the 20th century. These cards illustrate the irrepressible creativity of postcard producers and their constant efforts to get their product out and into the hands of a demanding buying public.

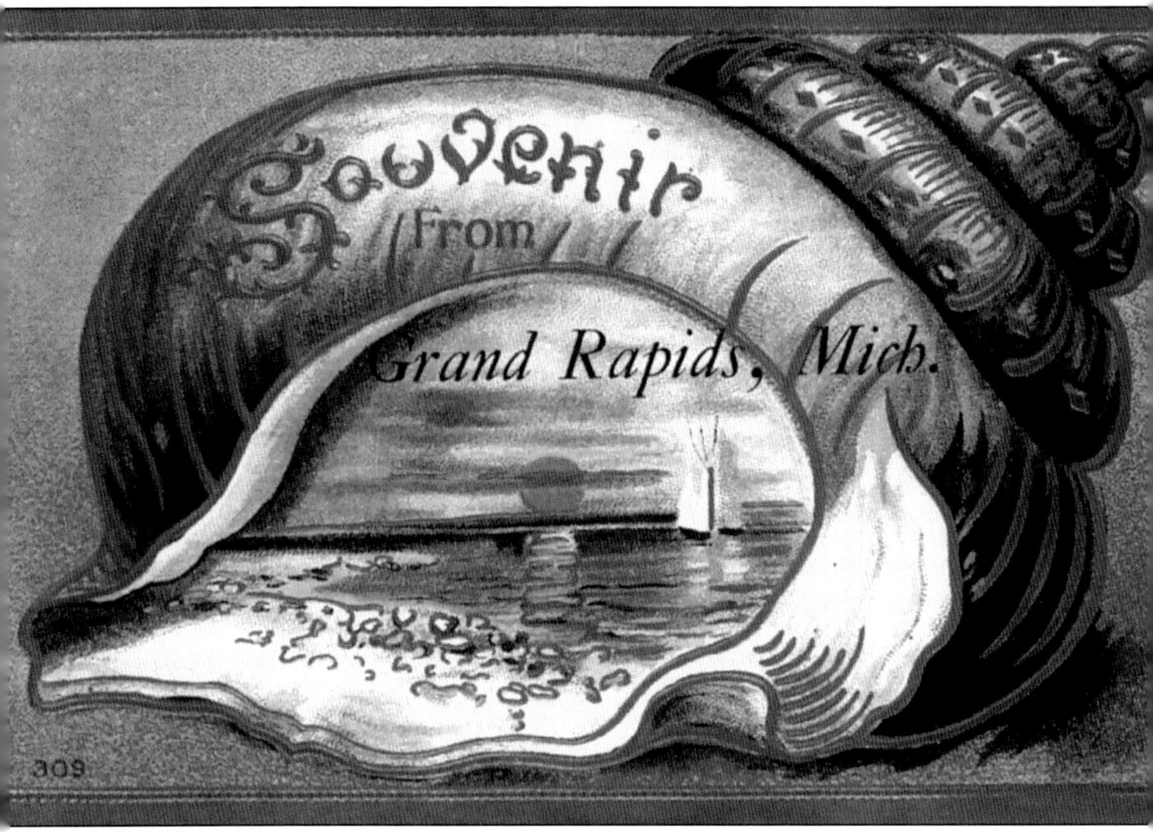

This is a stock tourist postcard, mailed in 1909 from Grand Rapids to the folks at home in nearby Caledonia. The seashell design was printed and embossed on a card without the local identification in huge numbers and then reprinted with the local "greetings" message for local sale. Such seashell cards were widely collected and were common in many parts of the country, including places where, like Grand Rapids, actual seashells were not part of the local landscape.

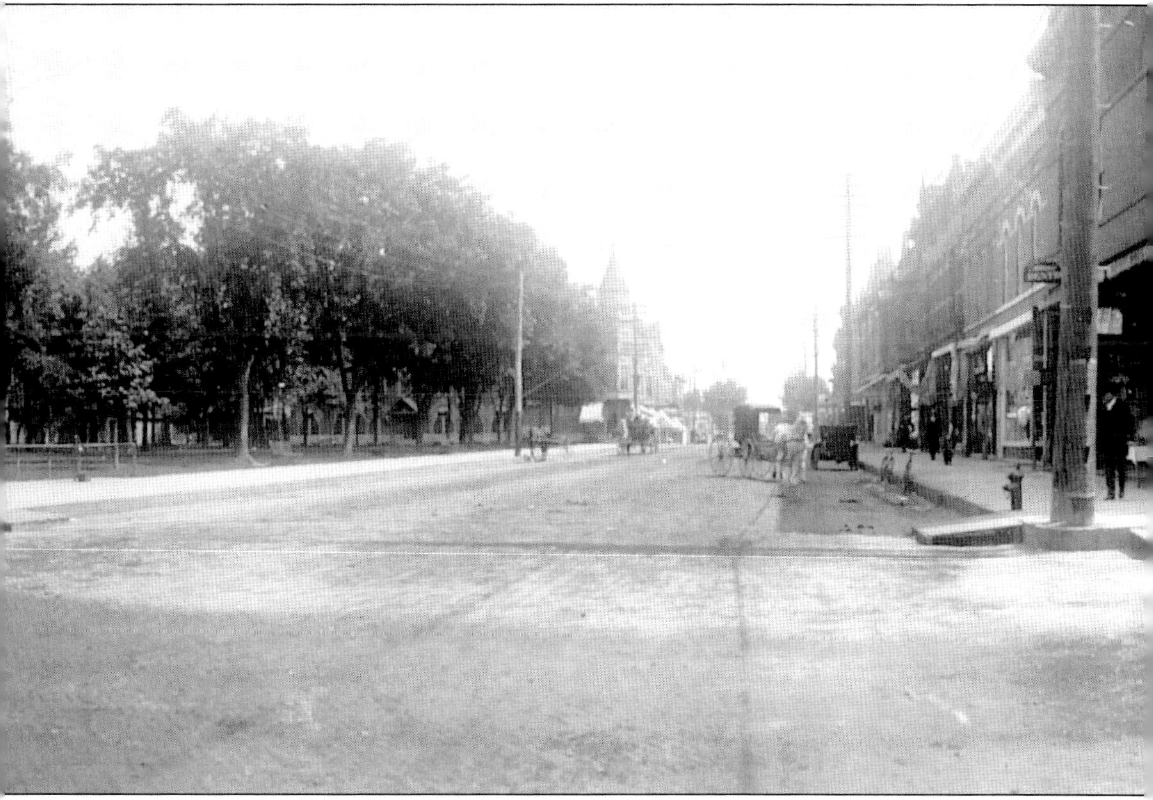

Even as printed "view" cards were at their zenith across the country and locally, the real-photo card began to appear, beginning in 1903 (though some professional real-photo cards came earlier), with the introduction of the Kodak folding pocket No. 3A camera. These cards carried images that were actual photographs, developed onto a postcard-sized card, which were then stamped with a postcard format on the back. This sort of postcard typically presented views of events or occasions that were quite personal or were made up for sale when a delayed, printed card would not do. This view, from 1912, is typical of real-photo cards of the era. It looks north up Division Avenue from the edge of Antoine Campau Park toward downtown. Although there is one motor vehicle parked at the curb to the right, most of the street traffic in this still predominantly residential area remains horse drawn.

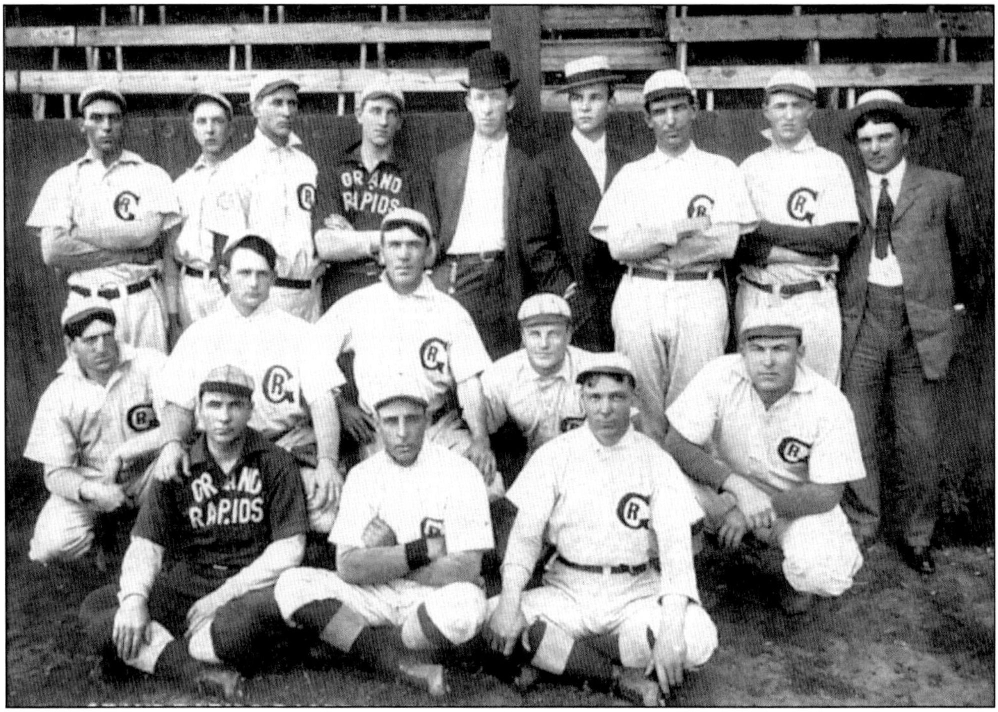

A team photograph of the Grand Rapids baseball team, from 1906, appears here.

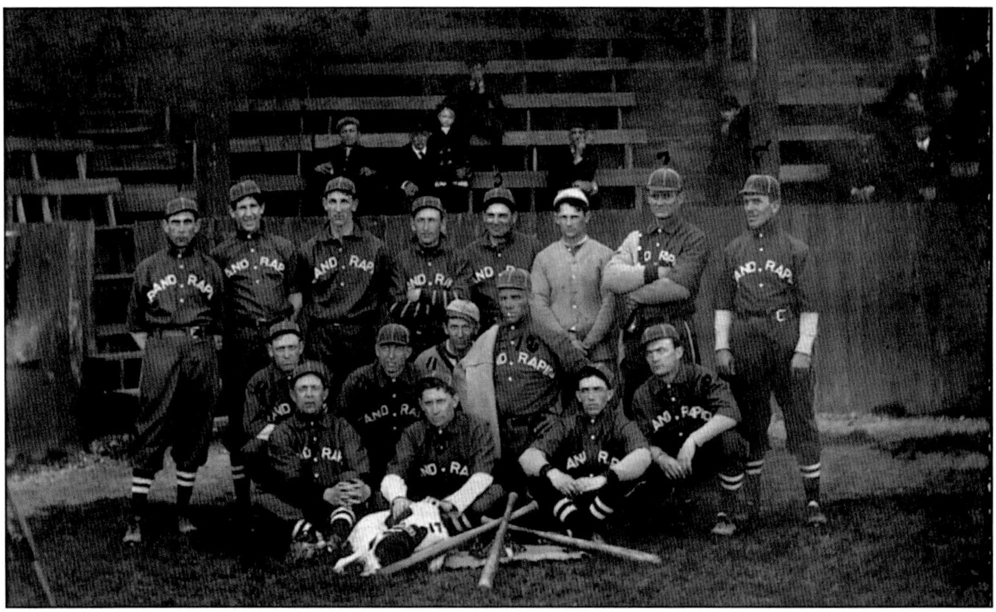

A rare real-photo view of the Grand Rapids baseball team, players in the Central League, from about 1910, this card was the property of Casey Hageman, the man sitting at the center of the front row with his hand on the dog. Hageman was a successful early professional player, later pitching for the Boston Red Sox, St. Louis Cardinals, and Chicago Cubs, between 1911 and 1914. Hageman prepared this card, listing each of the players (including the dog) by name, as a gift to his mother.

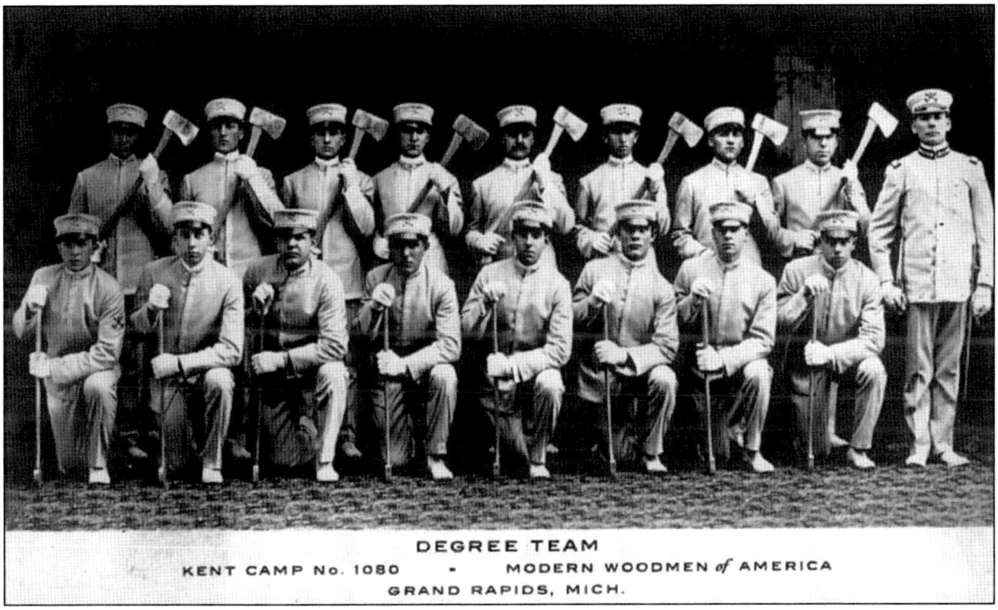

Another group photograph features the drill team of the local Modern Woodmen of the World chapter from around 1910. This fraternal group, like many others at the time, marched in local parades, including the homecoming parade in 1910.

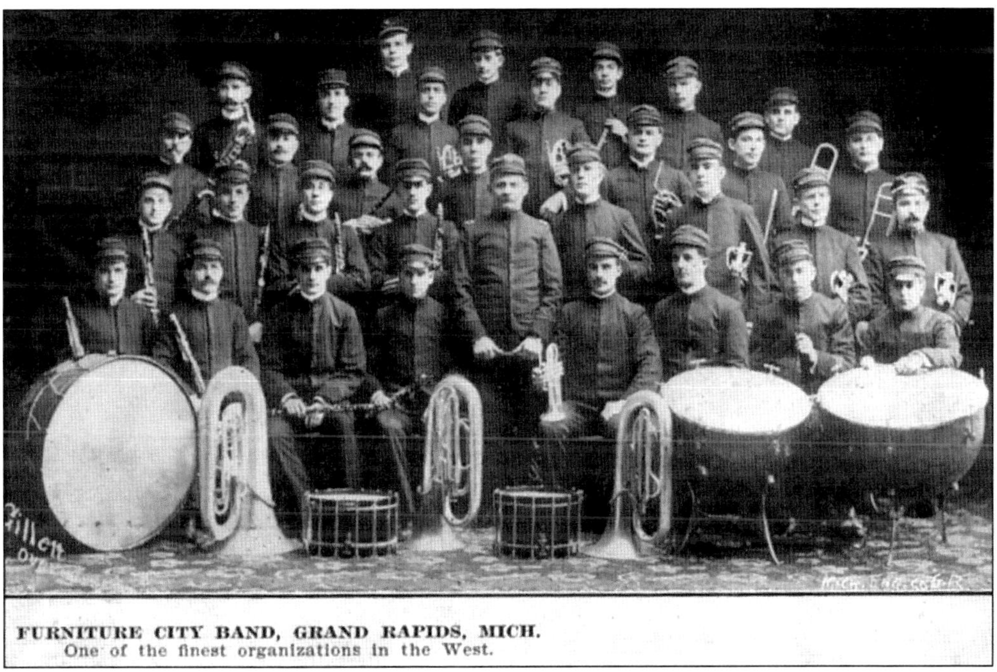

The Furniture City Band, a local musical group active in the opening decades of the 20th century, is pictured here in 1910. Groups like this one were popular attractions in the many parades that were staged in Grand Rapids at this time.

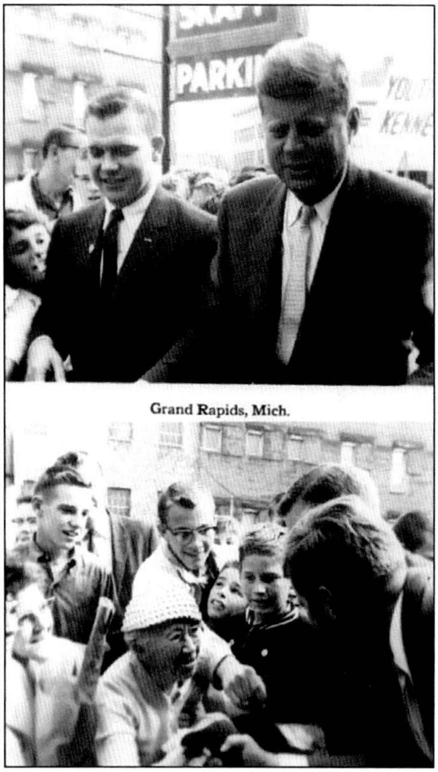

The next four postcards are very unusual modern real photo postcards, produced and sold in 1960. The cards depict the campaign visit of then senator John F. Kennedy, as he campaigned in the streets of Grand Rapids on October 14, 1960. The images show a motorcade through downtown Grand Rapids, where many local citizens had the opportunity to meet and shake hands with the future president. Here, in the top photograph, senator Kennedy is pictured with then Lt. Gov. John B. Swainson, who was then seeking election as the governor of Michigan.

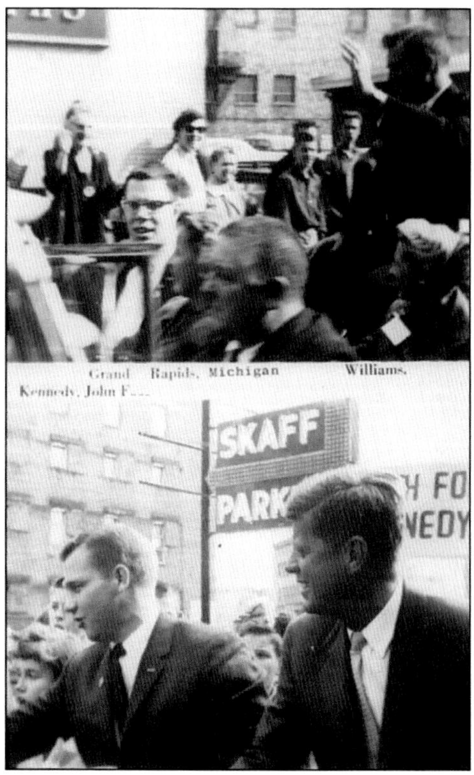

Another view of Kennedy and Swainson is featured in this photograph. The top photo shows then governor G. Mennen "Soapy" Williams and his wife Nancy in the back of a car in the motorcade, waving to the large crowd.

Senator Kennedy and Lt. Gov. Swainson meet and talk with local citizens.

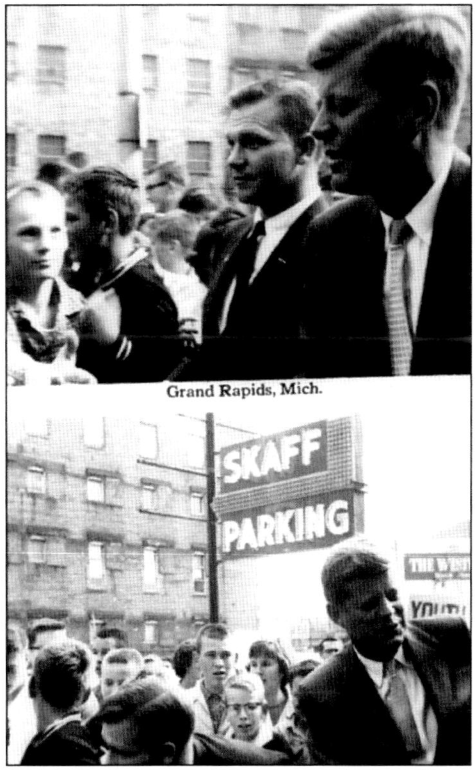

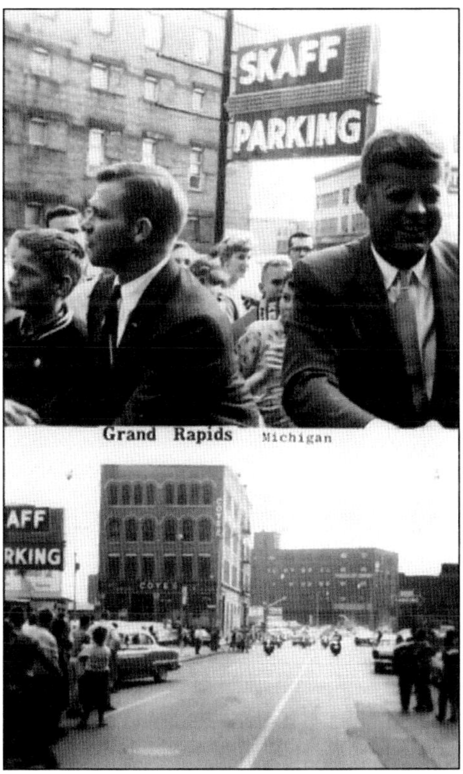

Yet another view shows senator Kennedy and Lt. Gov. Swainson, and the motorcade itself, as it proceeds downtown after the arrival of the candidates at the nearby Union Station.

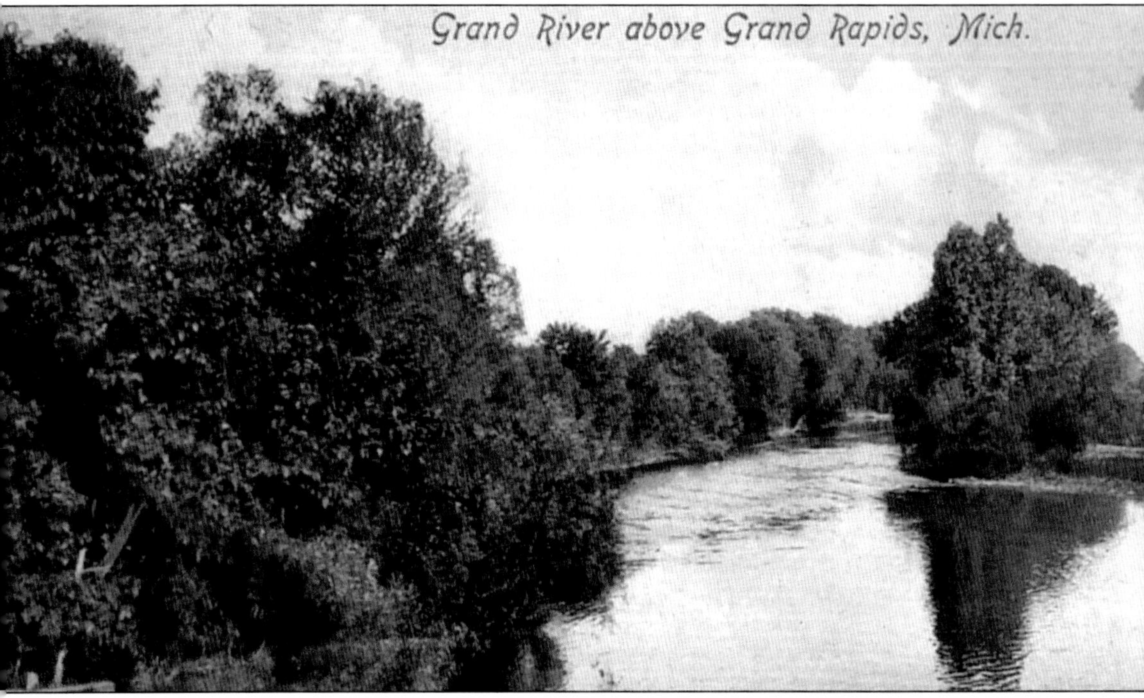

As the popularity of printed "view" cards grew in the first few years of the 20th century, publishers sought to expand their art by offering occasional panoramic views, which were folded at the

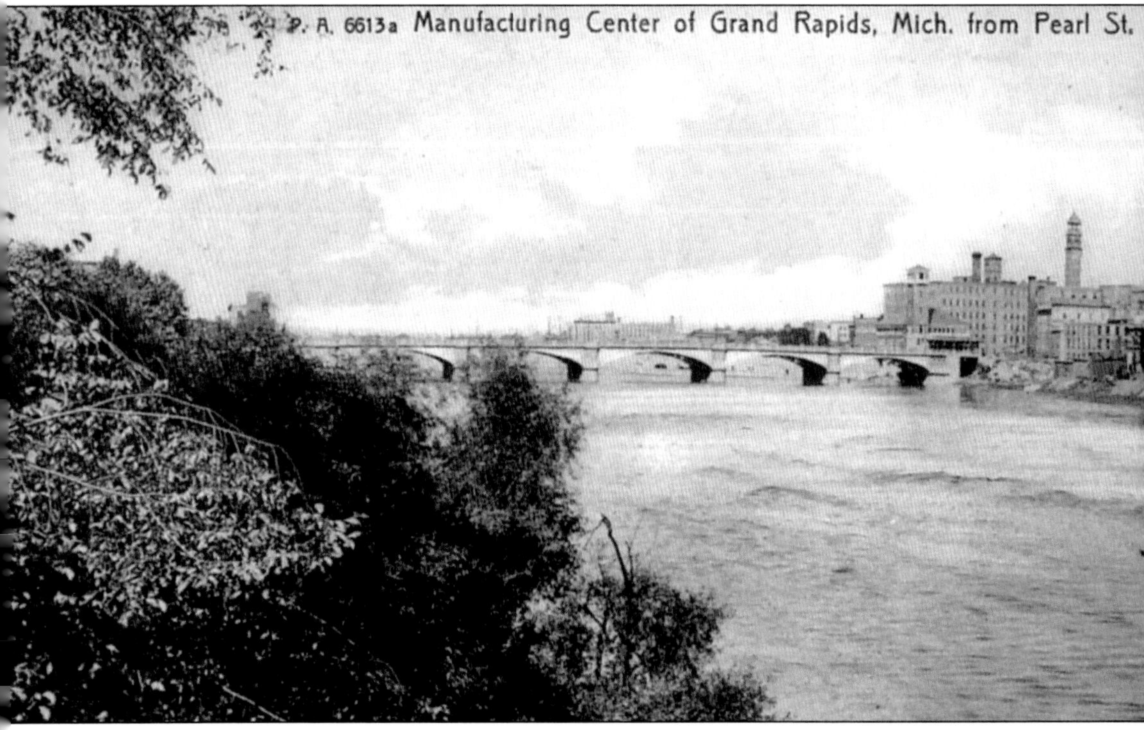

This is another double-card postcard from 1907, this time showing a view of the east bank of the Grand River, taken from the western end of the Pearl Street Bridge, the present location of

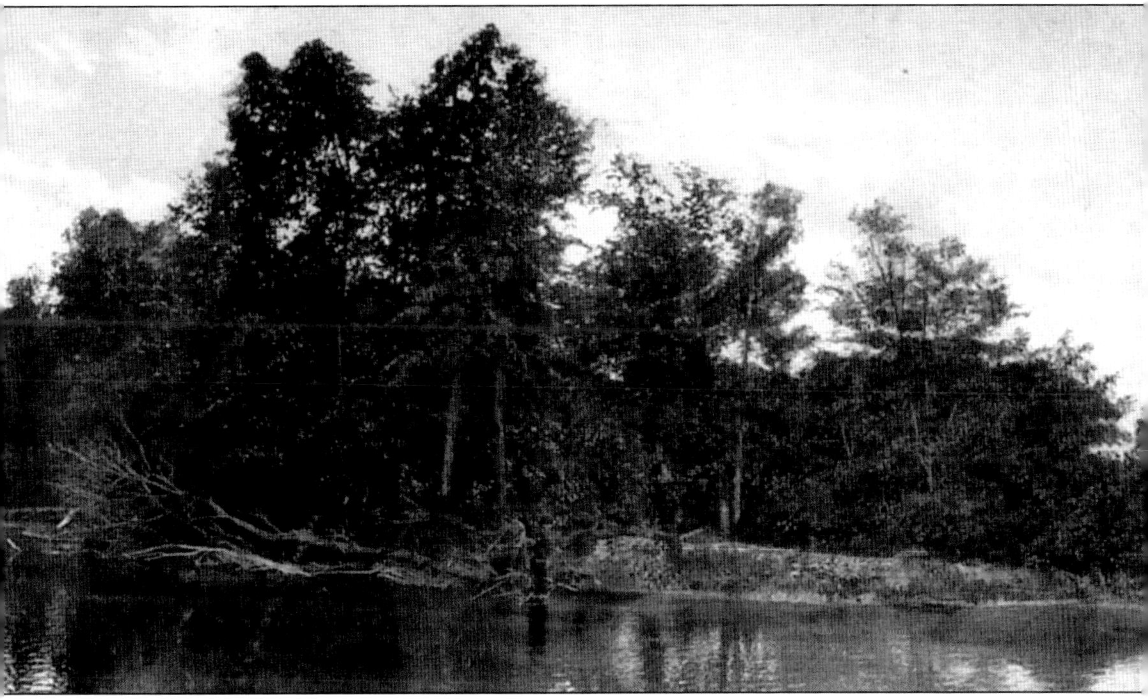

center for mailing, for 2¢. This card from 1907 depicts the Grand River just north of Grand Rapids. Here, just outside of the city, the banks of the river are still wild and undeveloped.

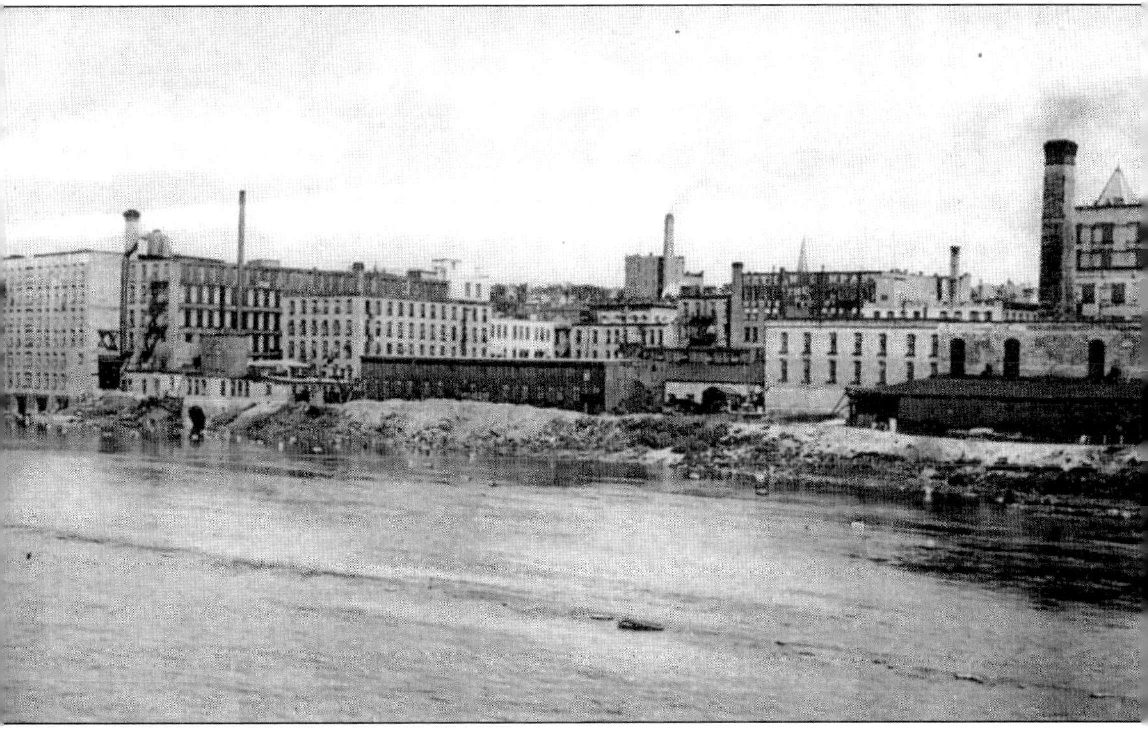

the Gerald Ford Museum. It is clear from this view that at the time at least the eastern bank of the river was dedicated to industrial use only.

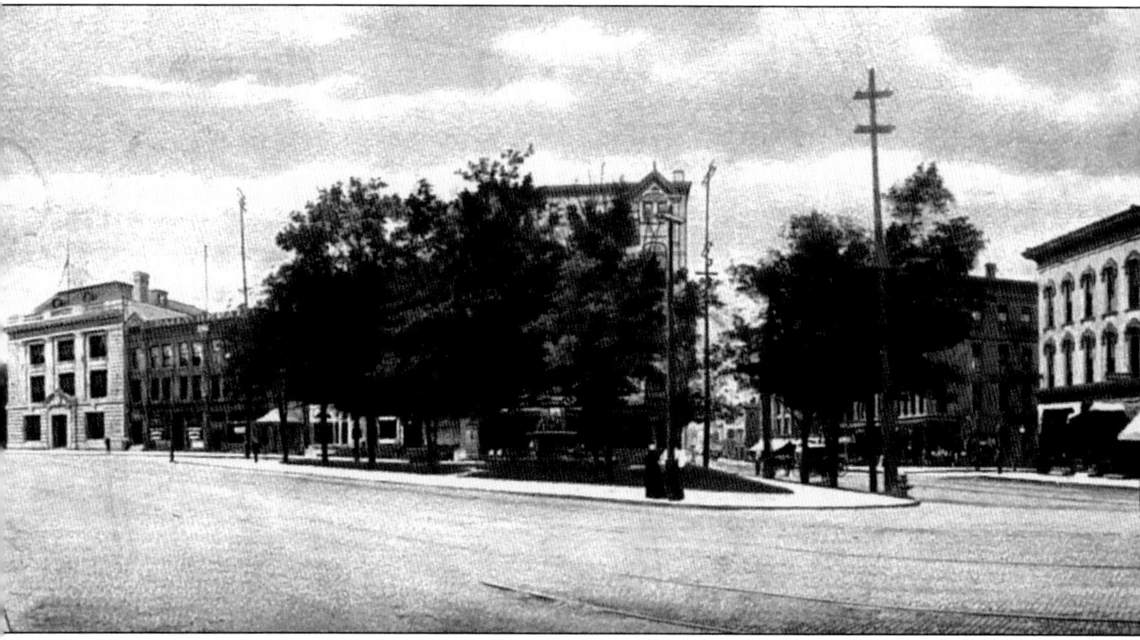

A panoramic double-card view of the intersection of Division Avenue and Monroe Avenue, from about 1910, appears here. In this instance, though foldable as a double card, the reverse of the card is printed as two separable postcards. It looks southwest down Monroe Avenue to the right, south on Division at the center, and up Monroe toward Fulton Street, at the left. The large building at

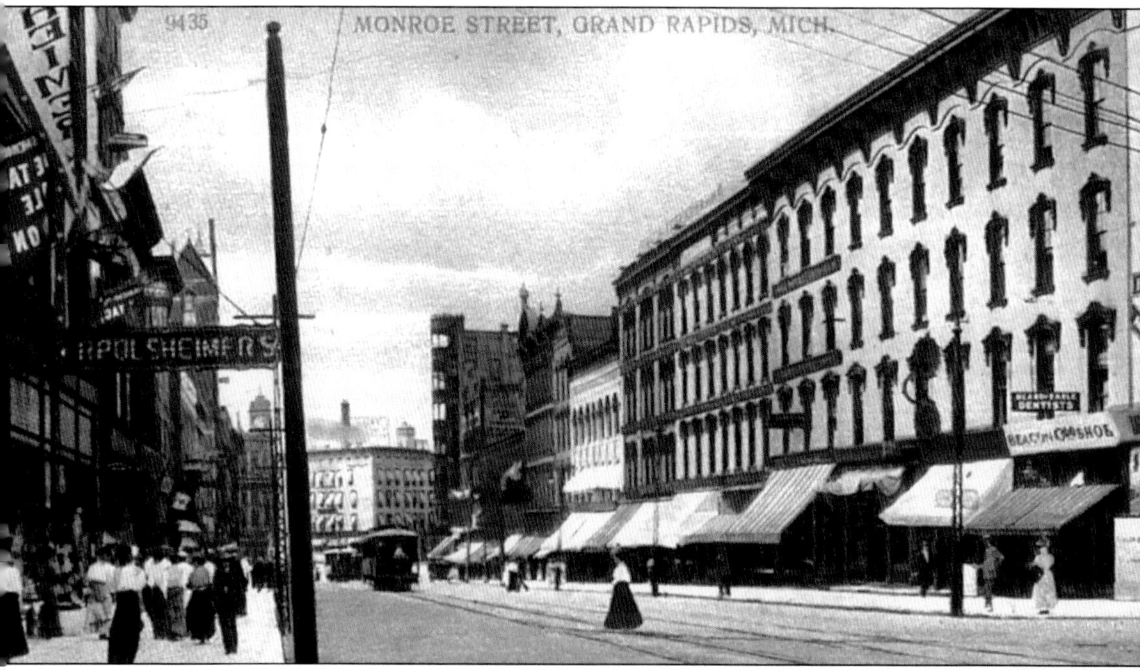

This is another panoramic view from 1910 of what is actually two cards that could be separated for mailing. Here the intersection of Monroe and Ottawa Avenues is seen. Looking north on Ottawa, to the right, the original Peninsular Club building sits at the corner of Fountain Street. Beyond it is the Young and Chaffee Furniture Store and still farther, looming in the distance,

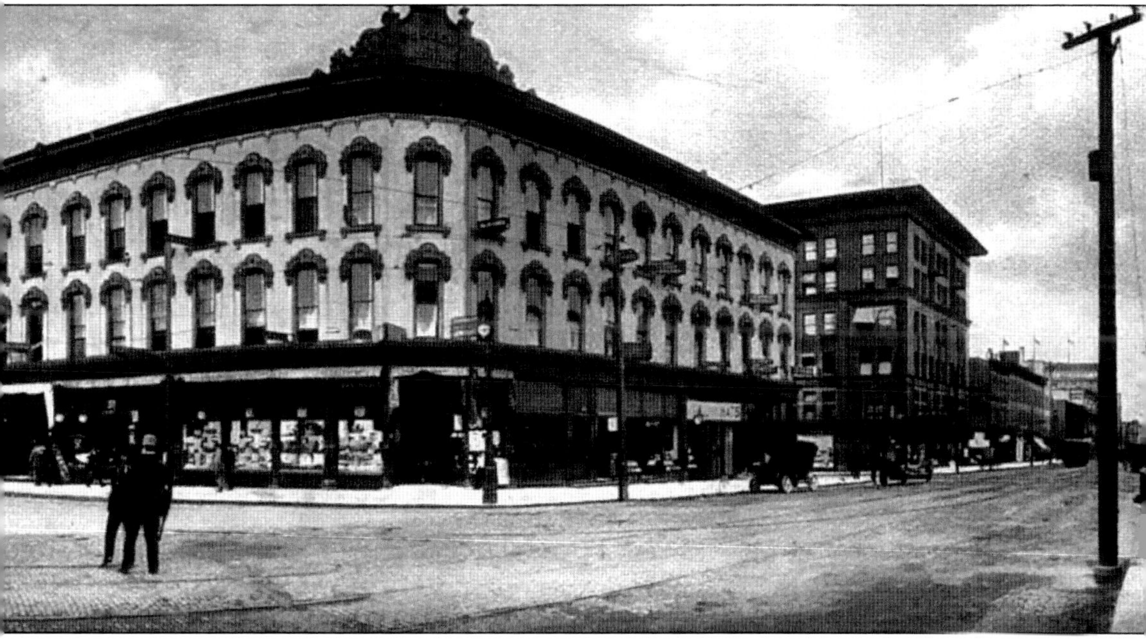

the center is the Porter Block, built in 1877 and used for general commercial and office space. It was replaced in 1949 with the new Herpolsheimer Store, which is today home to the Grand Rapids Police Department. The park at the left end of the photograph is Monument Park, with the (then) relatively new Civil War Memorial (erected in 1885) barely visible through the trees.

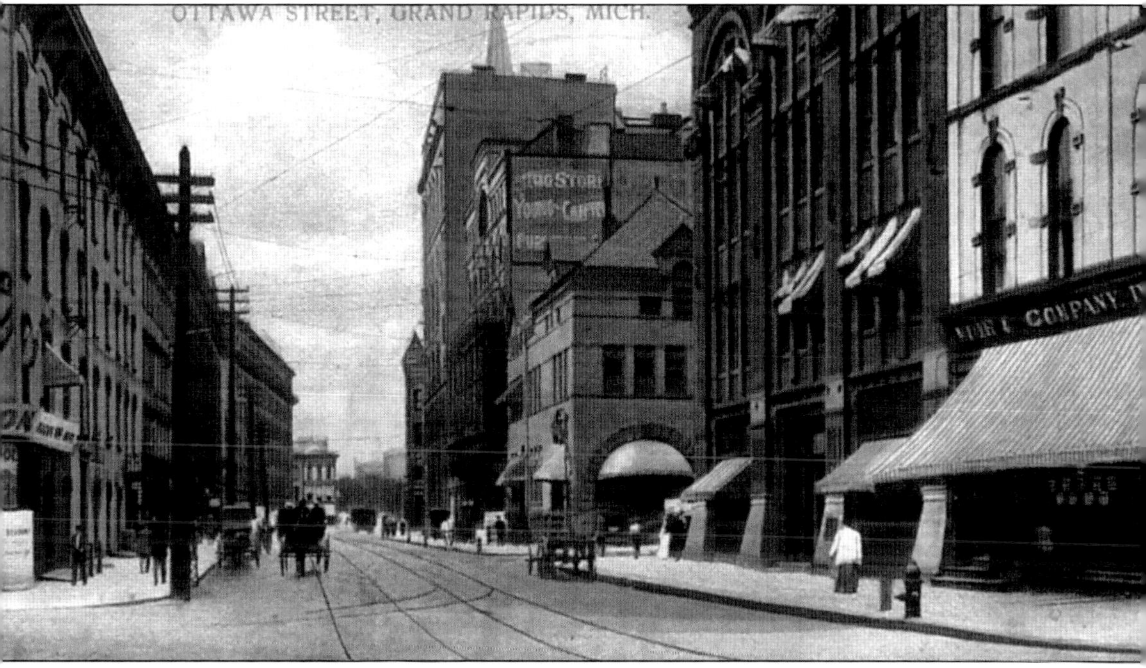

is the Michigan Trust Building, then the tallest building in the city. Looking to the left, down Monroe Avenue, the Wonderly Building, on the site of the present McKay Tower, is visible, as is the old Pantlind Hotel, due to be replaced within the next several years with the present structure at Campau Square.

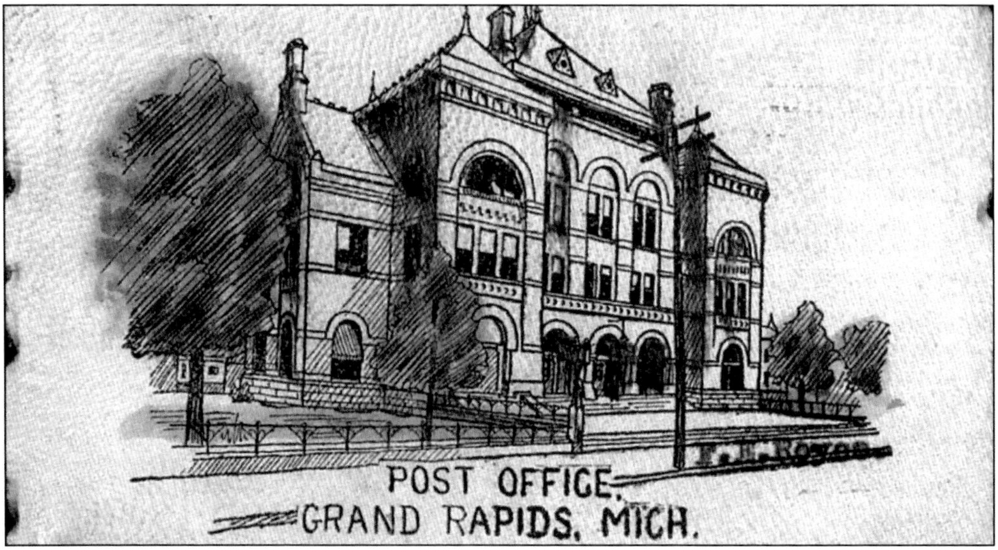

The four postcards on these pages, all dating from between 1905 and 1910, show sites of importance in the Grand Rapids area. They are all produced on tanned leather, rather than paper card stock, and represent examples of a limited and short-lived genre in early postcards, directed primarily at the tourist and collector market. Most leather cards feature whimsical greetings, with little or nothing in the way of an actual illustration, and though they could be, typically they were not mailed (although the first in this series was mailed for 1¢ in 1907 to Elkhart, Indiana). These four cards actually carry images of local sites, which have been pressed and burned into the leather. This is a view of the original United State post office and courthouse, located on Ionia Avenue between Pearl and Lyon Streets, from about 1907. The building was originally constructed in 1879 and was used until it was replaced on the same site in 1909.

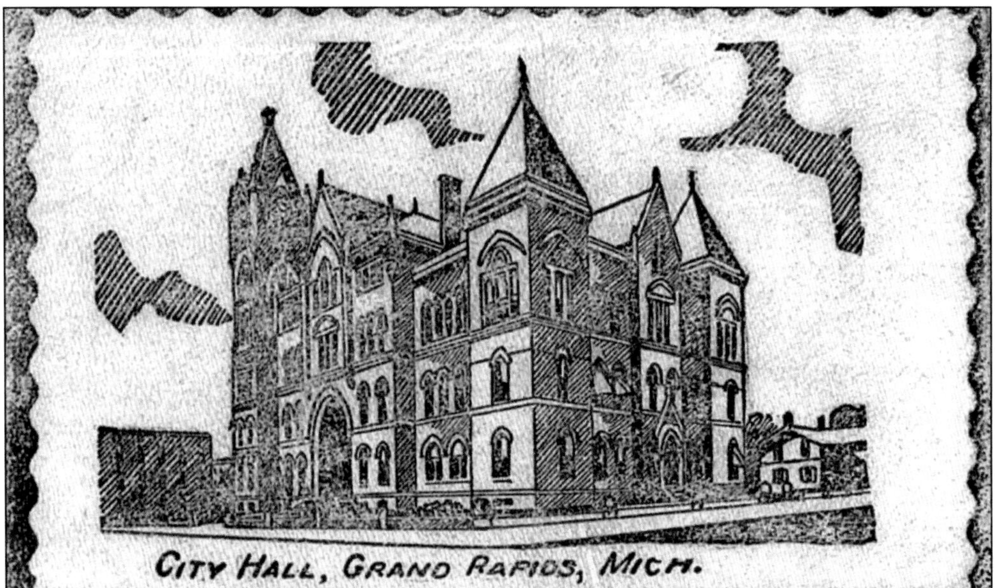

This view of the Grand Rapids City Hall, looking northwest from the corner of Lyon Street and Ionia Avenue, dates from 1910. The city hall, a grand Victorian Romanesque structure, was built in 1888 and continued in use until it was razed, amid much controversy, in the early 1970s.

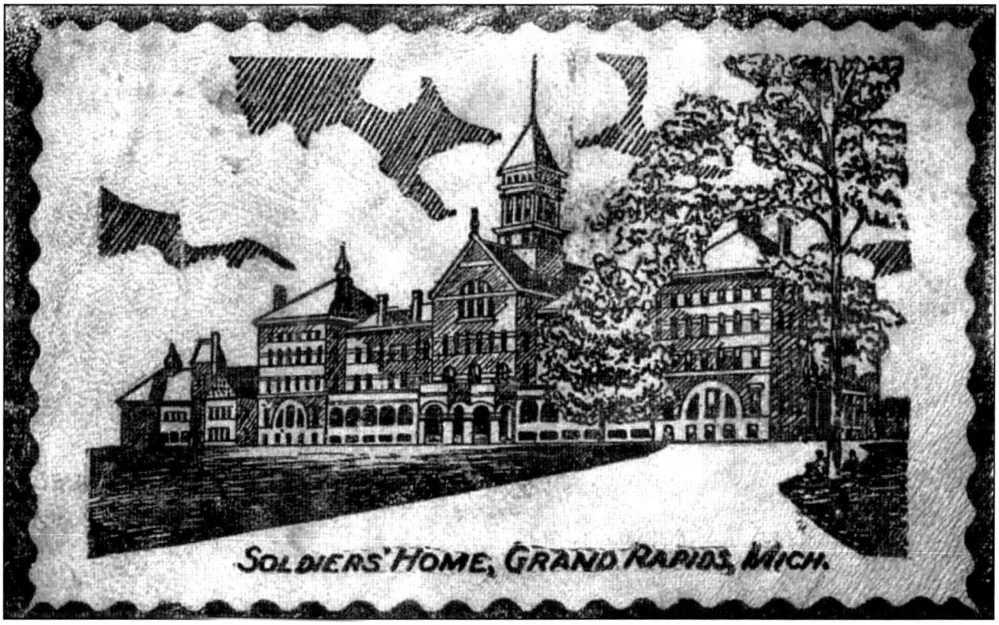

The main building of the Michigan Veteran's Facility, located on Monroe Avenue north of downtown, was built in 1886 as one of the first large-scale veterans' care facilities in the United States.

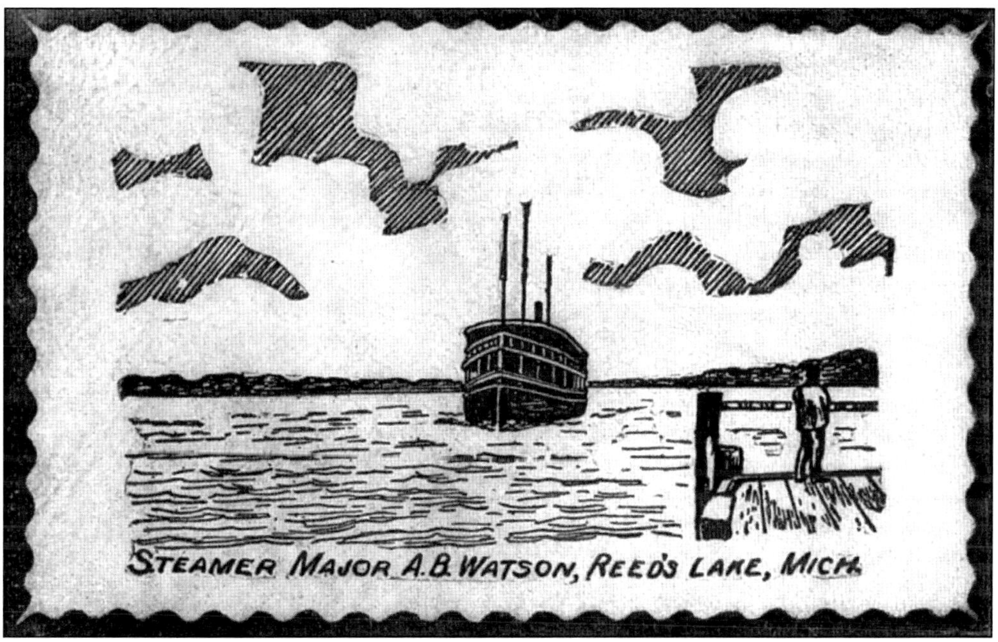

This is a view of the *Major Watson*, one of several steam excursion ships that plied the waters of Reeds Lake, east of Grand Rapids, between 1891 and 1921, during the most active and popular life of the Ramona amusement park, then located on the western shore of the lake. This steamer was named for local Civil War hero Amasa B. Watson but was known as the *Major Watson*, rather than as the postcard caption suggests.

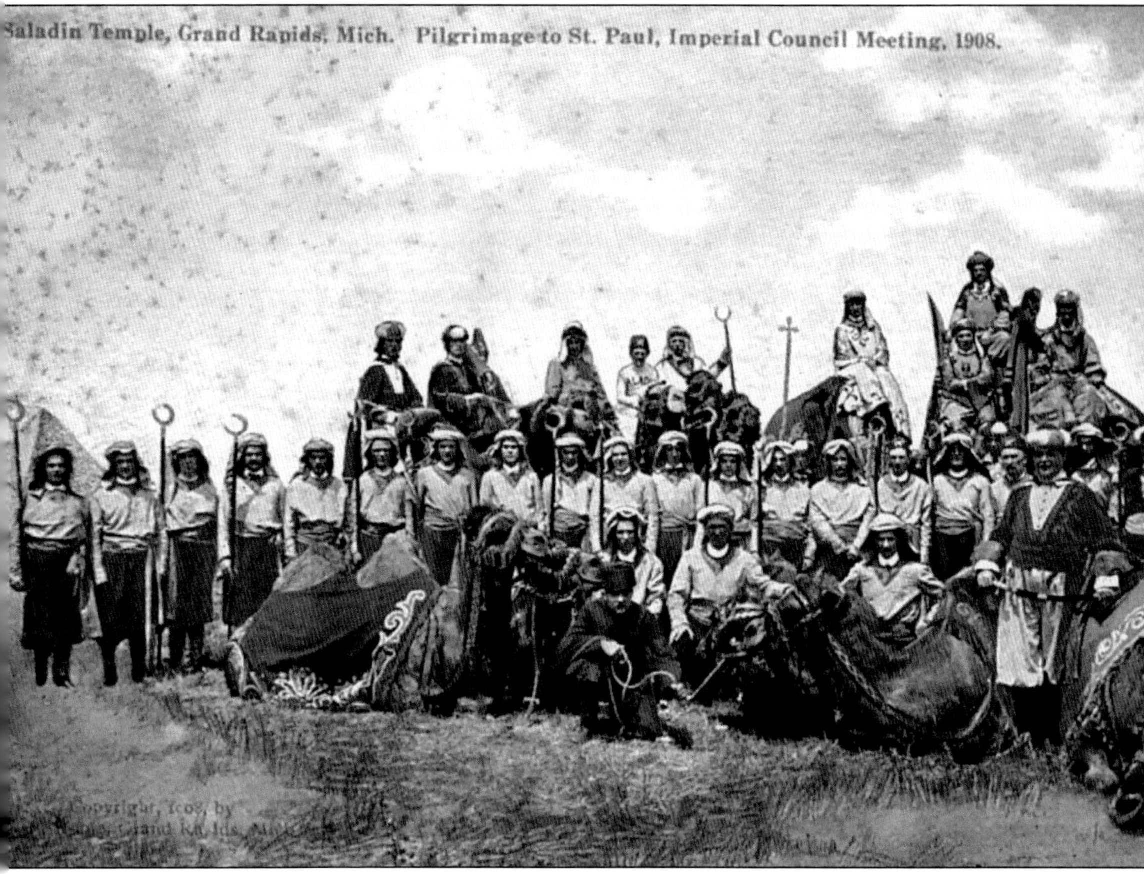

This extraordinary double postcard, commemorating the pilgrimage of the local Saladin Shriners to the Imperial Council meeting at St. Paul, Minnesota, was published in 1908. Given the

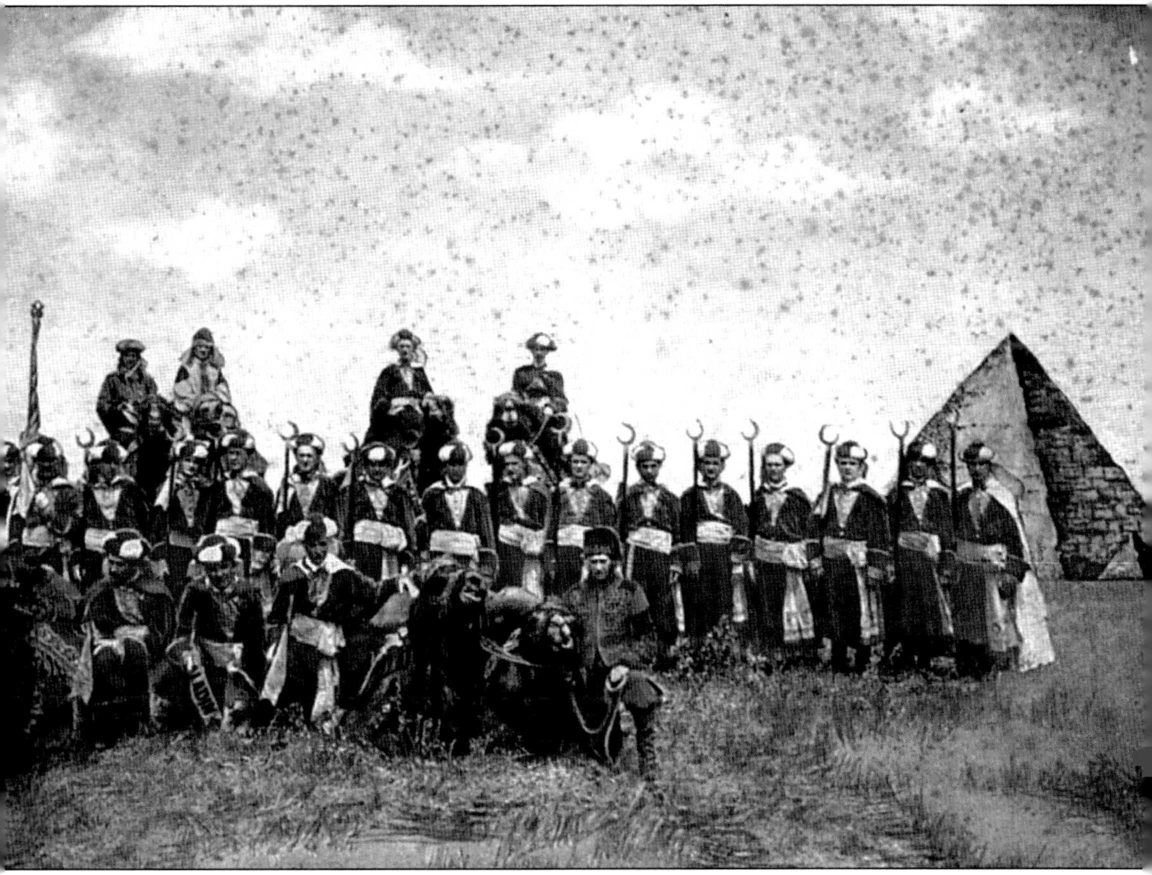

presumed absence of naturally occurring camels and pyramids in St. Paul, it is assumed that this photograph was thoroughly staged for the occasion.

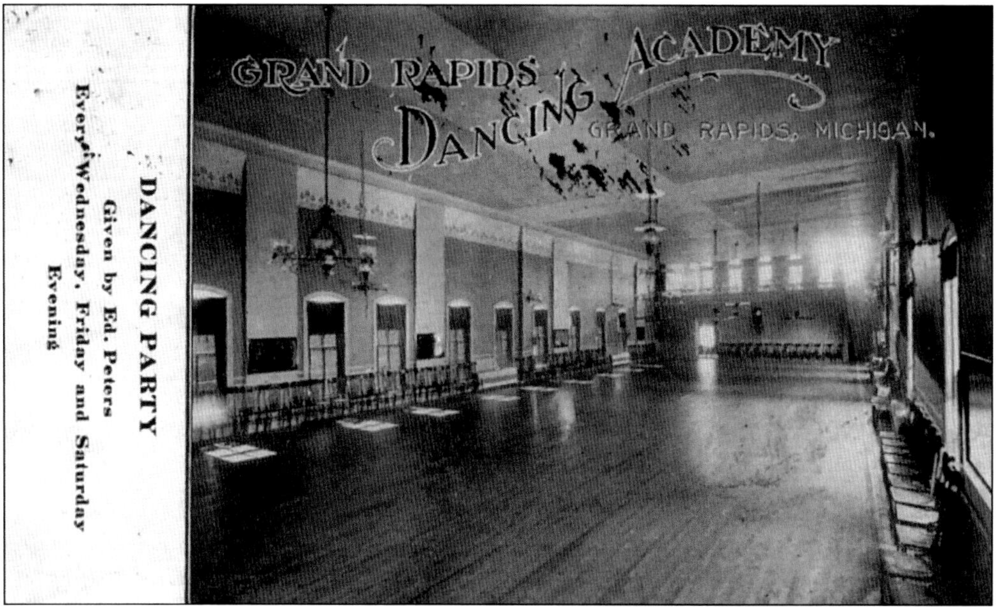

This is a promotional card sent out by the Grand Rapids Dancing Academy, located on Ionia Avenue in the Ashton Building, in 1914, announcing its weekly dances.

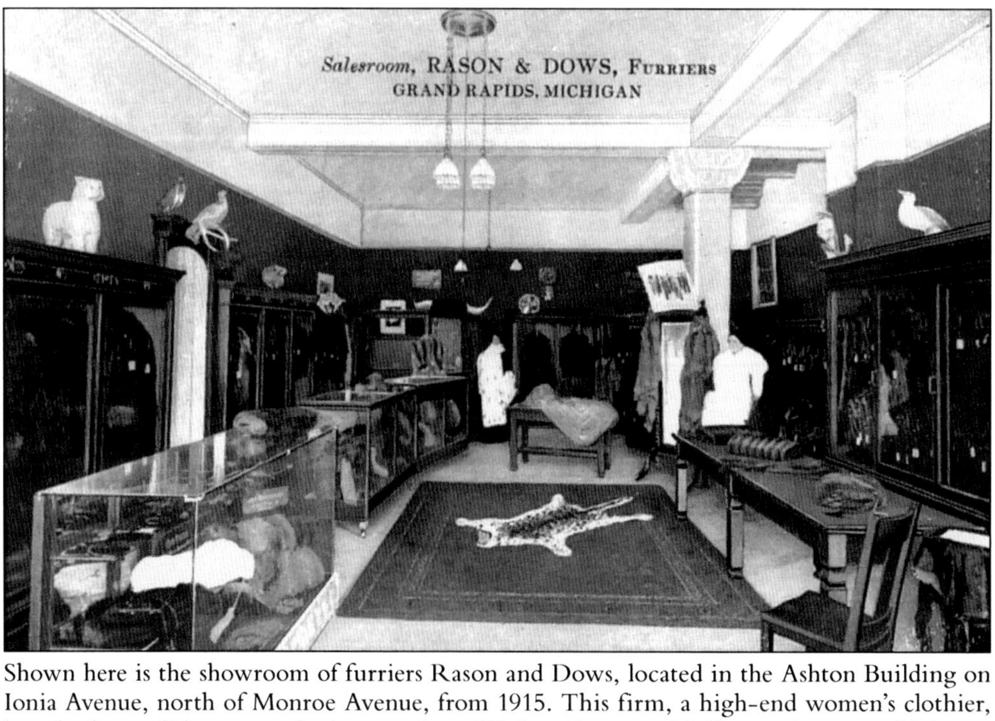

Shown here is the showroom of furriers Rason and Dows, located in the Ashton Building on Ionia Avenue, north of Monroe Avenue, from 1915. This firm, a high-end women's clothier, later built a stylish store at the intersection of Fulton Street and Jefferson Avenue, which was demolished in the early 1970s.

Two

Early Postcards in Business

Early on in the history of the city, life and business focused strongly around the river upon which the city was originally founded. In these early days, when business was booming, the Grand River was viewed and treated far more as a source of power and means of transport (and also a source of potable drinking water) than it was a beautiful natural resource. The banks of the river within the city teemed with businesses that needed the water in their production processes or relied heavily on the flowing currents to turn their mills. Only later, as the river banks became too crowded, and steam and electricity replaced water-driven mechanics, did the city begin to recognize the river as a place primarily of recreation and beauty.

As was the case in other cities, manufacturing and trade grew and prospered here, hand in hand. Goods, including vast amounts of household and business furniture, originally created for local consumption, quickly found national and, eventually, international markets. Still, the locals needed and wanted clothing and groceries and needed to build and outfit their homes. Local businessmen quickly stepped in to fill this need, opening in this era a large array of mercantile operations aimed at providing to local residents every item they could desire or buy from an out-of-town source or their current Sears and Roebuck catalog.

As commercial activity grew and prospered, merchants and manufacturers quickly recognized the usefulness of postcards for publicizing their companies and the goods they produced, and as a form of brief business correspondence, replacing the earlier, non-mailable trade cards of the late 19th century. Many of these early business postcards were used not just for publicity but for confirming orders and announcing the arrival of salesmen, and they all provide an interesting insight into the business environment of their day.

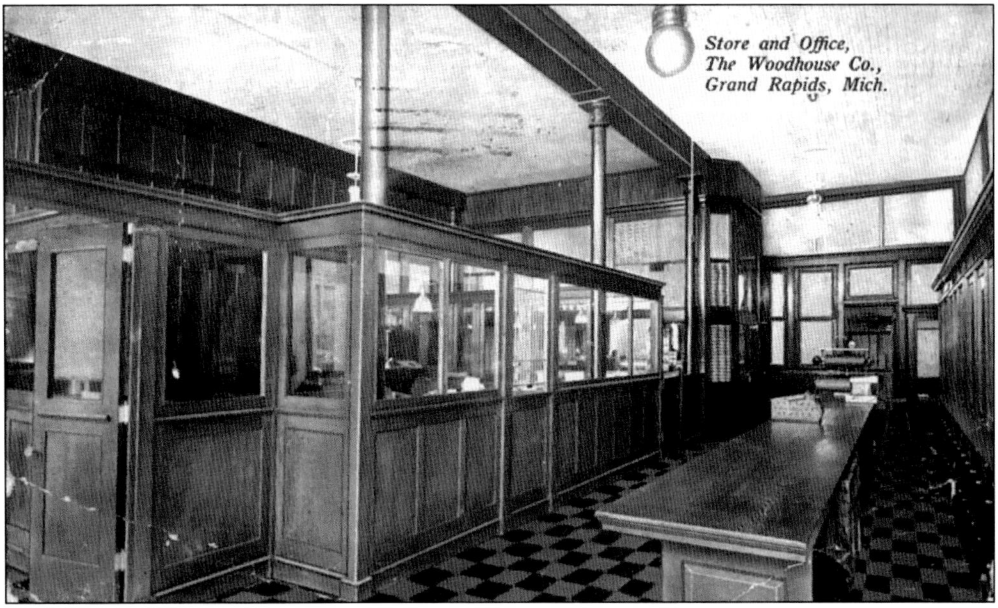

This view, from 1912, shows the offices of the Woodhouse Company, wholesalers of tobacco products, located at Ionia Avenue and Fulton Street. Cards such as this, depicting a business office, were typically used for brief and quick business correspondence. This card advised to a customer that a product he had ordered was no longer available.

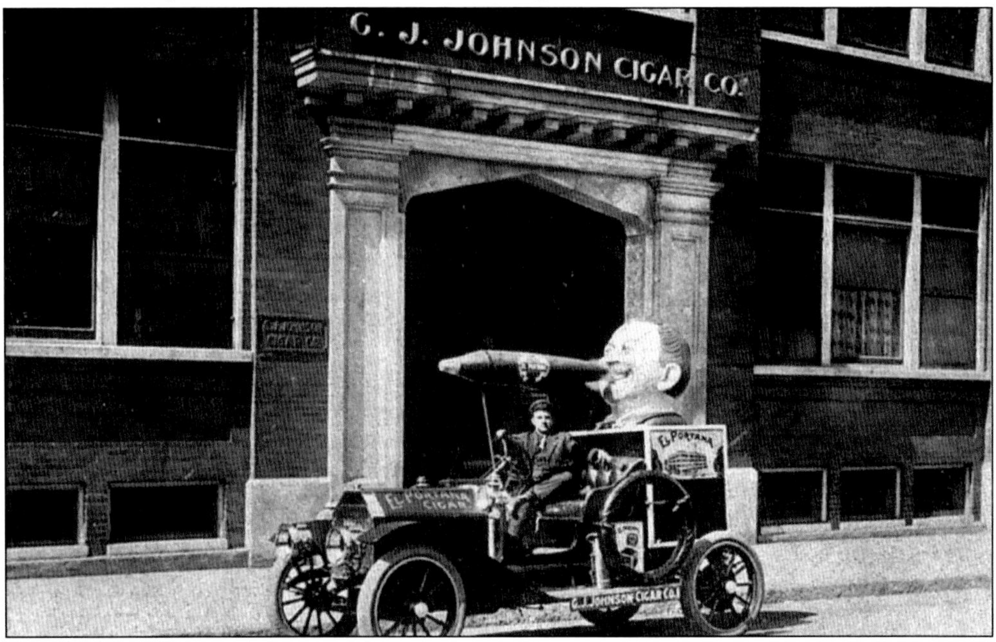

Presented by local postcard publisher Will Canaan in 1910, this card shows the front of the office and factory of the G. J. Johnson Cigar Company on Ottawa Avenue, north of downtown. This company originated the El Portana and Dutch Masters cigar brands and was later merged into the Consolidated Cigar Corporation, which continues to market the brands today. The float in the picture had very likely been prepared for participation in the homecoming parade, which occurred in August 1910.

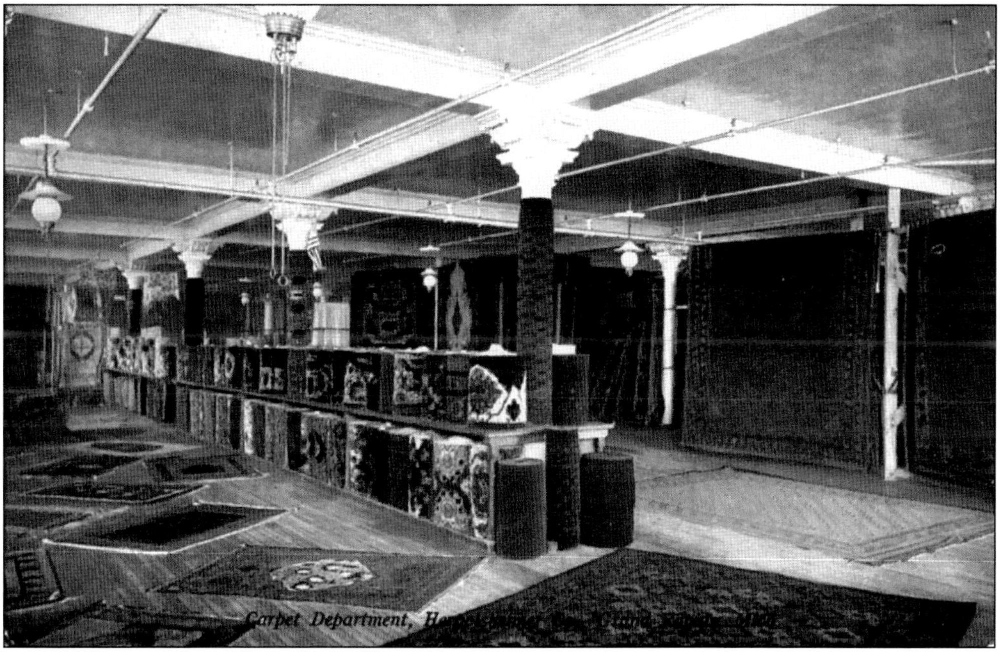

The interior of the Herpolsheimer Department Store, located on Monroe Avenue at Ottawa Avenue, is seen here from around 1910. The store began in 1881 in this location and much later, in 1950, moved to a larger and more modern building at Division Avenue and Monroe, where it closed in the late 1970s.

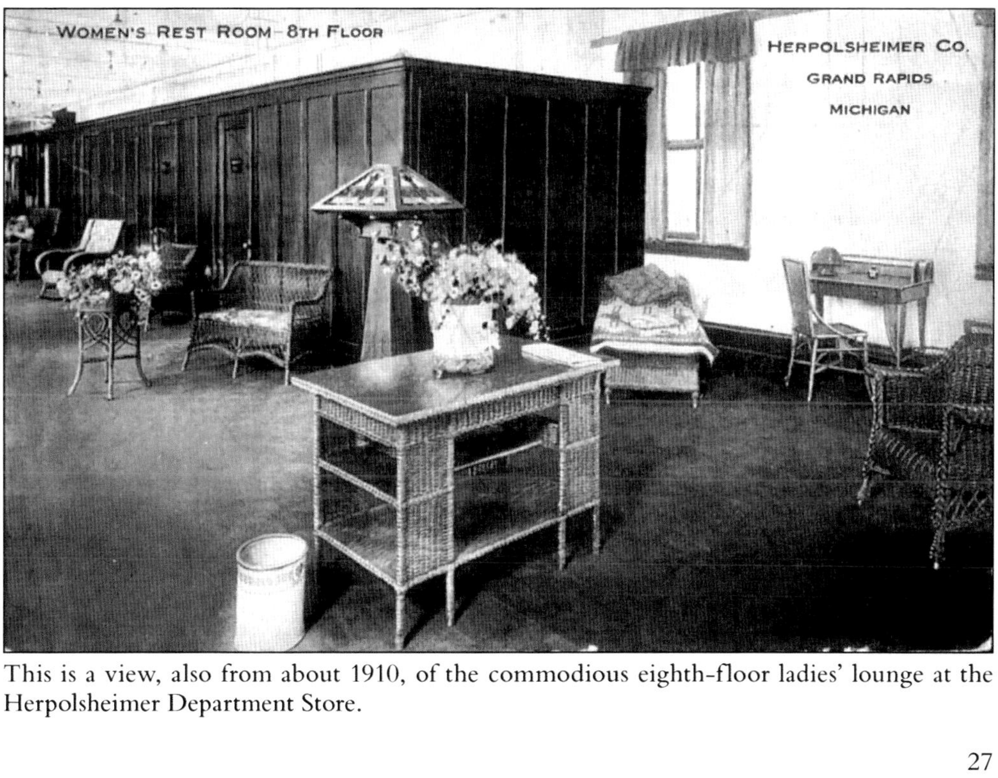

This is a view, also from about 1910, of the commodious eighth-floor ladies' lounge at the Herpolsheimer Department Store.

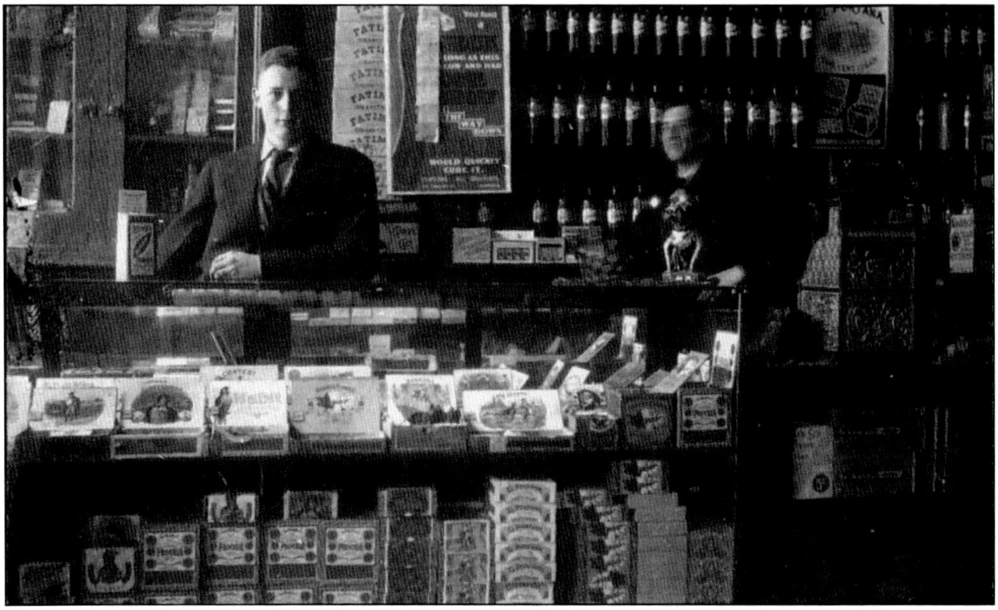

A real-photo view of the interior of an amply supplied cigar store located on South Prospect Avenue, from about 1912, is pictured here. The identity of the two men is unknown, but the placard over the left shoulder of the man on the right advertises El Portana cigars, the product of local manufacturer the G. J. Johnson Cigar Company.

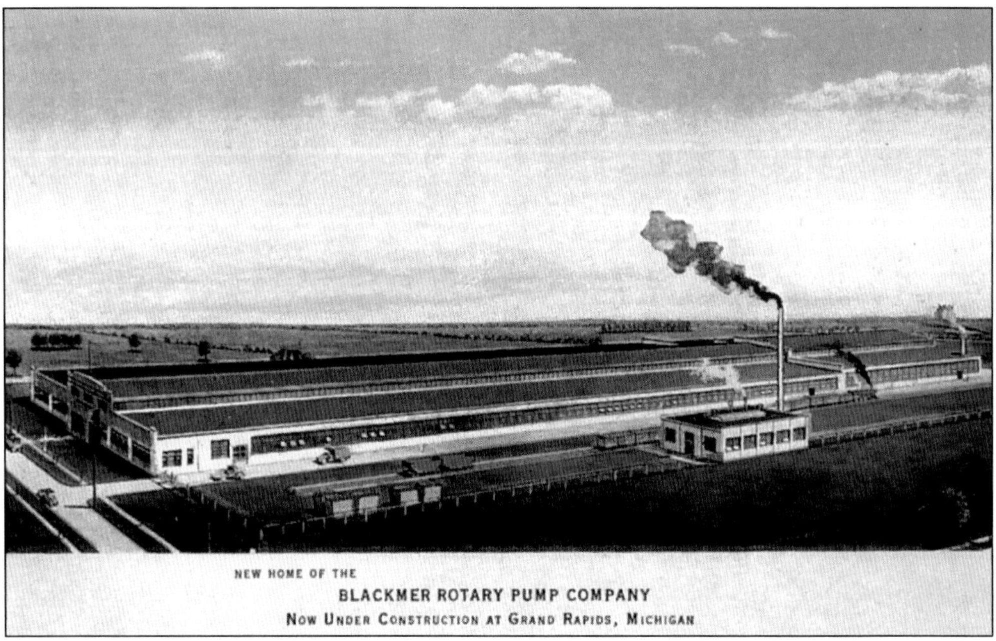

Shown here is a highly idealized view of the new factory of the Blackmer Rotary Pump Company, located on Century Avenue Southwest, from about 1915. Views like this, sometimes wildly inaccurate depictions of a facility, were common and were designed to highlight the prominence of the paying customer's factory. Two things about this card are certain: the factory was not as large as portrayed, and its surroundings were a good deal less bucolic than the card suggests.

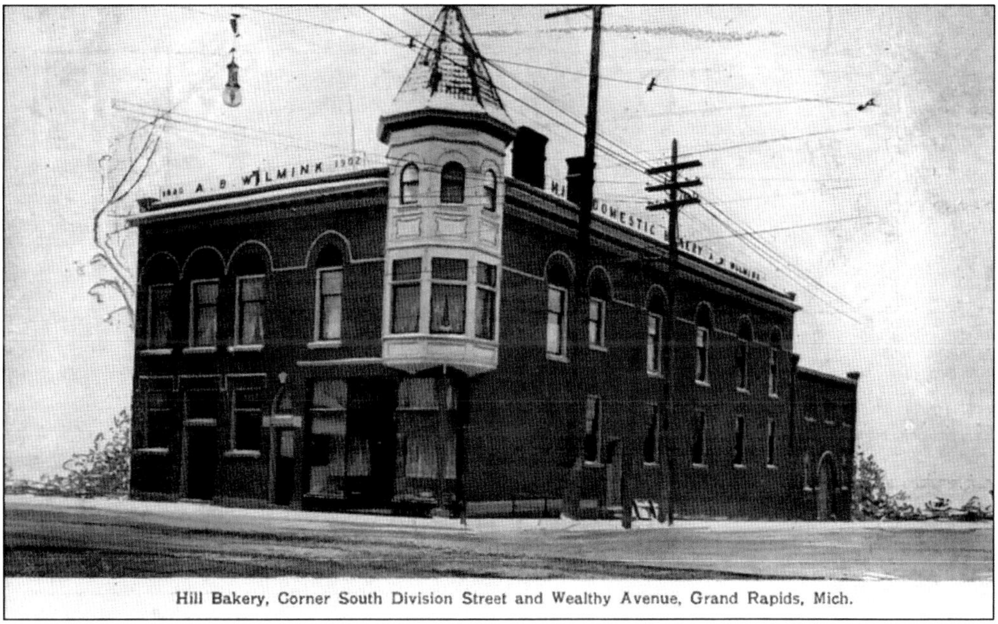

This is a view of the Hill Domestic Bakery, located at the corner of Division Avenue and Wealthy Street, from 1910. The view is fairly accurate, except for the cropping away of the neighboring buildings. Such cropping of the image was common and understandable. After all, the bakery proprietor was more interested in publicizing his own business than those of his neighbors.

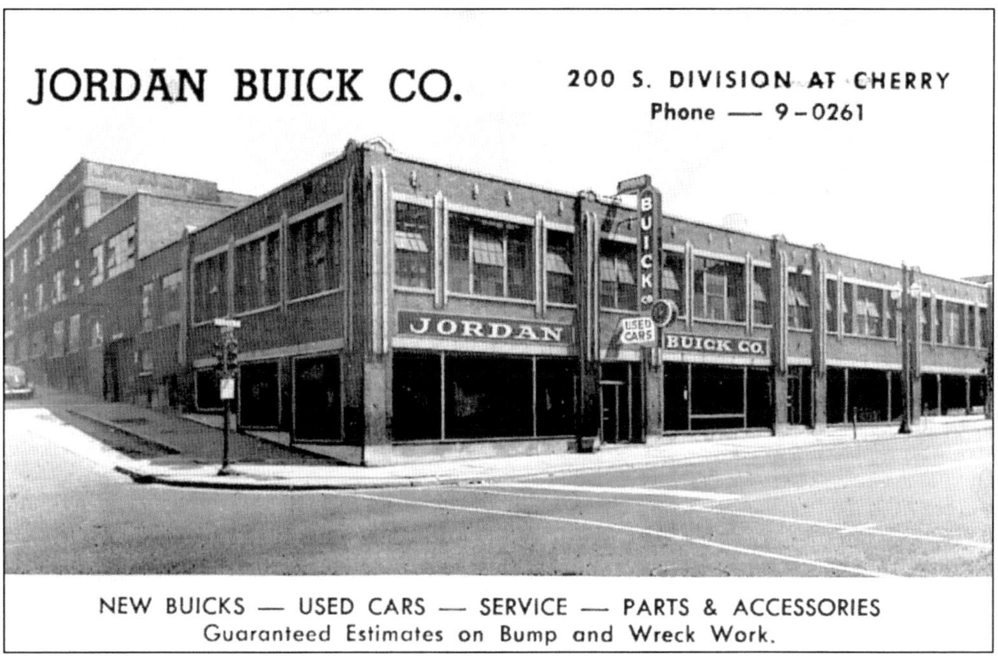

This view from 1955 features the showrooms of the Jordan Buick Company, located at the corner of Division Avenue and Cherry Street. Though the building still stands, it is today used for other purposes. Most car dealerships in Grand Rapids, formerly located in the downtown area, moved out to larger suburban spaces on the north or south ends of town in the 1950s and 1960s.

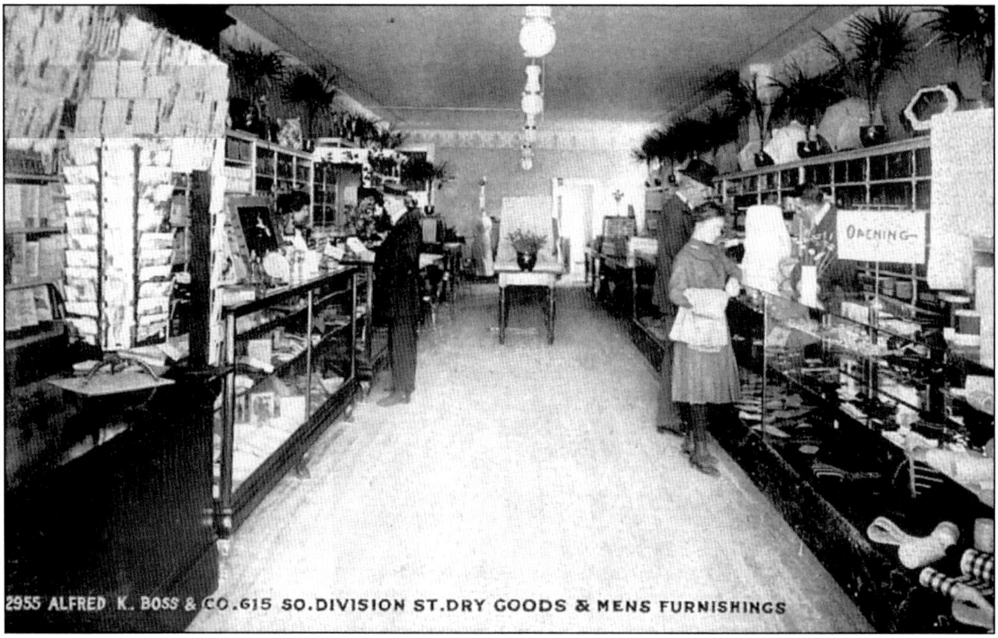

An interior view of the Alfred K. Boss and Company dry goods store, located on Division Avenue just south of downtown, from about 1920 is seen here. Note the rack of postcards for sale on the counter to the left.

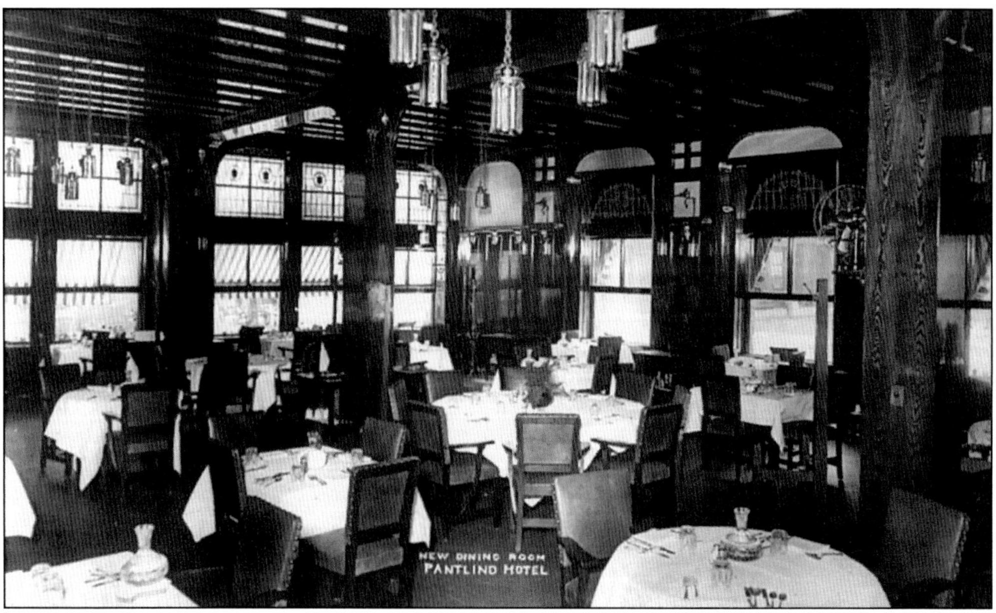

This is a rare real-photo view of the interior of the "new" Pantlind Hotel from about 1915. This hotel building replaced an older, much smaller building on the same site, and secured the prominence of the Pantlind name as the premier hotelier in Grand Rapids for decades thereafter.

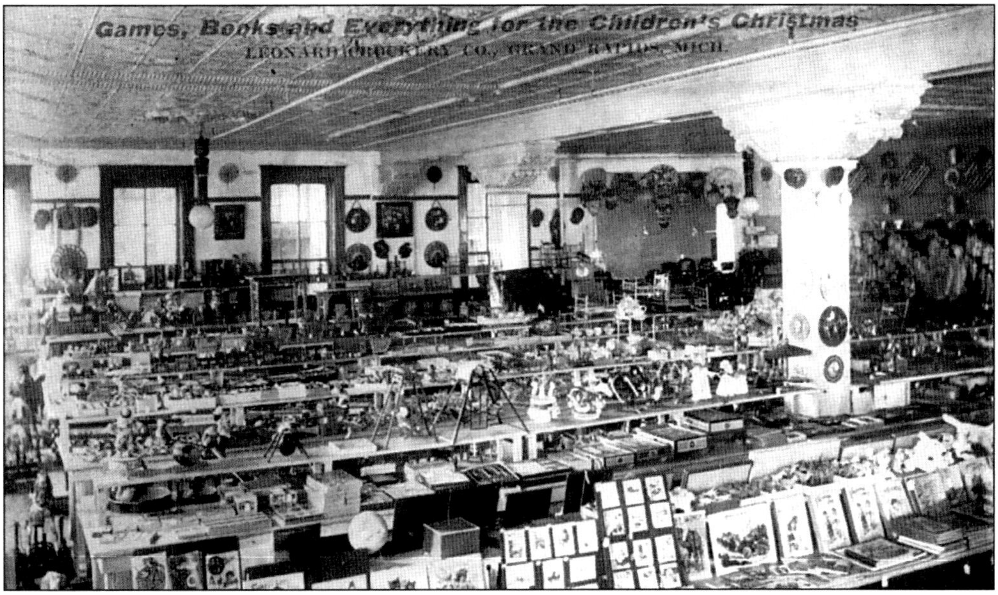

The interior of the H. Leonard and Sons Store, at Commerce and Fulton Streets, from 1907 appears here. The Leonard store was first opened in 1842 by Heman Leonard and was located on Monroe Avenue, near Campau Square. The Leonard store was the first in Grand Rapids to use the new electric lights. Later Leonard was joined in the business by his three sons, who greatly expanded the business over the following years, finally undertaking the manufacture and sale of the highly successful Leonard Cleanable Ice Box and, ultimately, refrigerator. The company was later merged into the Kelvinator Company and American Motors.

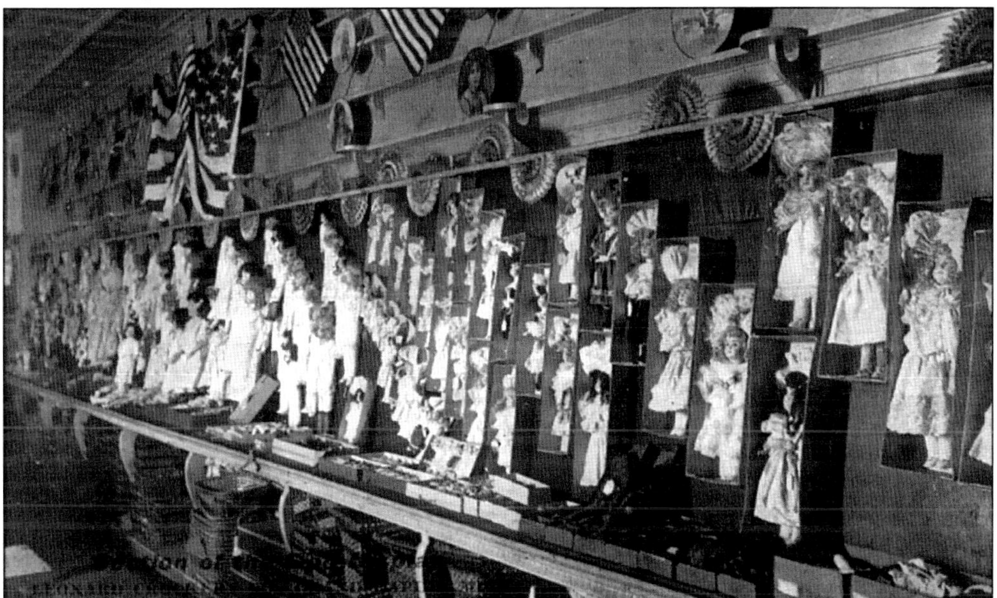

This is another view of the interior of the H. Leonard and Sons Store, from around 1910, this time showing a large selection of dolls available to wholesale customers. This and the previous card are actually promotional mailings sent to retailers in small Michigan towns in advance of a visit from a Leonard company salesman.

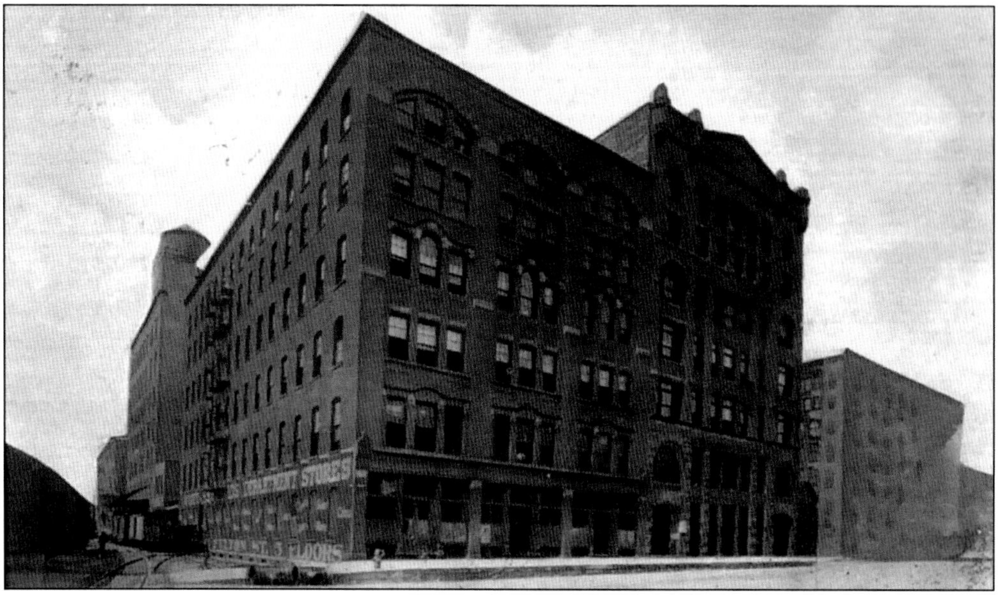

This card features a view of the two buildings built side by side by the Leonard family in the late 19th century to provide exhibition space for the growing furniture market in Grand Rapids, undoubtedly including the successful Leonard Cleanable Refrigerator that they manufactured here at the time. The buildings were located on Ottawa Avenue, between Louis and Fulton Streets, and remain today, though completely renovated and refaced, as office space. The date of the view is 1911.

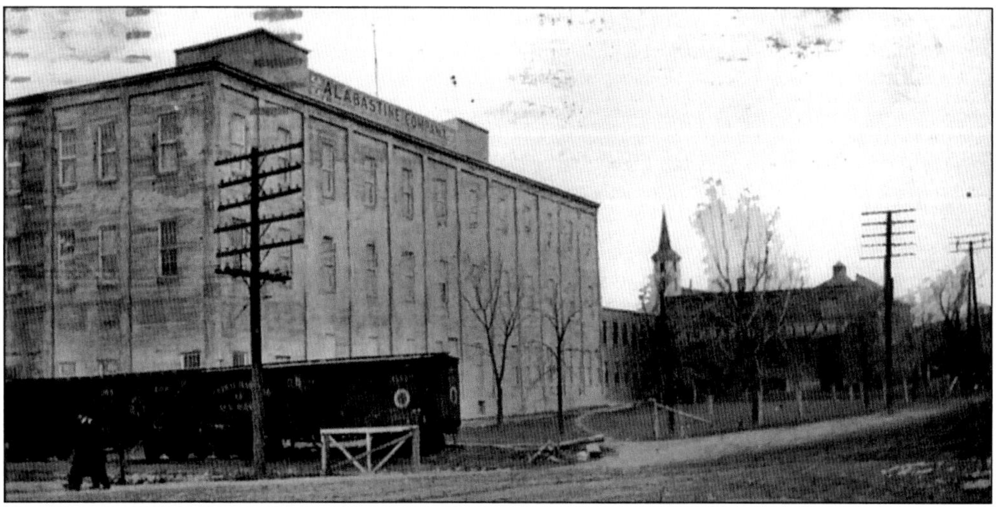

Pictured here is the factory of the Alabastine Company, a local gypsum-plaster processor and manufacturer, located on Hall Street, south of downtown, at the Pere Marquette Railroad tracks, from 1918. This company, founded in 1879, engaged in the mining and processing of the very high quality gypsum found underground, south of town. Gypsum and the fine plaster made from it were among the first natural resources located and exploited in the Grand Rapids area. The first mines were begun in 1841 and soon made the city the "gypsum center of the world." The Alabastine product, a thin wall covering available in dozens of then fashionable colors, was wildly successful and supported the operation of the company until a change in fashion forced the closing of the operation in 1943.

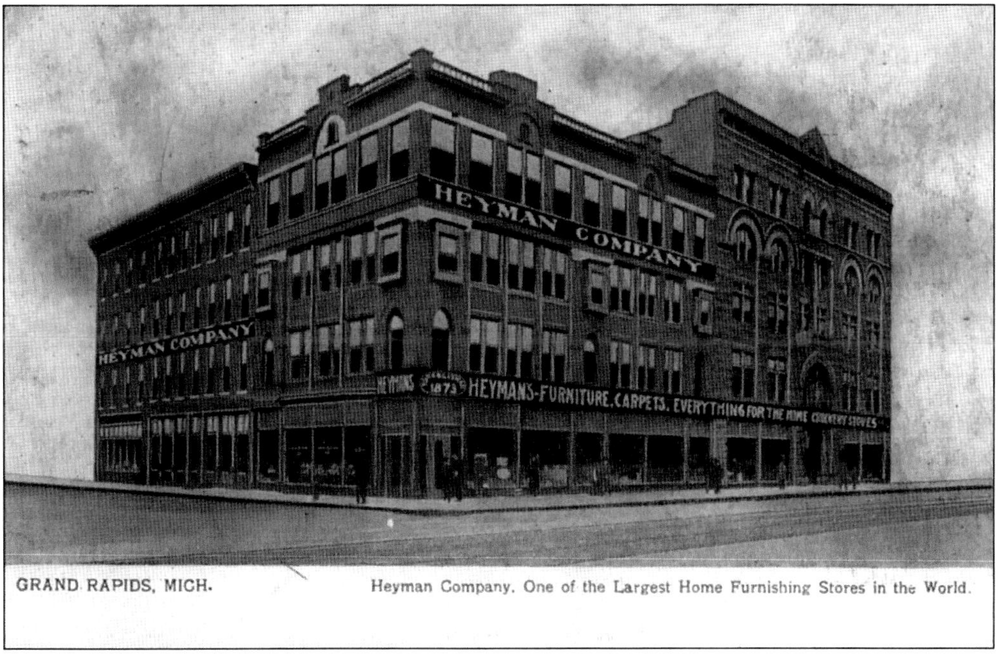

A picture of the Heyman home furnishings store, located on Monroe Avenue north of Campau Square, from 1909 is seen here. This card was sent out to promote the "Spring Opening" of the store and promised to make a visit there "interesting and exciting."

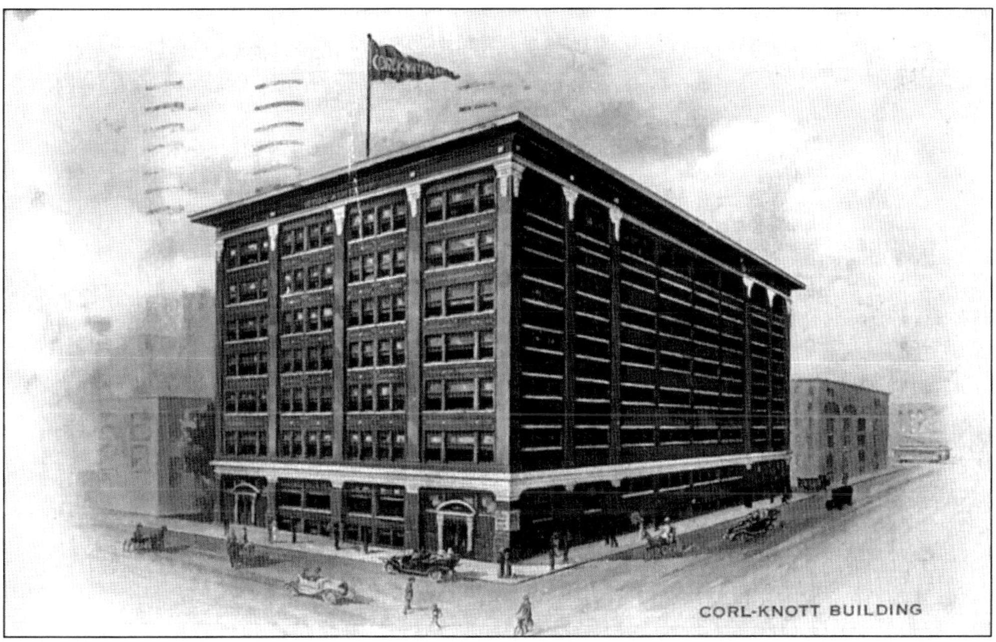

The Corl-Knott Company warehouse was located on Commerce Avenue, south of Fulton Street. This company was a successful wholesale and retail millinery firm, supplying the hat ware needs of ladies locally and throughout the Midwest. The view is from 1913.

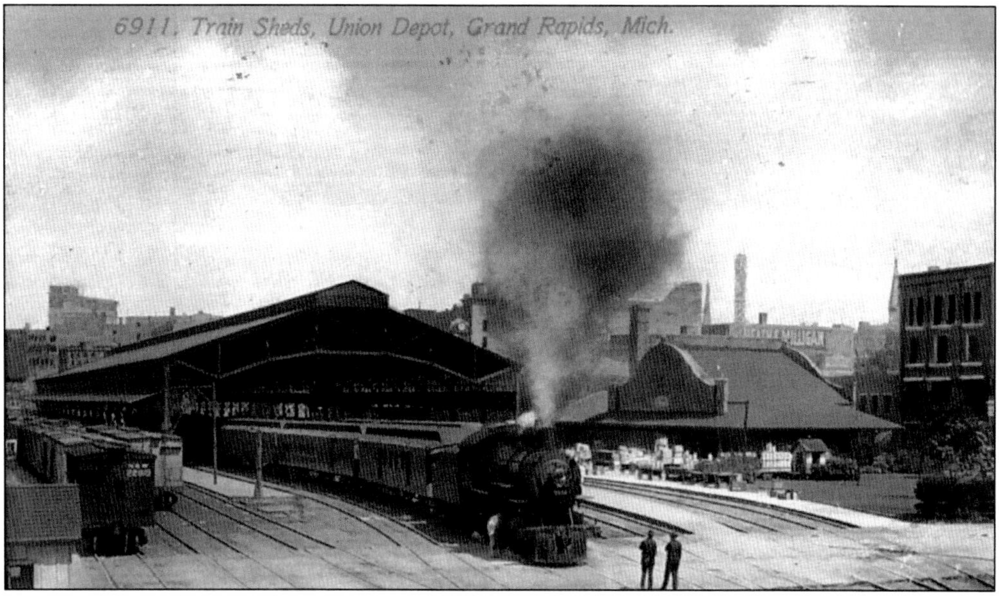

This is a 1912 view, looking northeast over the train shed at the rear of Union Station on Ionia Avenue, south of Fulton Street. The Van Andel Arena is now located on this site. The then still-developing skyline of the downtown area is visible in the background. At this time, and in the decades before, train traffic through Grand Rapids was heavy, including thousands of passenger and freight trains each year.

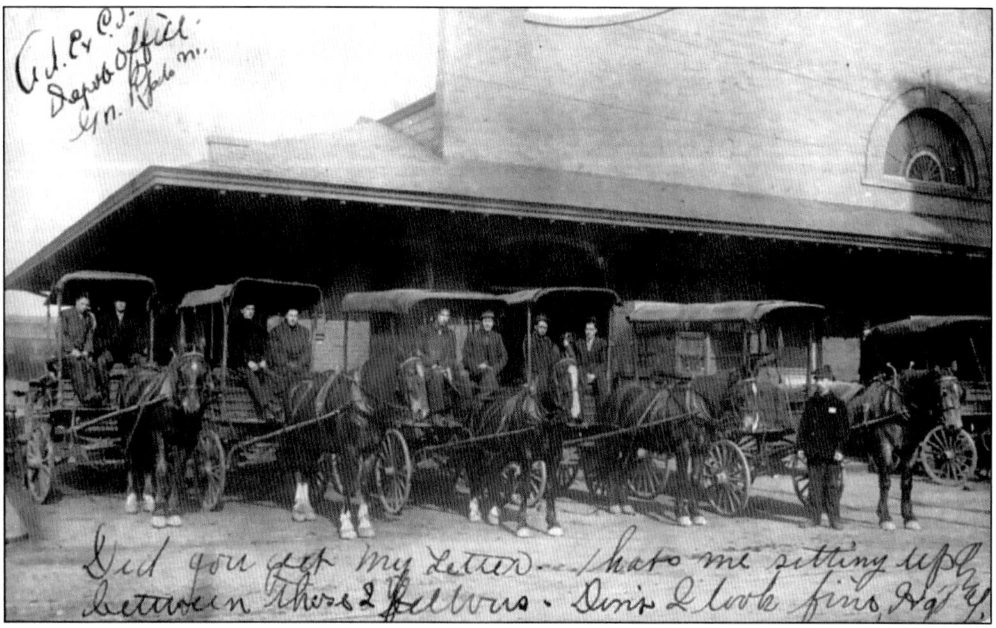

A real-photo view of the Ionia Avenue front of the freight terminal at Union Station, from 1907, is seen here. The message written on the front of the card jokingly refers to the dog sitting in the wagon at the center of the photograph. The message was written on the front of the card because postal regulations at the time still prohibited anything other than an address from being applied to the other side of the card. This restriction was changed later in the year that the card was mailed.

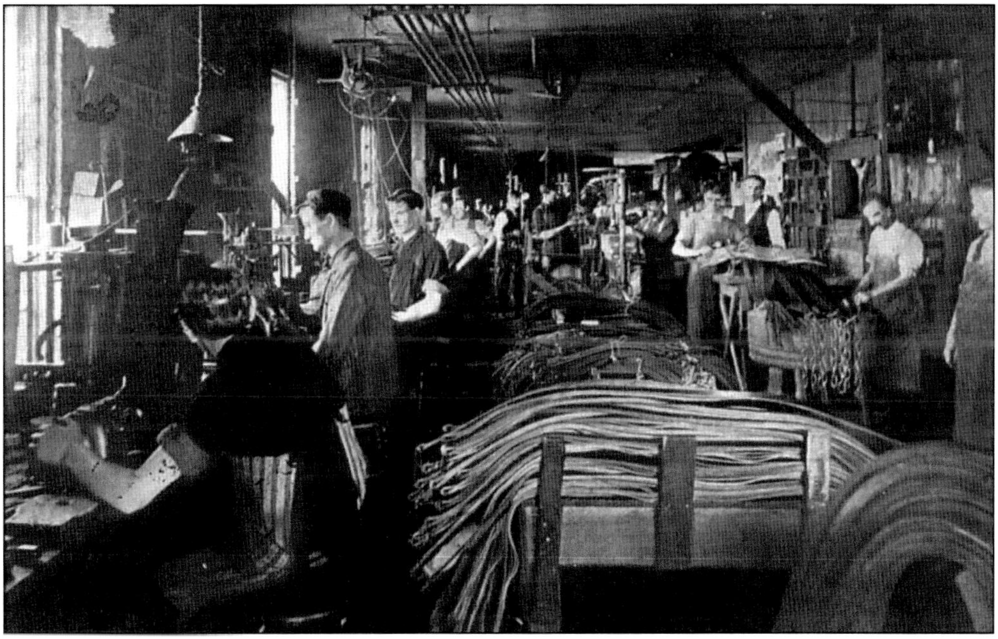

This is a "will call" postcard printed for the Brown and Sehler Company in 1908, to be used by salesmen to announce to customers when they would be making a sales call. The photograph depicts the firm's factory, located on Bridge Street on the west bank of the river. The company offered a full line of harnesses and related leather materials.

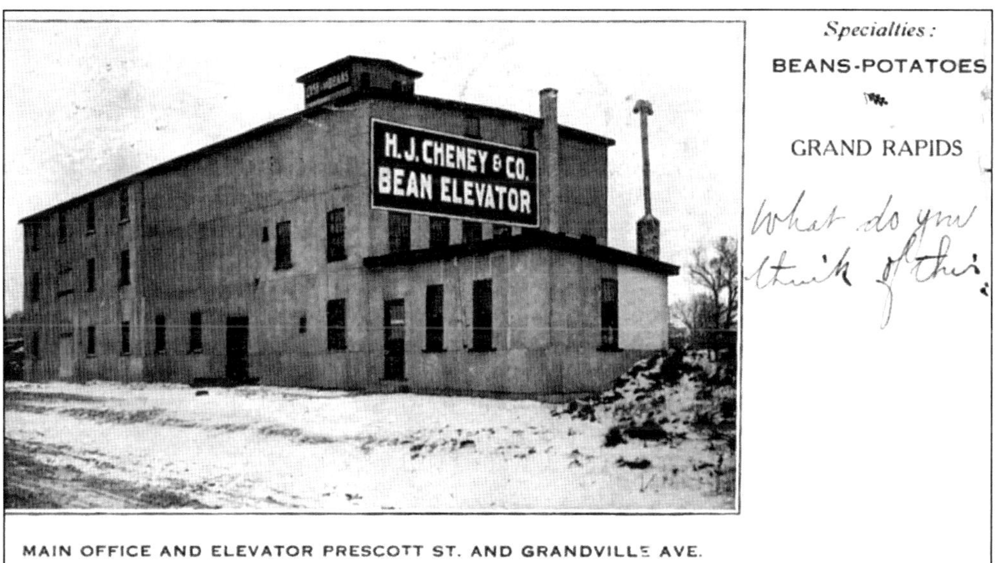

This 1909 postcard, actually a trade advertisement, depicts the office and elevator of the H. J. Cheney Company, suppliers of seeds, located on Grandville Avenue, south of downtown.

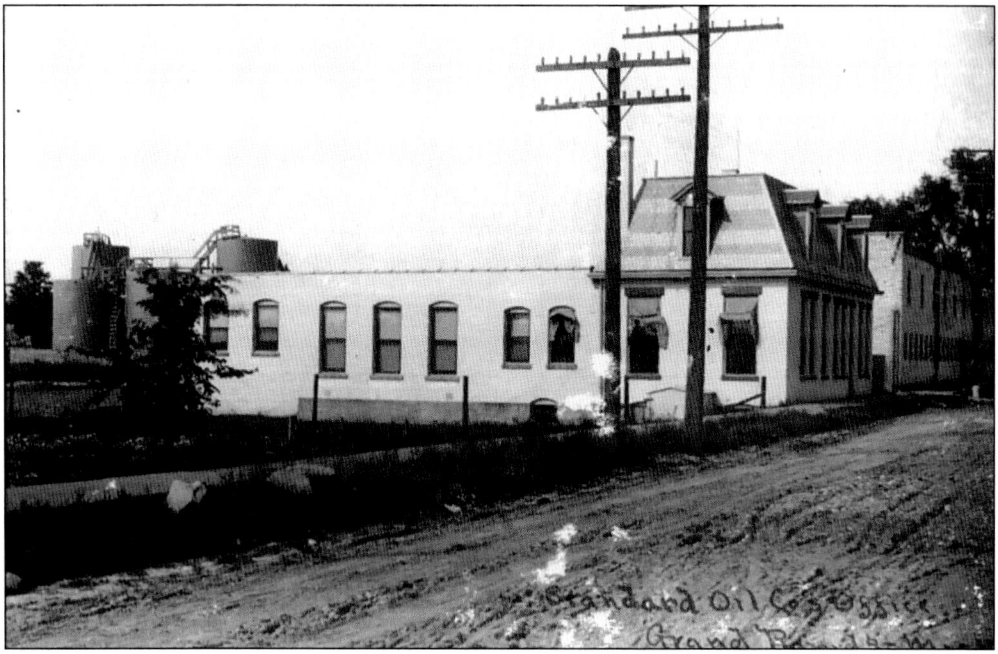

The local office and warehouse of the Standard Oil Company is shown in this real-photo postcard from about 1910.

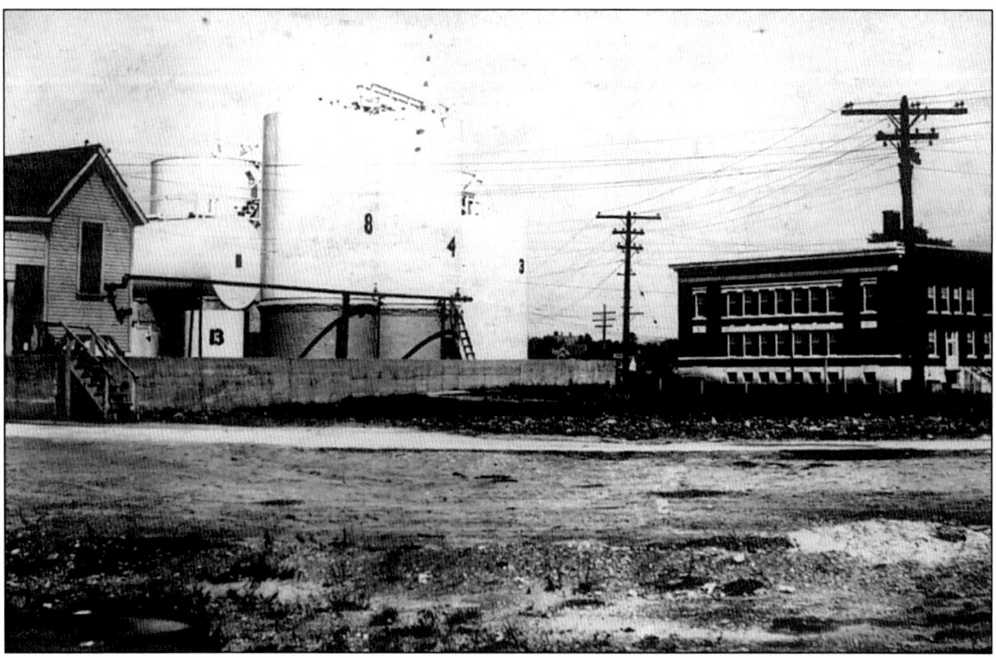

A 1916 picture of the Standard Oil office, located on Butterworth Avenue in southwest Grand Rapids, is seen here.

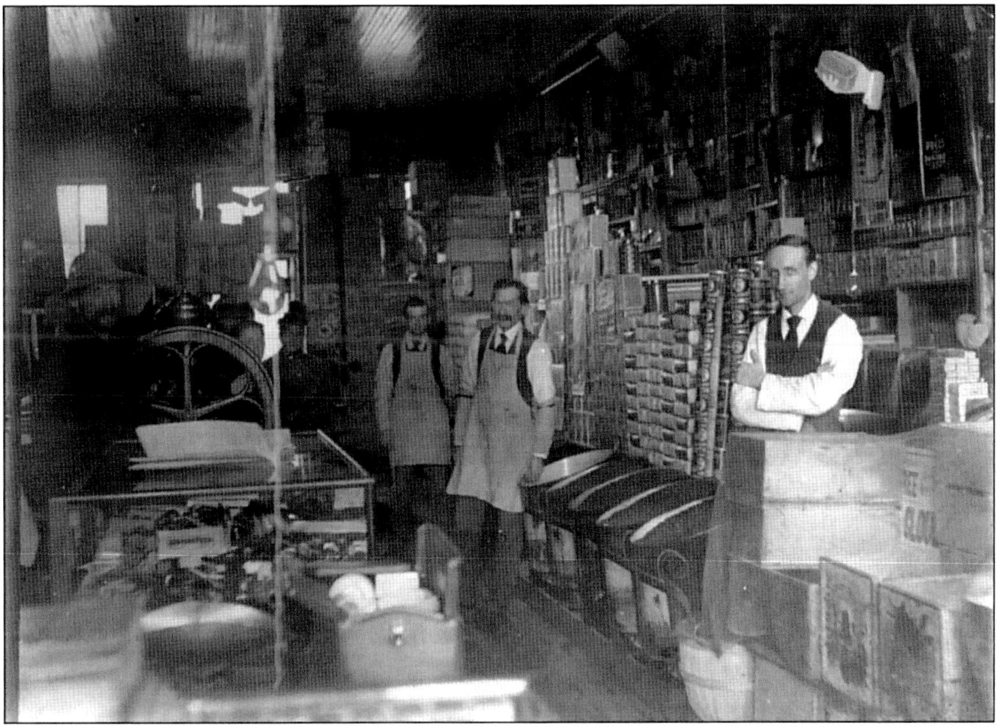

This real-photo will call card depicts an unknown local grocery and was sent out by George A. Newhall, a traveling salesman for the Judson Grocery Company, a local wholesale grocery supplier, announcing his intended arrival at the store of a customer in 1907.

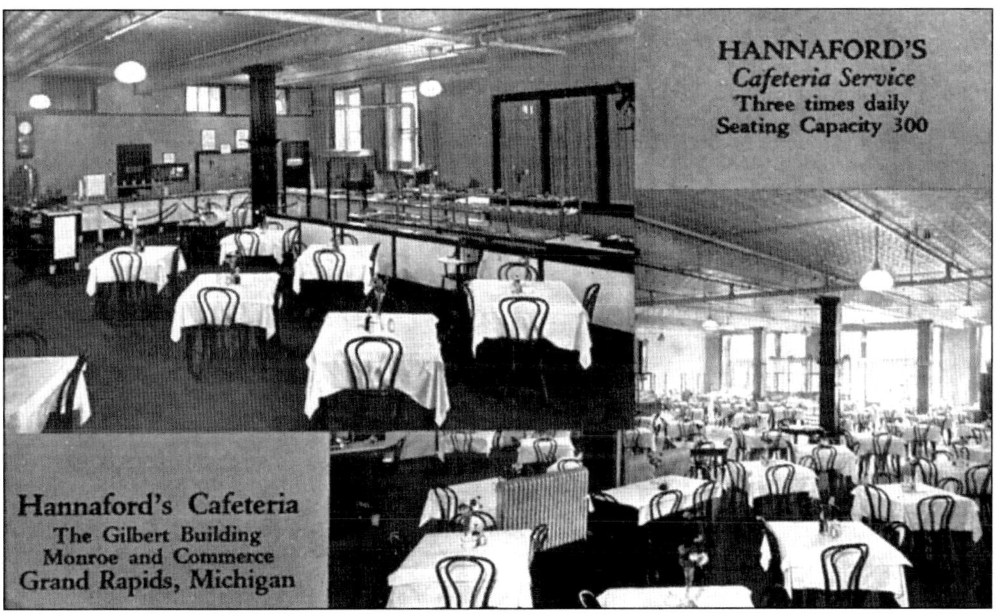

This view of the interior of the Hannaford Cafeteria, located in the Gilbert Building at the corner of Monroe and Commerce Avenues, is from about 1920.

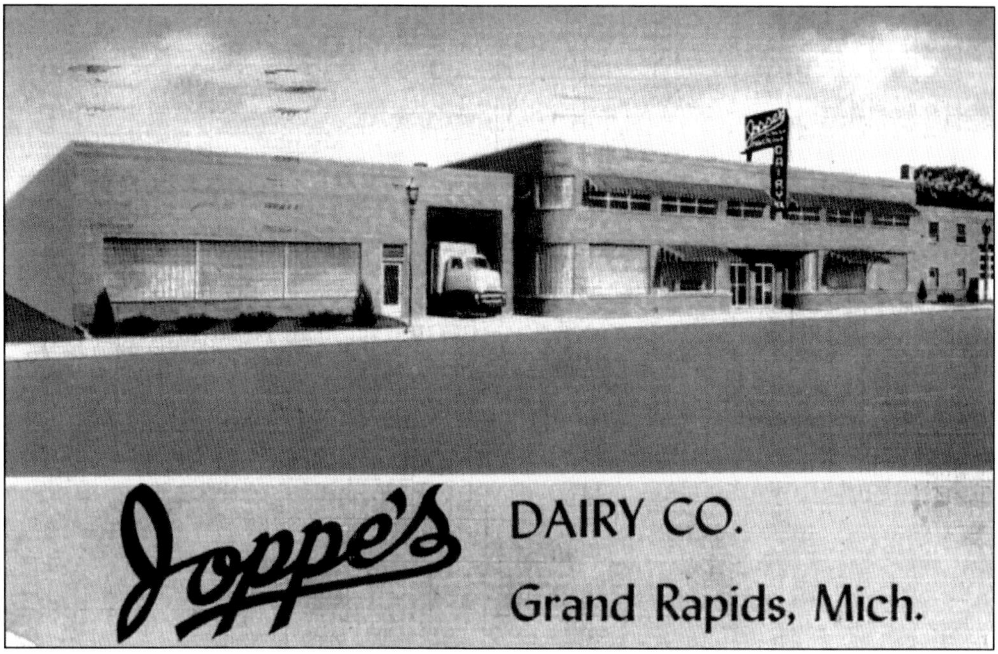

A commercial card sent out in February 1952 commemorates the opening of the new Joppe Dairy, located on Division Avenue just north of Wealthy Street. The dairy continued in business until about 1970. The building still stands, though now put to other uses.

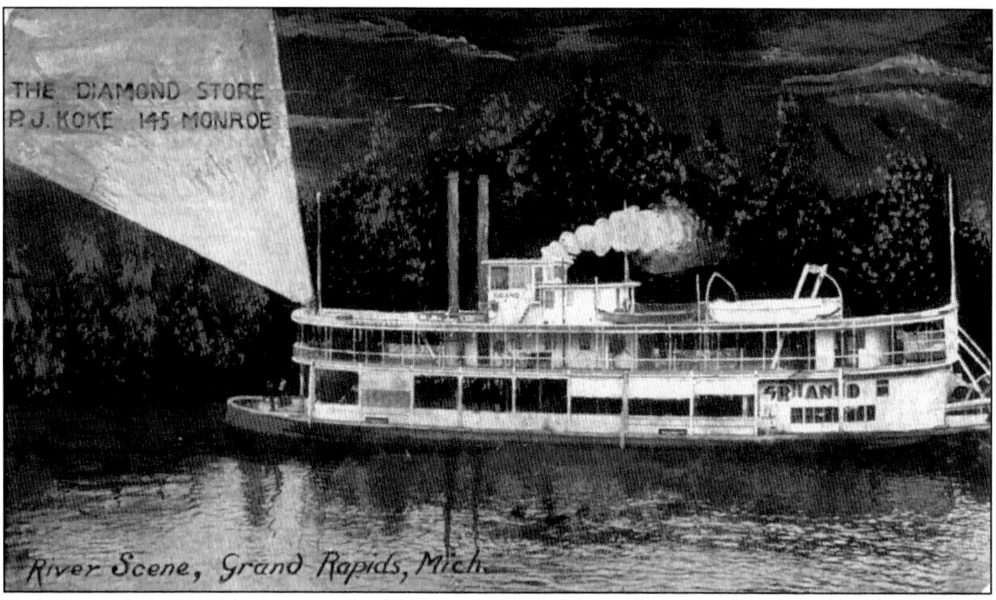

This is an advertising card sent out to promote the Diamond Store, a jeweler located on Monroe Avenue, around 1905. This style of card, bearing an exaggerated, often humorous image, became popular at this time and demonstrates the effectiveness of the postcard as an inexpensive commercial advertising device. This image is only partly imagined. The ship depicted is the *Grand*, one of the last two commercial passenger vessels that ran the Grand River between Grand Rapids and Spring Lake between 1905 and 1908.

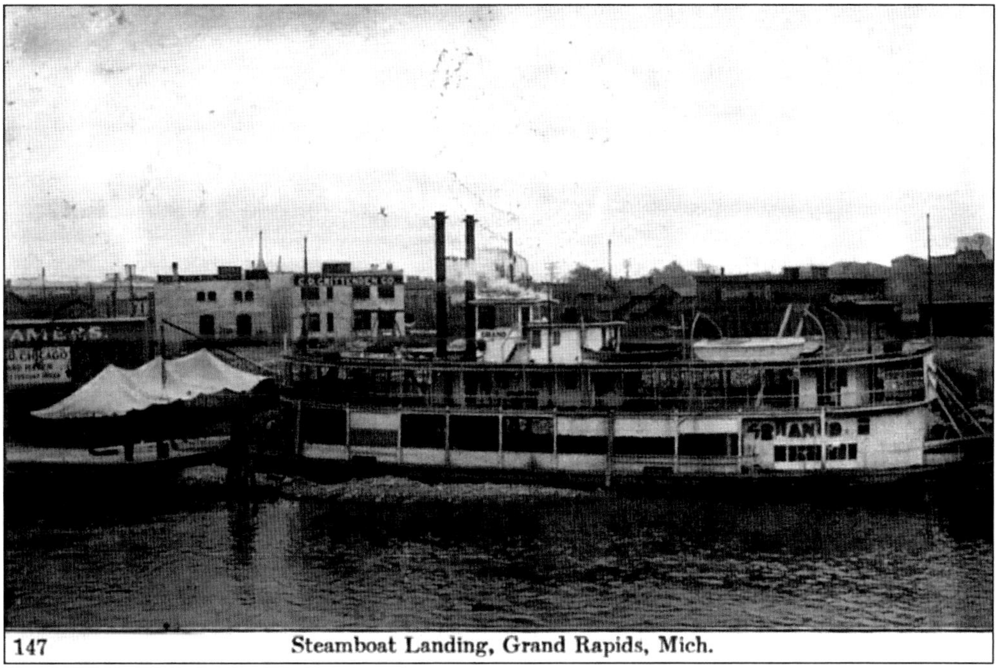

Another view of the steamship *Grand*, from about 1908, shows a landing at Fulton Street on the river. This card was sent to a rural retailer by the Powers and Walker Casket Company, announcing the arrival of its salesman, a Mr. Chappell, 10 days hence.

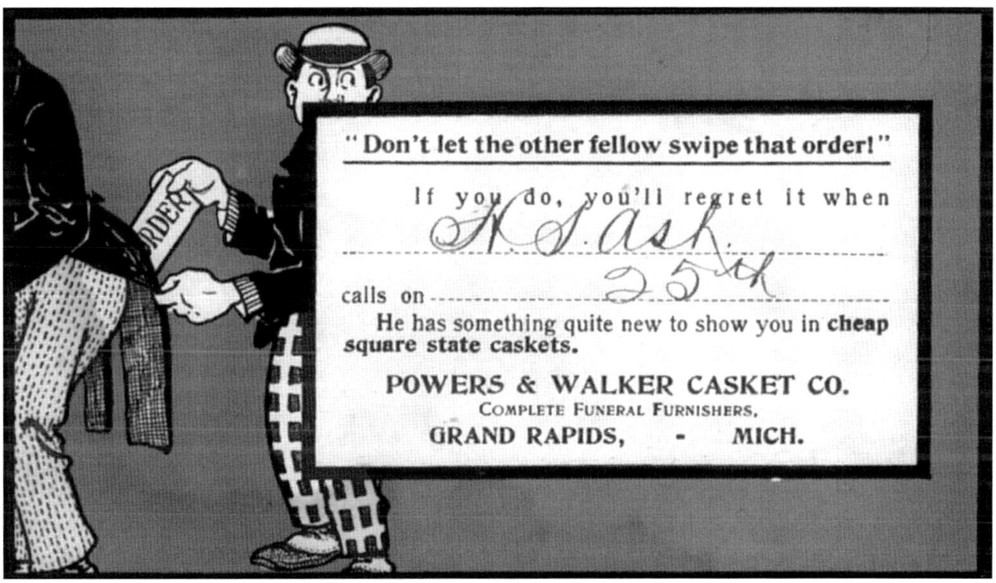

Another mailing by the Powers and Walker Casket Company alerts a customer of the impending arrival of the company representative. Unlike the previous card, which had a conventional picture-postcard appearance, this card was intended only for a business purpose.

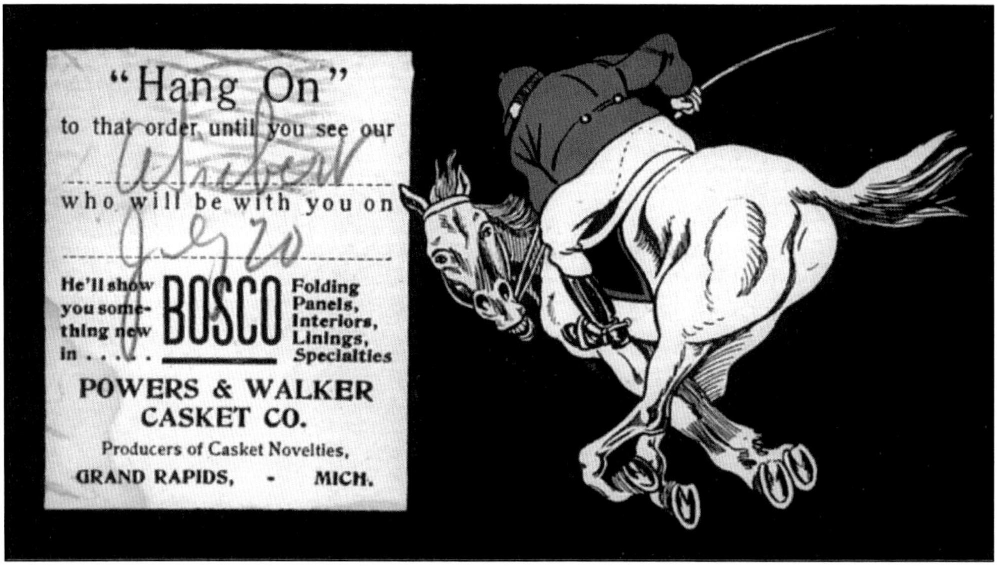

Yet another will call card sent by Powers and Walker asks the recipient to "hang on" to its orders until the salesman arrived. This and the previous card, both mailed in 1903, strongly resemble the non-postcard Victorian trade cards that were very widely used to publicize and promote businesses before the advent of the mailable postcard.

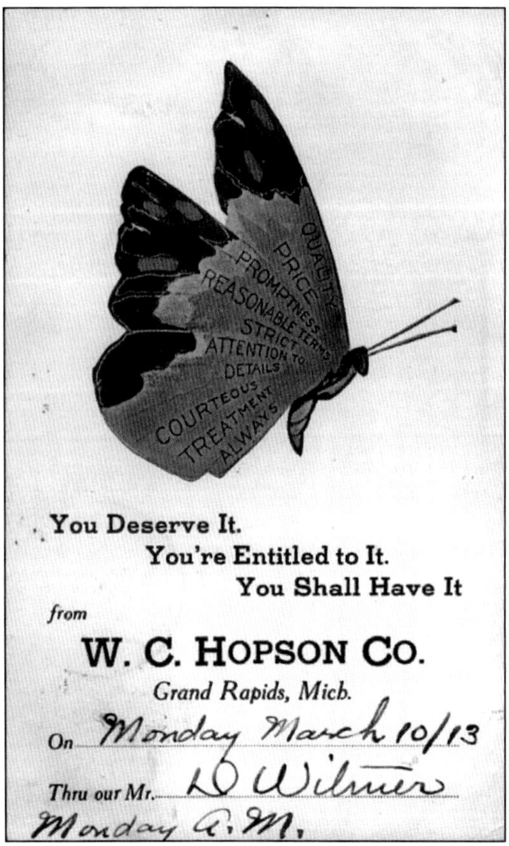

The W. C. Hopson Company, local manufacturers of sheet metal products, sent out this advance announcement of the arrival of its salesman in 1913.

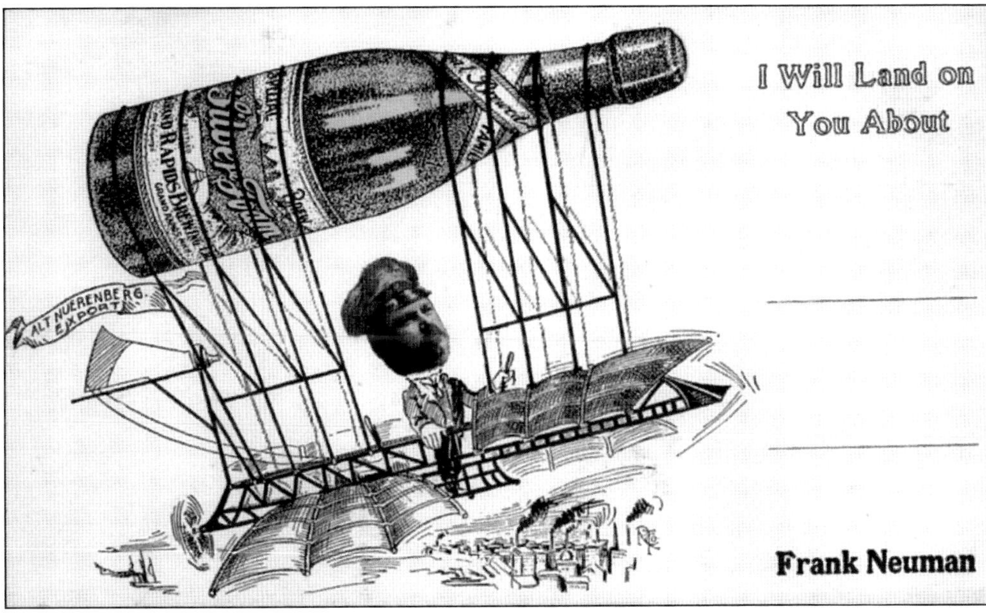

The Grand Rapids Brewing Company, local brewers of Silver Foam beer and other products, produced this card in about 1905. It is unique in that it carries not only the printed name of the salesman, but also his photographic portrait.

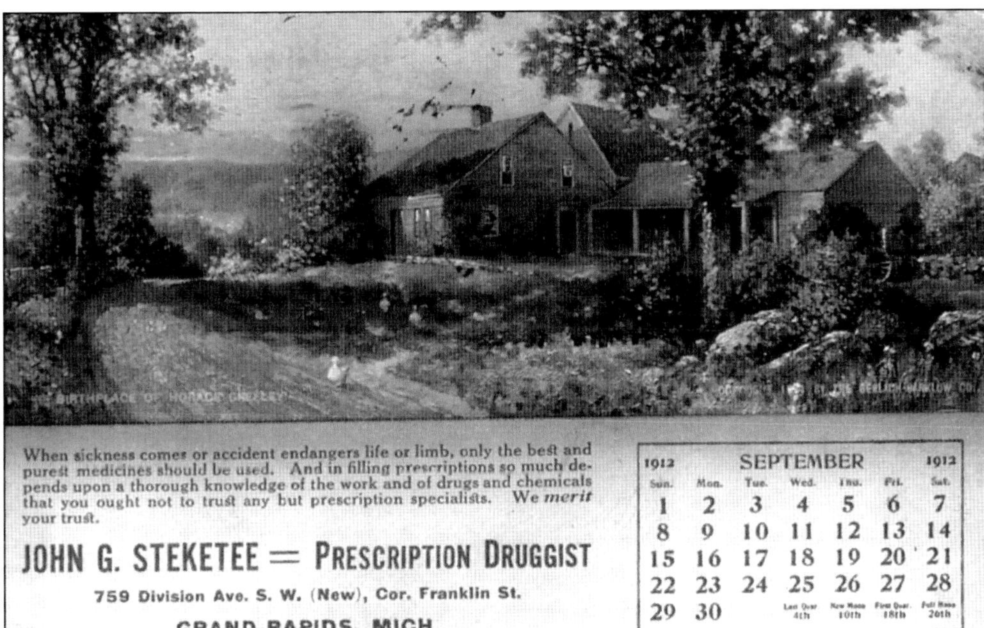

This card, preprinted and sold in bulk to a local druggist and then reprinted with his name and address, is typical of many from the era when it was mailed, in 1912. The image has no local importance, but the card, which strongly resembles other sales promotional devices such as blotters and trade cards, carries a calendar for use by the customer, thereby making it more likely that the recipient will hang on to it when it is received.

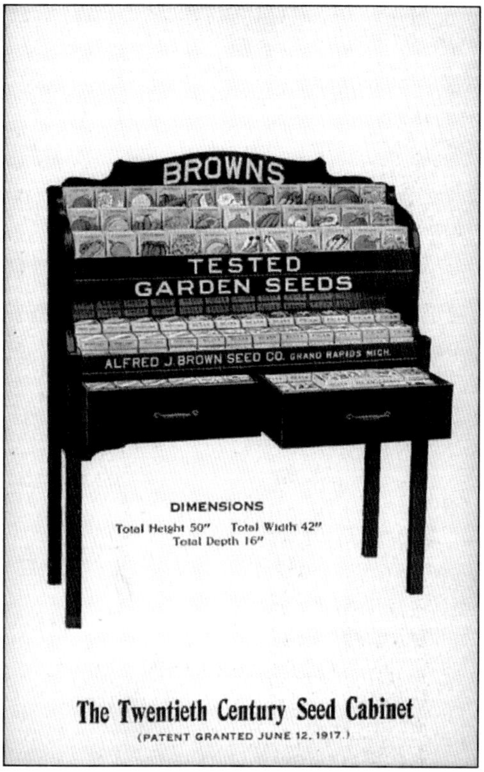

The Alfred Brown Seed Company, purveyors of garden seeds and supplies, sent out this will call card in 1917. This card was printed locally and shows the retail customer to whom it was mailed the newly patented "seed cabinet" offered by the company to market its product.

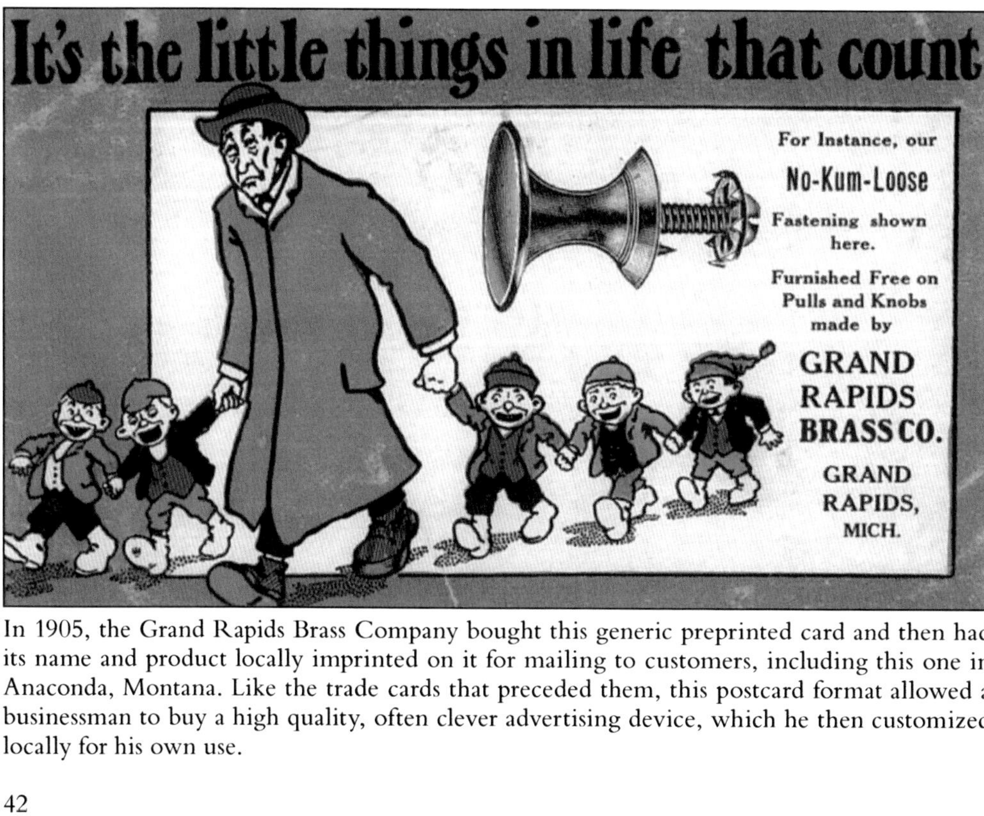

In 1905, the Grand Rapids Brass Company bought this generic preprinted card and then had its name and product locally imprinted on it for mailing to customers, including this one in Anaconda, Montana. Like the trade cards that preceded them, this postcard format allowed a businessman to buy a high quality, often clever advertising device, which he then customized locally for his own use.

This image from about 1910 is typical of the many advertising images used at that time and before, this time for the Fox Typewriter Company, located at the time on the west bank of the Grand River in downtown Grand Rapids.

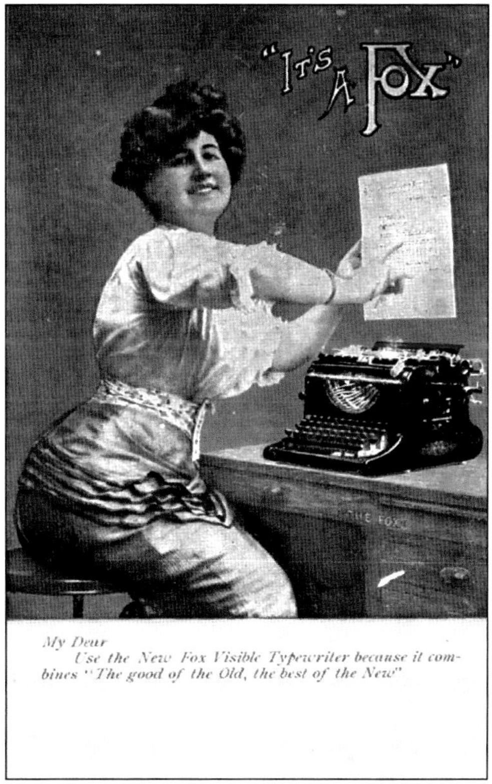

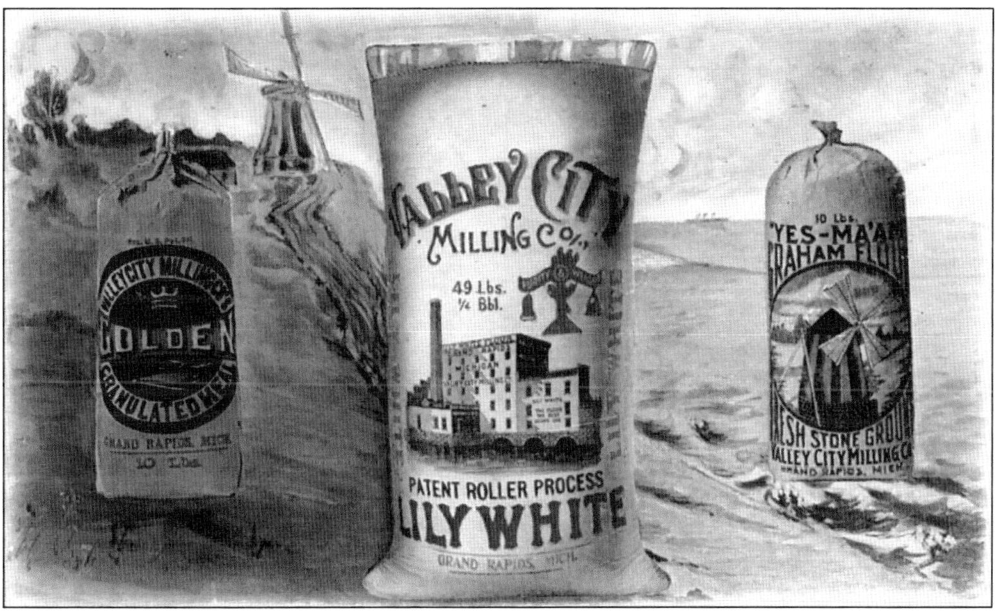

Unlike some of the other commercial postcards of this time, this card from the Valley City Milling Company, dated 1915, shows no hesitation in using the card to depict its commercial product, Lily White Flour. The card was mailed to a rural retail customers, soliciting sales.

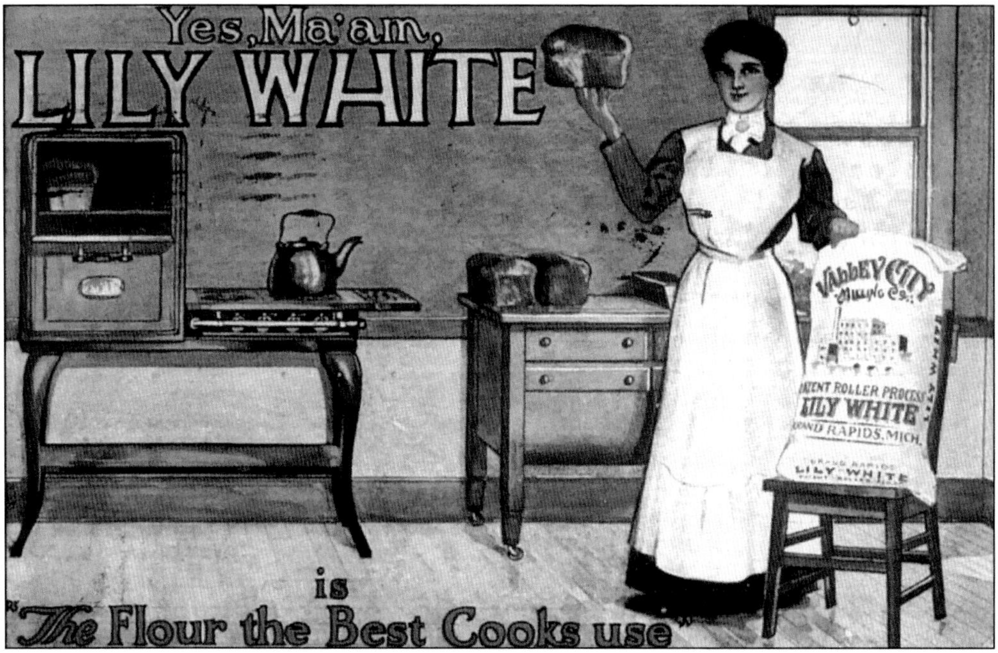

Another mailing by the Valley City Milling Company, this time is visually extolling the domestic use of its flour. This card was not intended for use in the wholesale trade, but rather was mailed to a housewife to promote her personal use of the product.

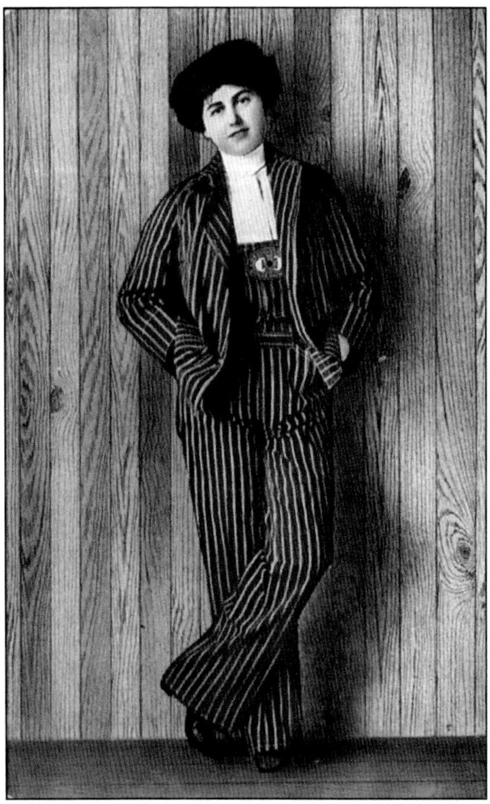

This striking and unusual commercial postcard was sent out by the Ideal Clothing Company, local manufacturers of work clothing, in 1911. The advertising image of the company's work trousers being worn by a woman, for whom they were never intended, must have attracted some attention.

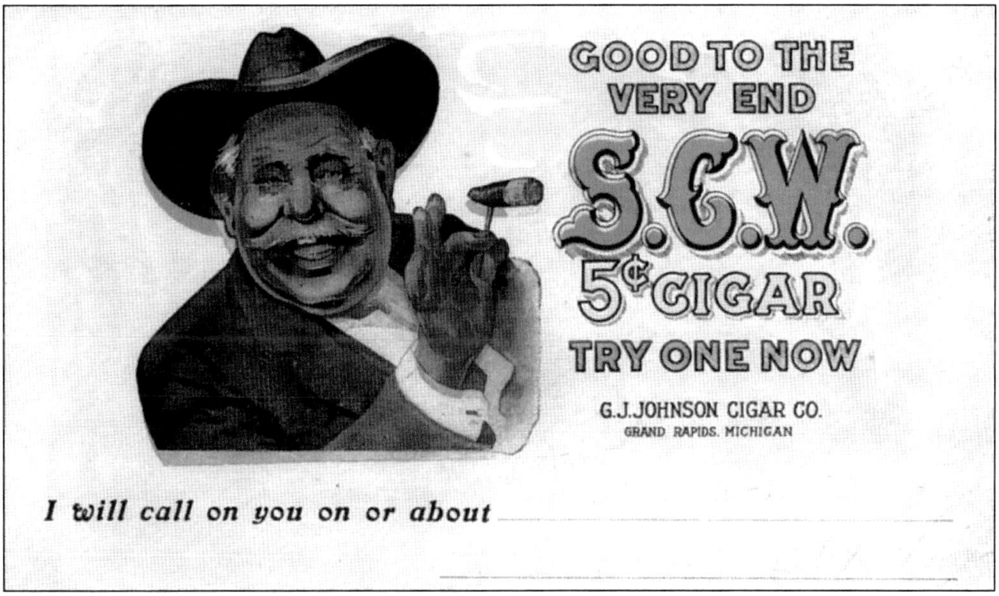

This rare will call postcard was sent out by the G. J. Johnson Cigar Company, a large local wholesale manufacturer of cigars, in 1909. This card was actually issued (and printed with postage) in blank by the post office and then later printed with the company image on the back. Although the blank on the front of the card was not filled in, its intended use to was to announce the impending arrival of the company salesman.

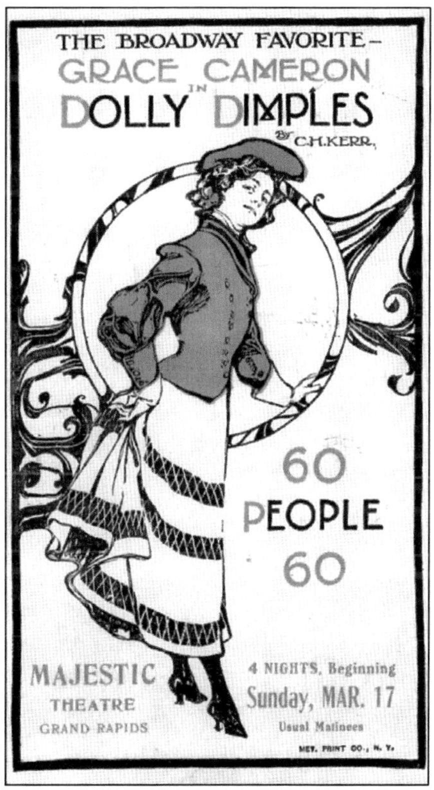

In about 1905, actress Grace Cameron and her company of 60 other actors came to the newly opened Majestic Theater in Grand Rapids to perform for four nights only. This card, doubtless preprinted and provided to the local management by Cameron's agents (as they did at every stop on the tour), allowed the local promoter to have it imprinted with the local theater and performance dates, and then mailed to prospective patrons.

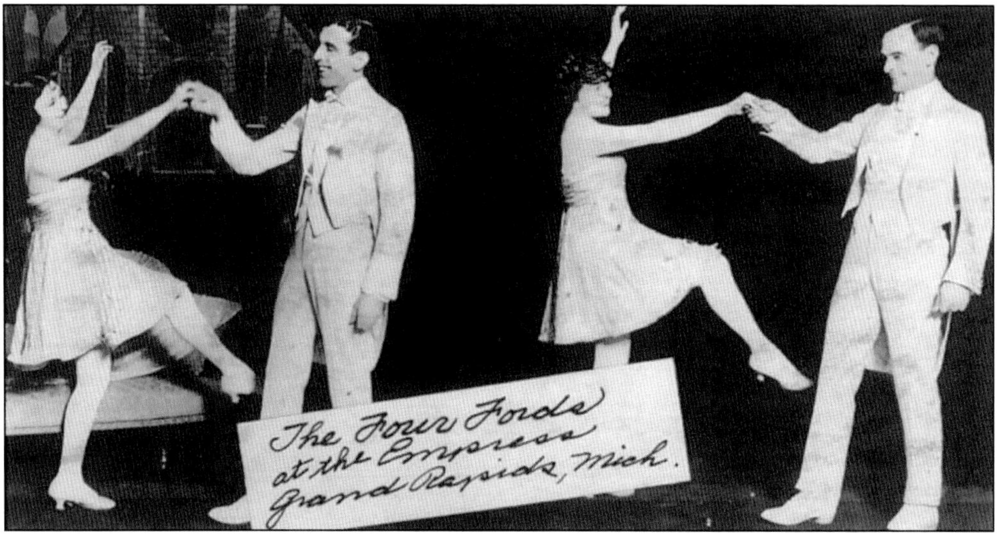

Like the previous card, this real-photo postcard from around 1910 was mailed out to promote a troupe of entertainers that was appearing at the Empress Theater, a local vaudeville house located on Pearl Street, just east of Monroe Avenue.

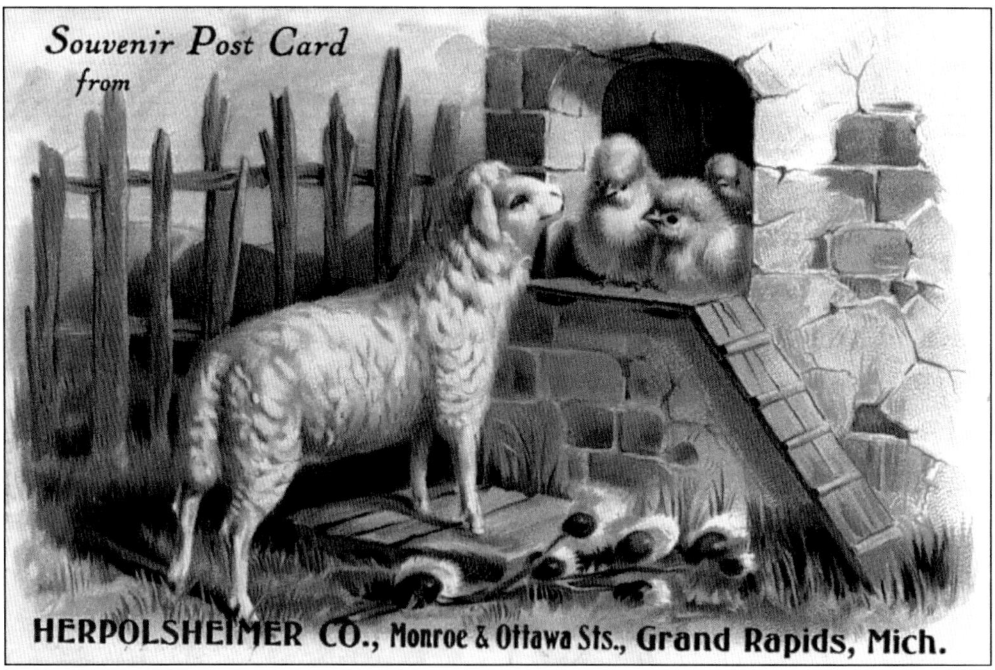

Some of the early commercial postcards were identical to the earlier trade cards so common in the 1890s, except that these could be mailed. This card and the following, produced by local dry goods retailer the Herpolsheimer Company, was distributed to store customers as a "souvenir post card."

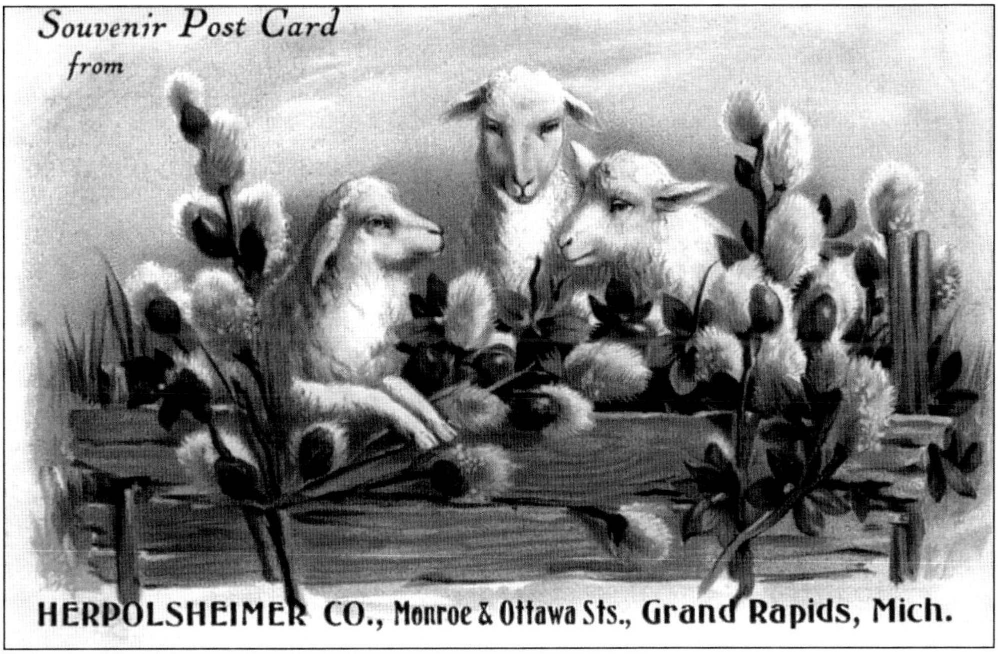

These commercial cards were issued in a progressive series in the same way many trade cards had been issued, designed to promote return trips by the customer to the store. The customer was then free to keep or send the card, thereby further promoting the Herpolsheimer business.

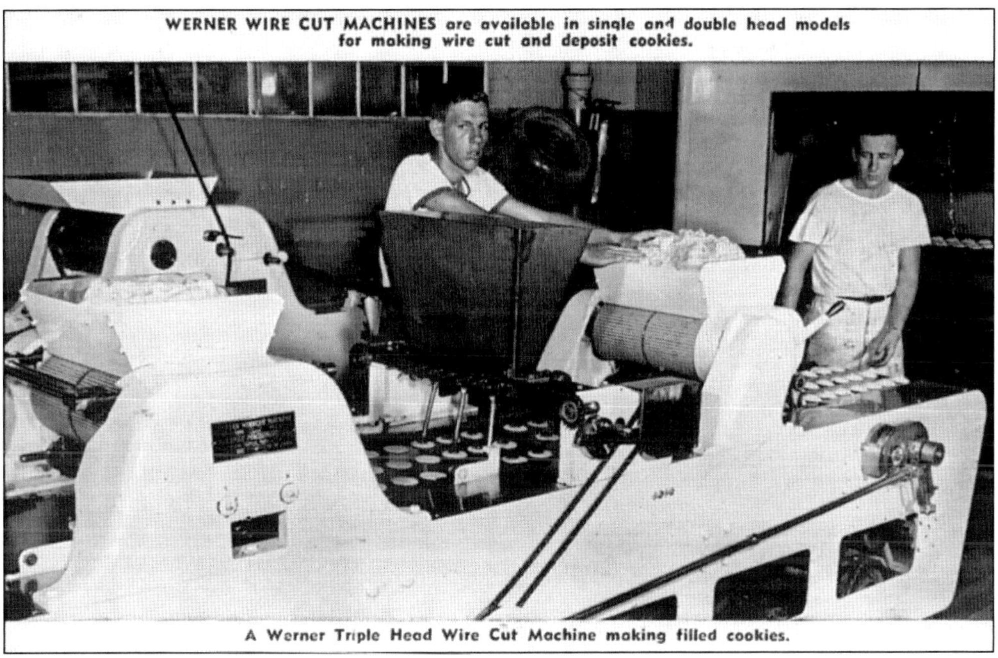

Though the commercial and advertising use of the postcard fizzled in the decades after World War I, as new, more effective forms of advertising developed, a few examples of this inexpensive mode of publicity persisted. This card, sent out by the Werner Machinery Company in 1950, promoted its mechanized cookie forming machines.

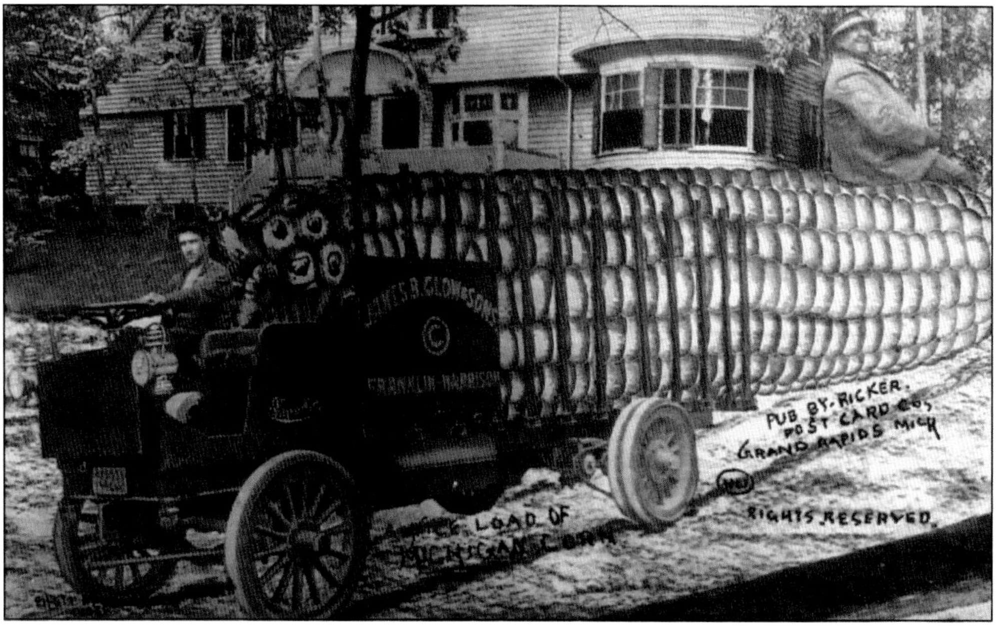

Another fine and rare example of the exaggeration/promotional postcard genre, this card was published by the local Ricker Postcard Company in about 1910.

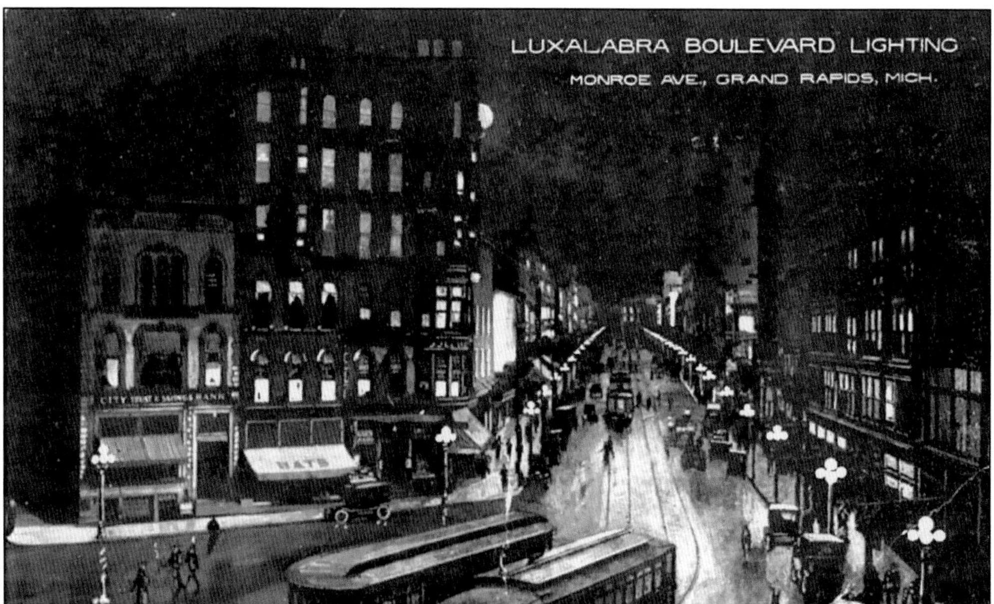

This postcard, published by the A. B. Knowlson Coal Company of Grand Rapids, is a commercial mailing card from about 1914. The image is a night view looking up Monroe Avenue and featuring the new Luxalabra streetlights recently installed to light the downtown streets.

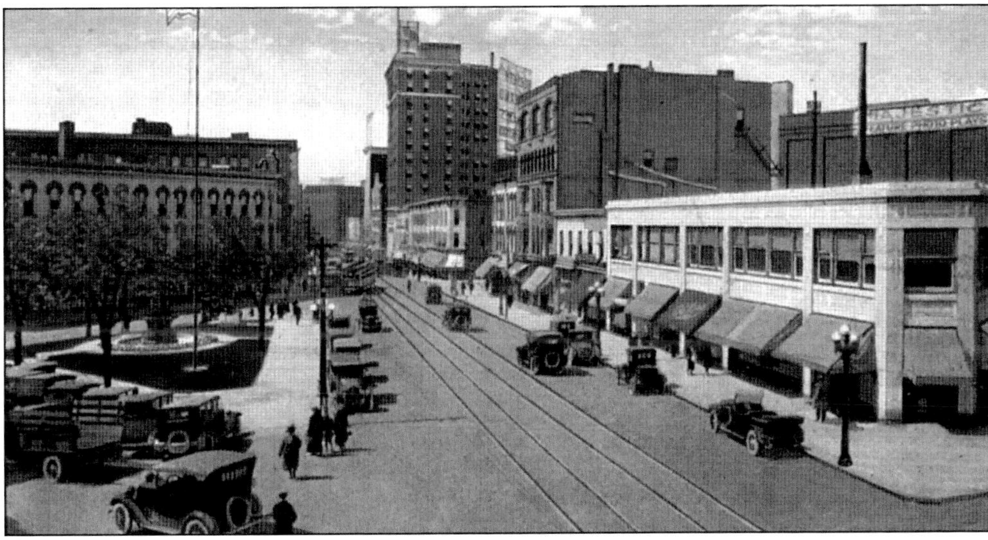

This is a 1923 view looking northwest down Monroe Avenue. The wide street, with angled parking and streetcar tracks, is visible.

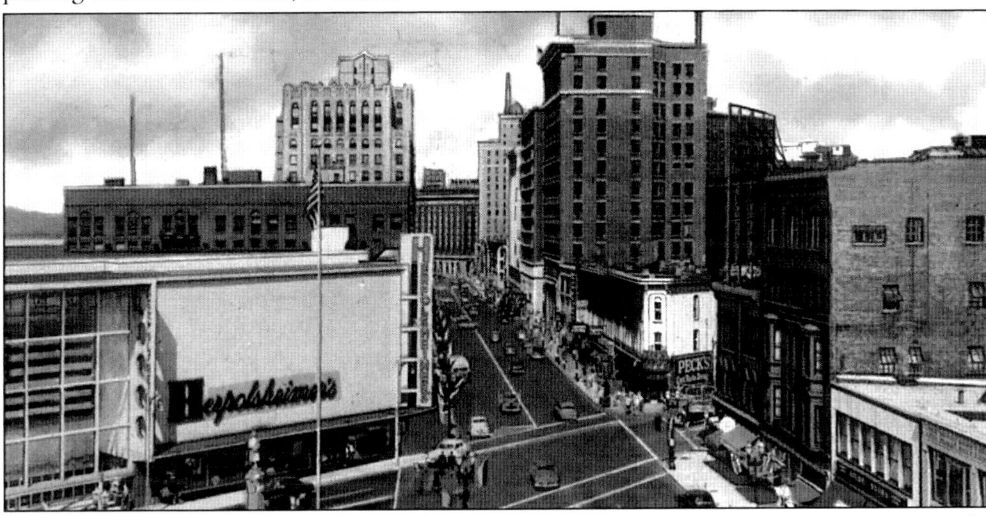

A later view of Monroe Avenue, from 1959, taken from approximately the same spot as the previous card (probably the upper stories of the Grand Rapids Press Building), shows a changed downtown but with many of the same features as 36 years earlier. The large building at the center of both views is the Peoples Building, originally the Grand Rapids Savings Bank, built around 1915. The new Herpolsheimber Store is also visible, opened in 1951, with the top of the Michigan National Bank Building, built in 1926, visible beyond it. Not all of the promotional postcard activity in the growing city was purely commercial. Beginning in the late 1840s, a movement directed at the display of agricultural products and the means of their production was organized and resulted in a number of annual "fairs" being held at various locations around the city. Early efforts at these fairs were sporadic and were initially entirely agricultural, but by the beginning of the 20th century, the West Michigan Fair had become an annual event, held on a fairgrounds just north of the city at Comstock Park. These fairs offered the usual variety of farm animals and produce but also came to include amusements to attract a large share of the local population. The promotion of local annual fairs made successful use of flyers, buttons, and other types of printed ephemera, as these postcards attest.

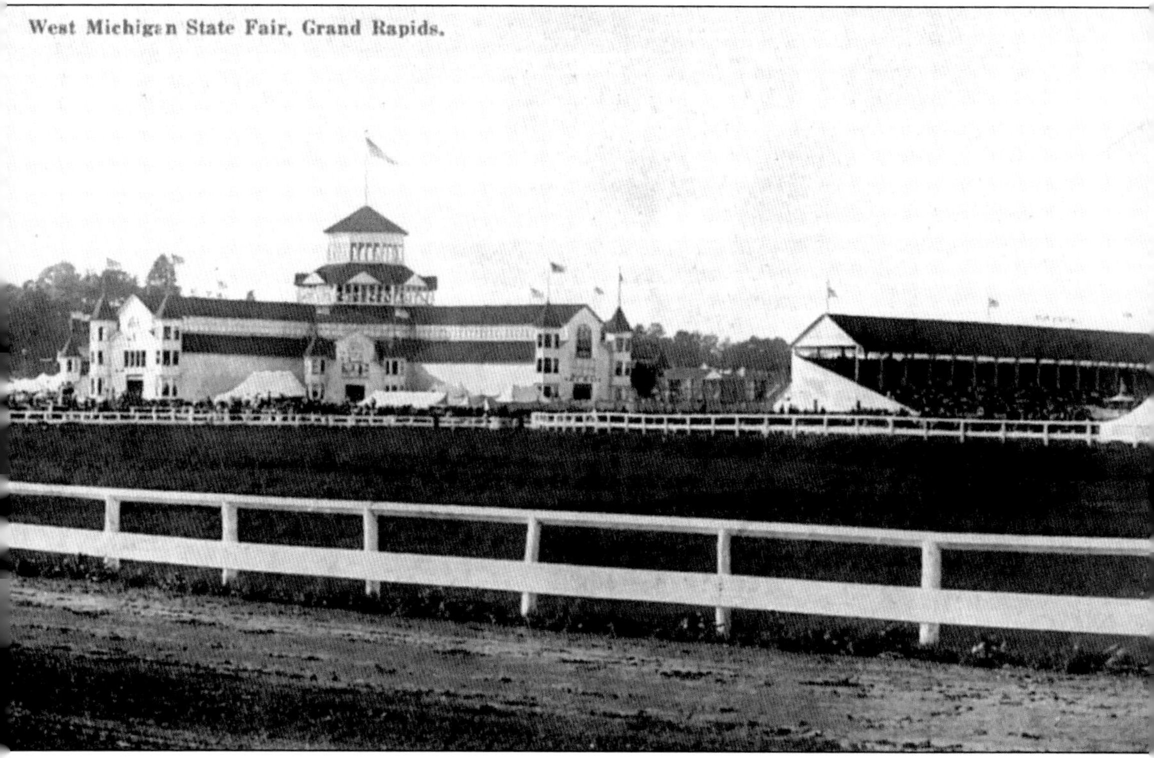

This double postcard from about 1908 provides a panoramic view of the fairgrounds, including the attractive grandstand built at the side of the racetrack where horses in harness were raced. At the right is a balloon whose ascension would have been a much-attended scheduled attraction.

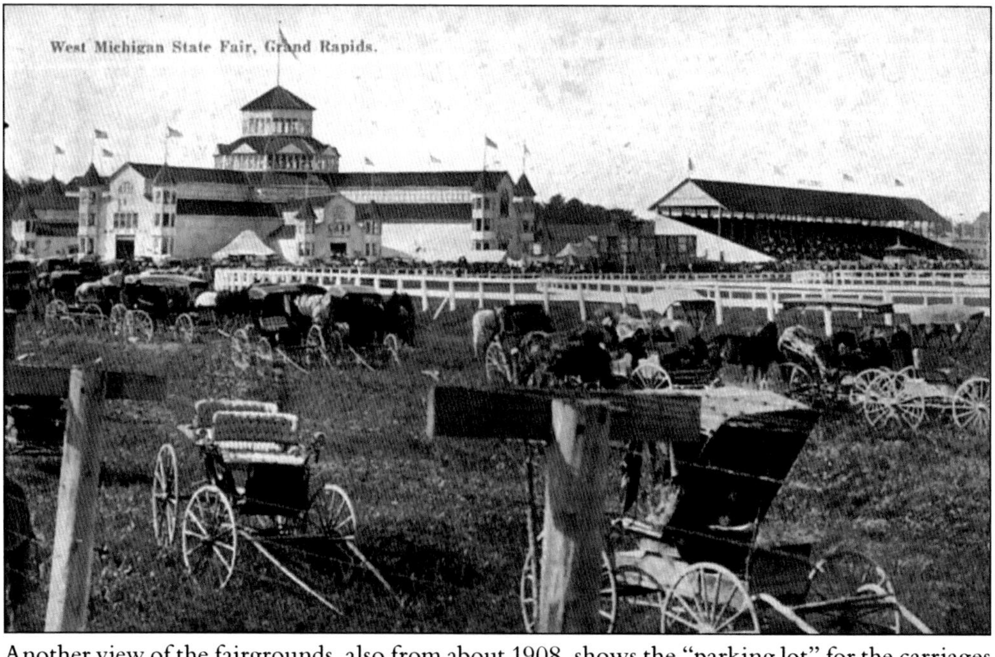

Another view of the fairgrounds, also from about 1908, shows the "parking lot" for the carriages of attendees.

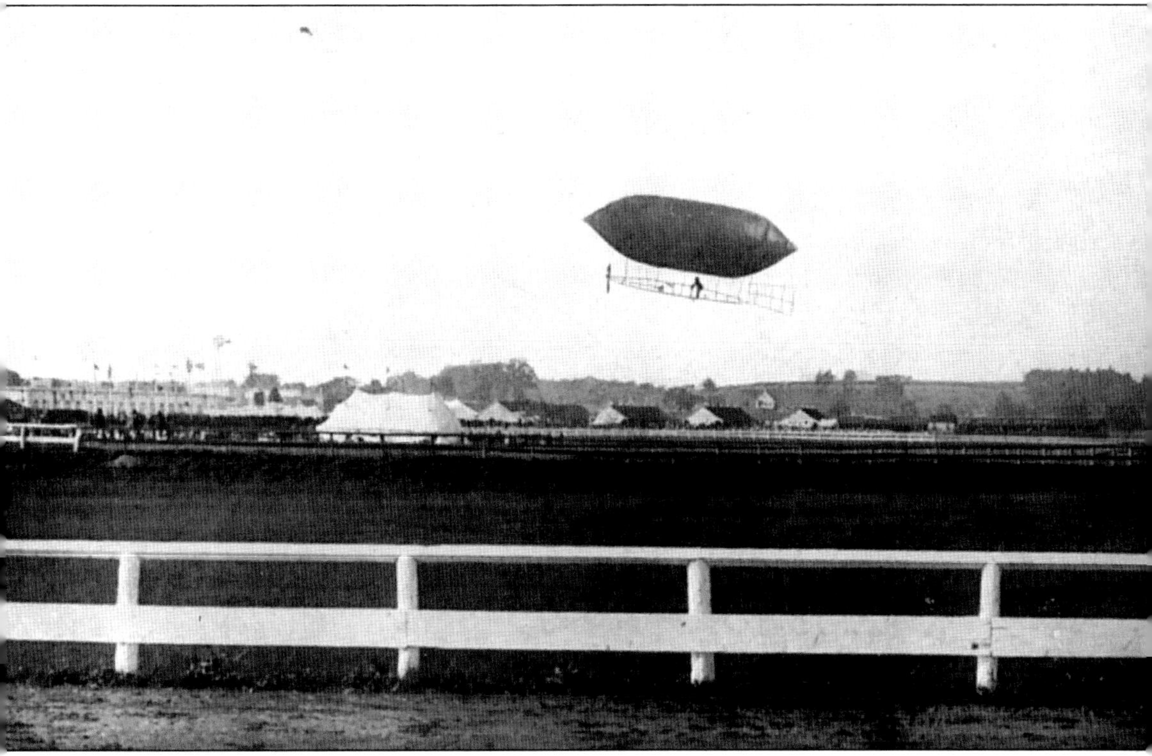

The balloon is powered by a bicycle-type device ridden by the man just visible below the balloon itself.

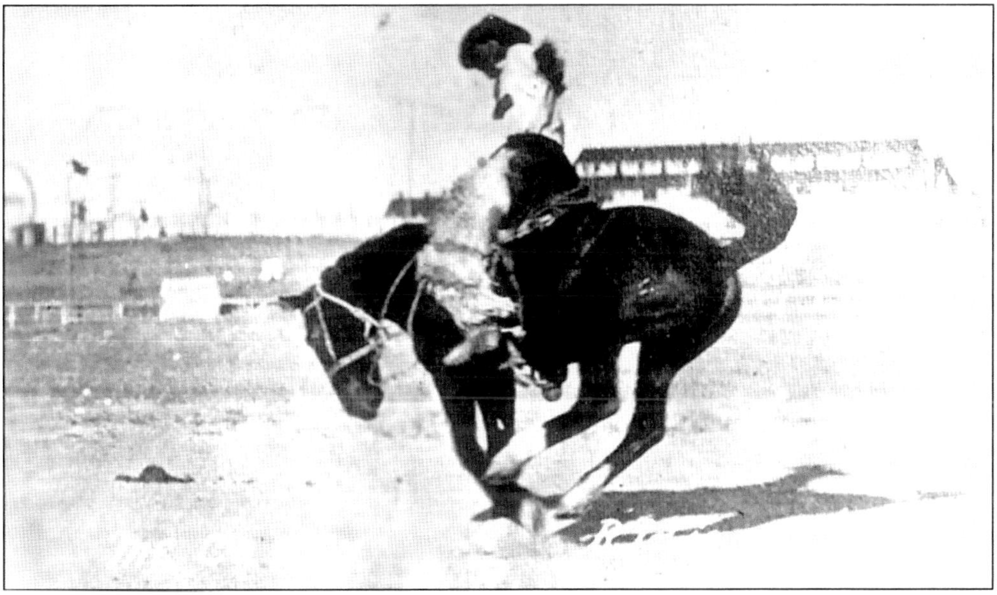

As the character of the fair changed over the years, professional performers such as this rodeo rider replaced harness racing and other local entries. This card, a real-photo postcard, dates from the summer of 1926, late in the history of the fairgrounds. The grandstand visible in previous cards is seen here in the background.

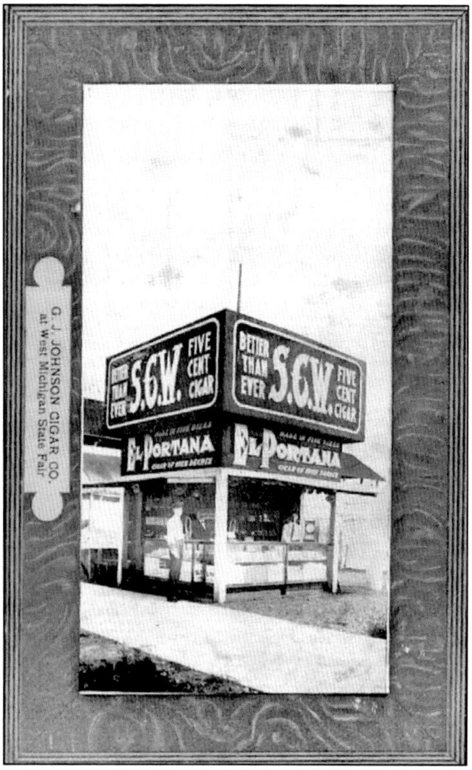

This card, one of a packet of views sold to tourists, shows the stand of the G. J. Johnson Cigar Company at the fair, from about 1910.

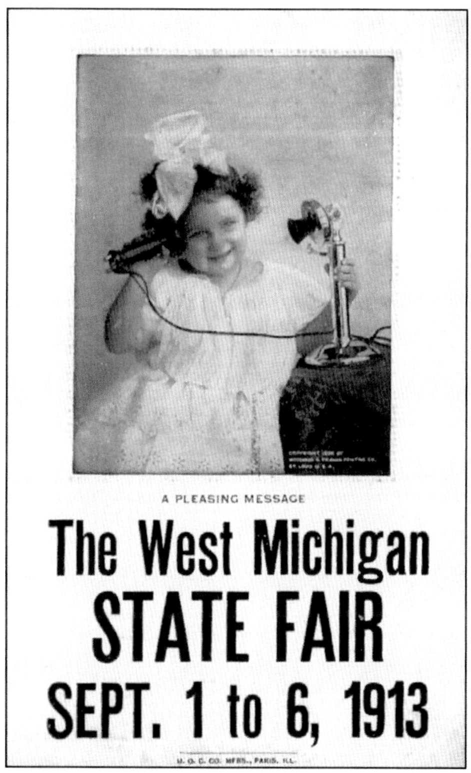

This is a publicity card produced by the fair promoters in 1913. As the city became more urban and less agricultural in the opening decades of the 20th century, fair attendance and support declined, and despite efforts to prevent it from closing, the fair was discontinued in the mid-1930s. The land was then sold off, first to a flying school and then was used briefly as a "speedrome."

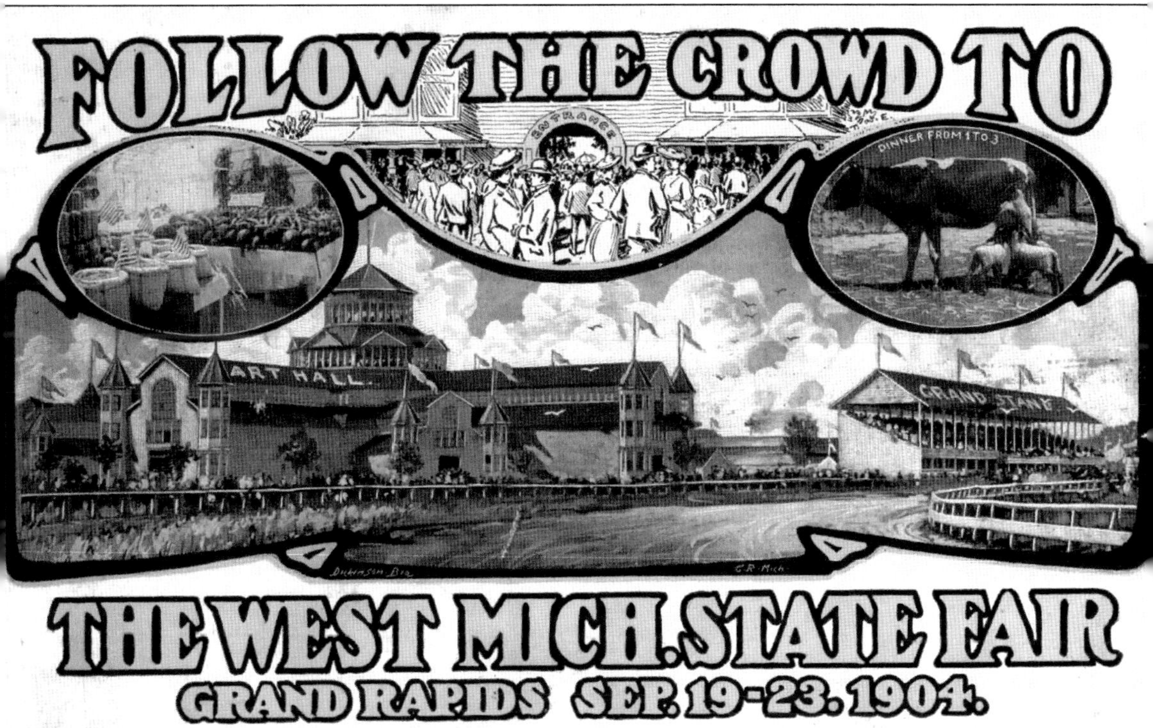

Though not really intended as a conventional postcard, this very rare handbill promoting the fair in 1904 was actually addressed and mailed as such to a friend in Elbridge, Missouri. Produced and printed locally by the Dickinson Brothers Company, the card depicts the grandstand and display halls that were present on the Comstock Park site (approximately where the West Michigan White Caps play today) at the fair's peak in the early 1900s.

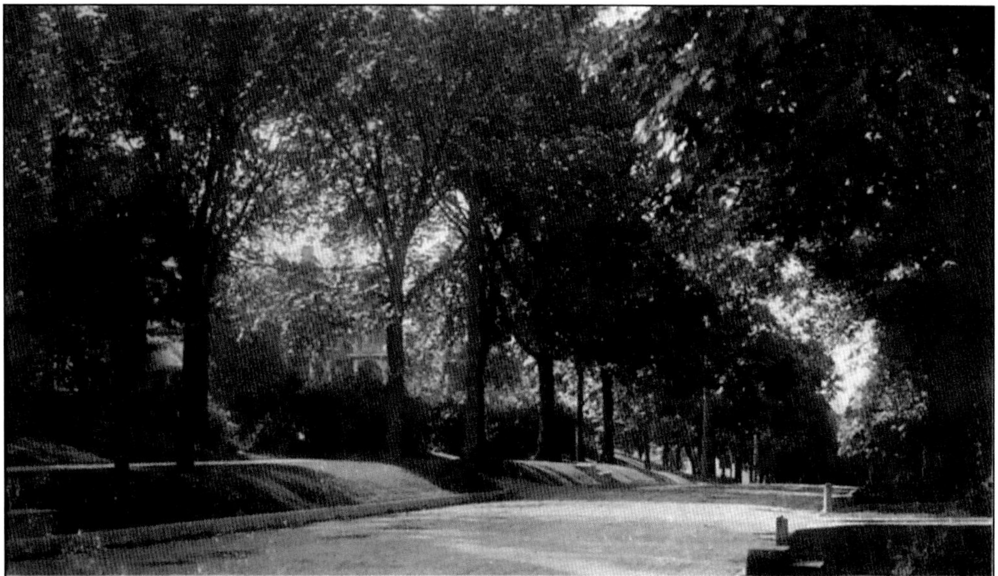

North Lafayette Street, Grand Rapids, Mich.

One of the most beautiful and historic residential areas of the city is the Hill District, located east of downtown between Jefferson Avenue and Union Street. This postcard from 1907 shows a shady North Lafayette Avenue, on which an increasing number of large and elaborate homes began to appear in the last decades of the 19th century.

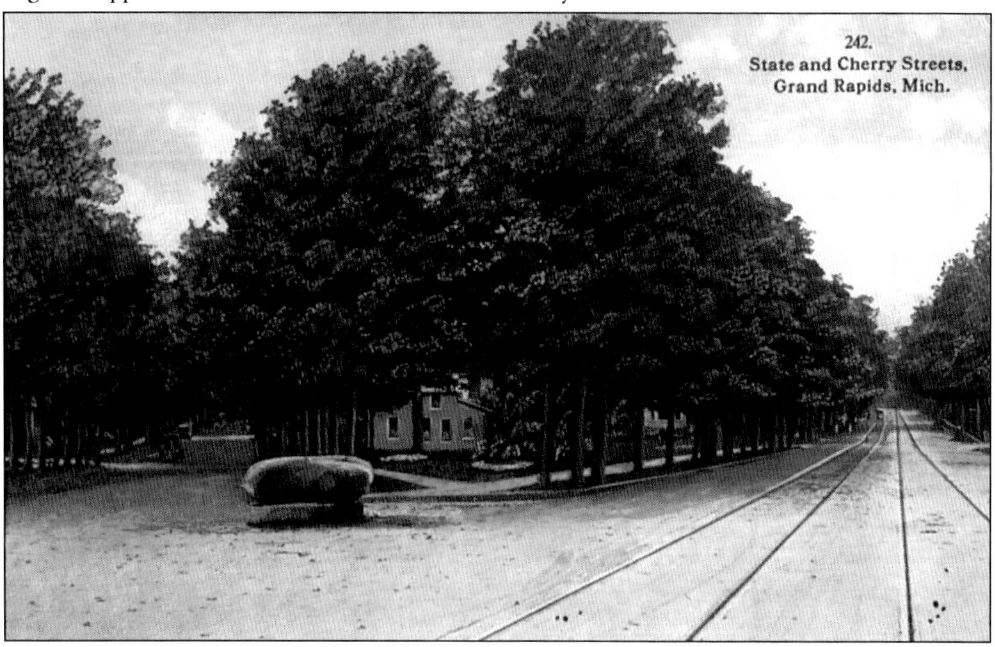

This is a 1910 view of the intersection of State (right) and Cherry Streets, looking west toward downtown. The streetcar tracks on State Street represented an important improvement to the city at this time, allowing many residents of the Hill and districts farther east easy and economical access to downtown. The area depicted later became a small commercial hub for the neighborhood, including shops and the park at the center of this photograph.

Three

The City's Neighborhoods

As is true of most cities, some of the most visible growth in Grand Rapids over the years was evident in the development and expansion of neighborhoods beginning in the late 19th century. Initially most of the population lived and worked within shouting distance of the center of the city. As the population grew and the need to create working and living spaces expanded, so too did the neighborhoods of Grand Rapids expand, both inside and outside the city limits.

Initially all of the nonurban postcard views of the city depicted only the Heritage Hill area, just east of downtown, where the homes of the elite were located. As growth continued in the early part of the 20th century, Madison Square, Easttown, and Ottawa Hills, all more modest neighborhoods in the southeast end of Grand Rapids, began to fill.

Largely vacant at first, with streets laid out on which there were no houses, the empty lots gradually filled, and each of these areas became a microcosm of the city itself, equipped with a commercial district with grocers, butchers, bakers, and dry goods shops. They usually had one or more public schools and a number of churches within an easy walk, and were frequently provided with branch banks, libraries, and post offices. Later a system of streetcars, first horse drawn and later electrified, gradually worked its way out from the center of the city and made traveling about, whether for work or other reasons, easy and relatively cheap.

The initial arrival, and later pervasive private ownership of automobiles in the 1920s brought big changes to urban and suburban neighborhoods. Streets had to be widened and household garages provided, and the former limitations on travel to accomplish household errands disappeared. Neighborhood stores, formerly a local convenience within walking distance, now competed with destination retailers like large grocers, which would draw customers from a far wider geographical area than was previously possible. Still the neighborhoods survived and, though changed, prospered as identifiable residential districts, well known to local residents today.

Many of the neighborhoods that were formed during this time have escaped serious documentation in the postcards of the day. But several of these areas were the subjects of postcards that were both sent through the mail and collected in the early 20th century.

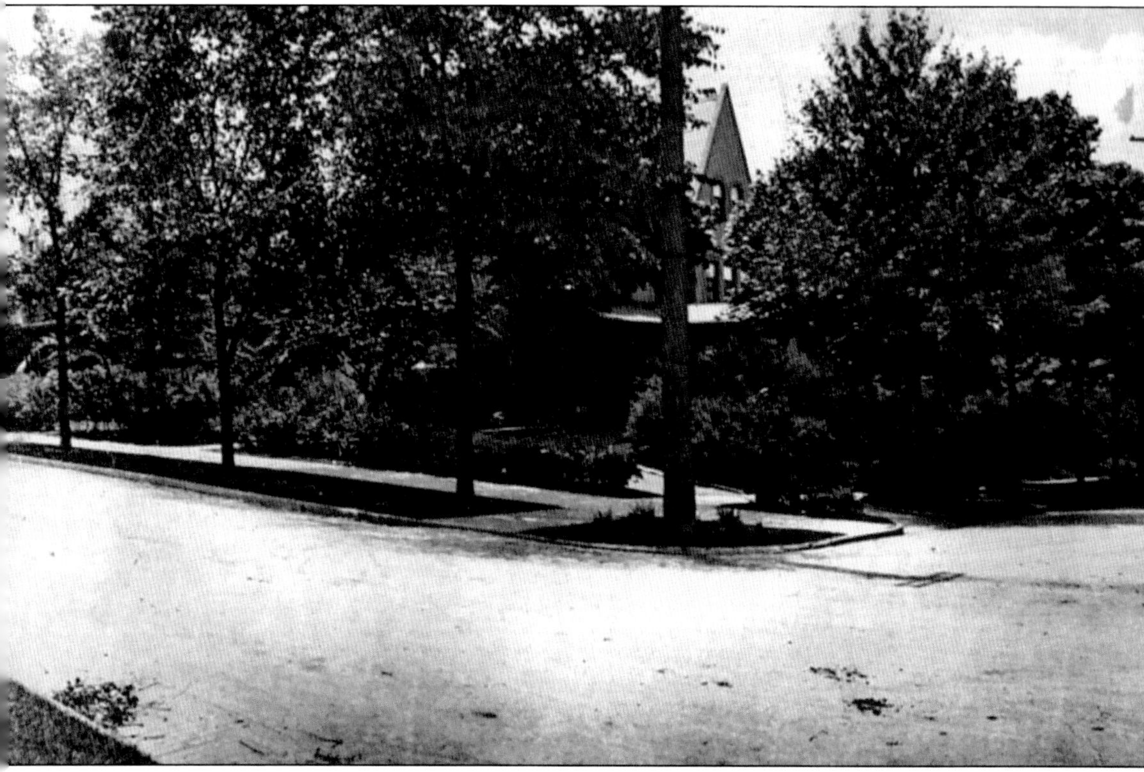

This 1908 double card depicts a summer afternoon at the corner of College Avenue and Washington Street, in the very heart of the Hill District, looking west down Washington Street. On the left is the home of Edward and Susan Blodgett Lowe, benefactors of Butterworth Hospital. This card

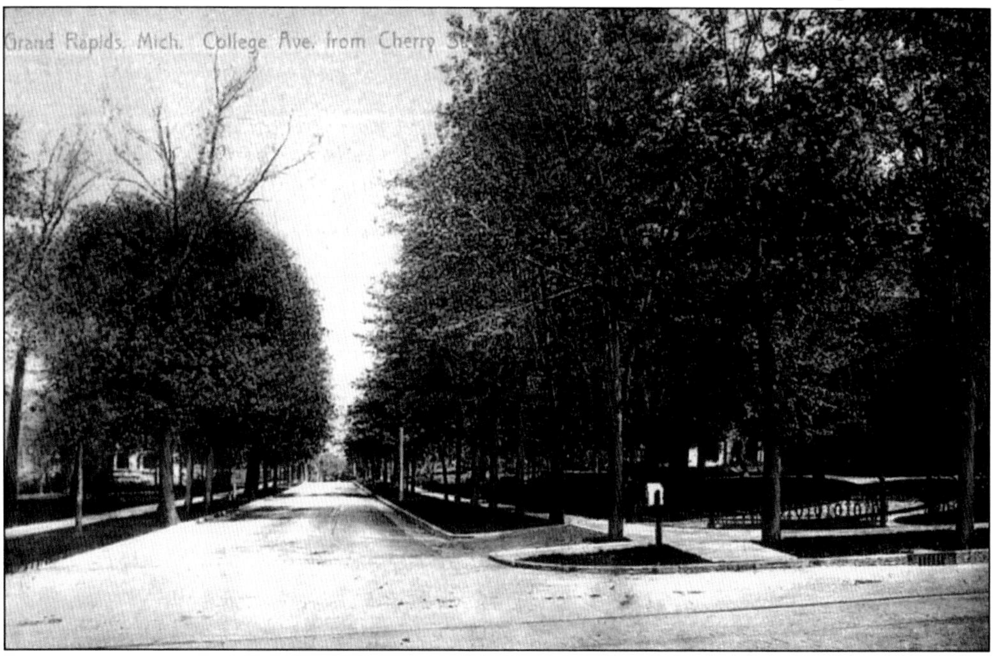

This view of College Avenue looks north from the corner of Cherry Street around 1911

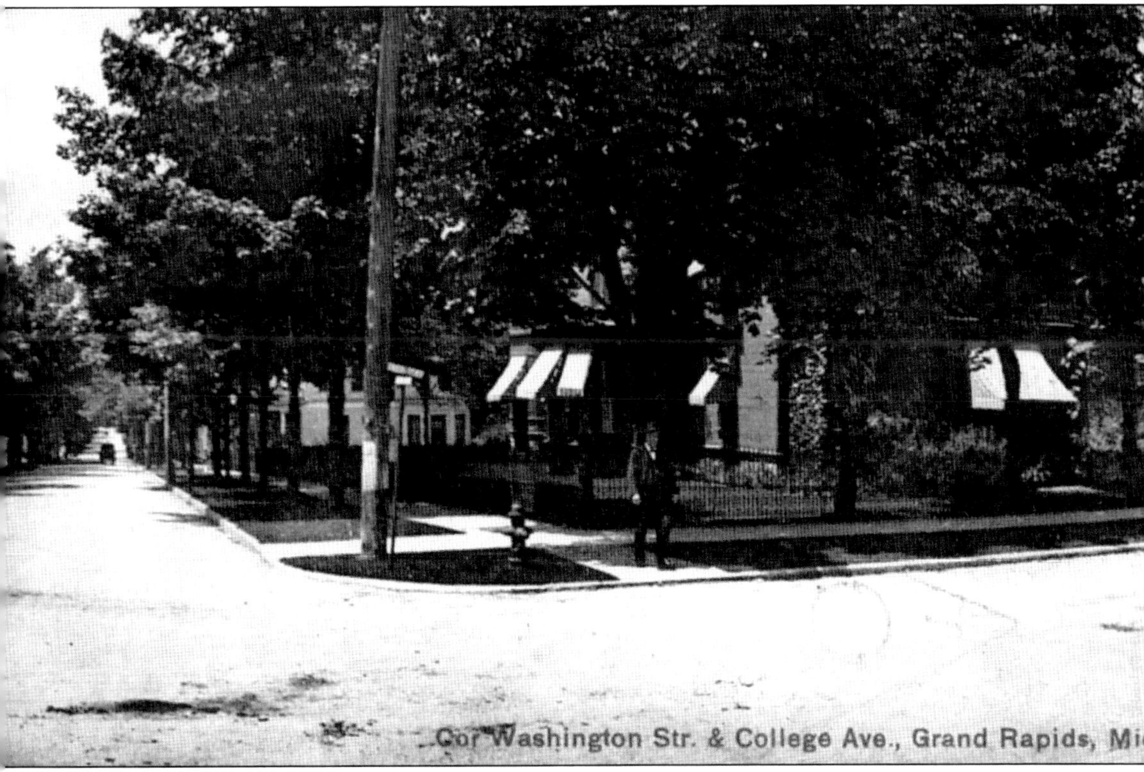

was actually sent out as an announcement of the convention of the Michigan Electric Association in advance of its convention in Grand Rapids in August 1908.

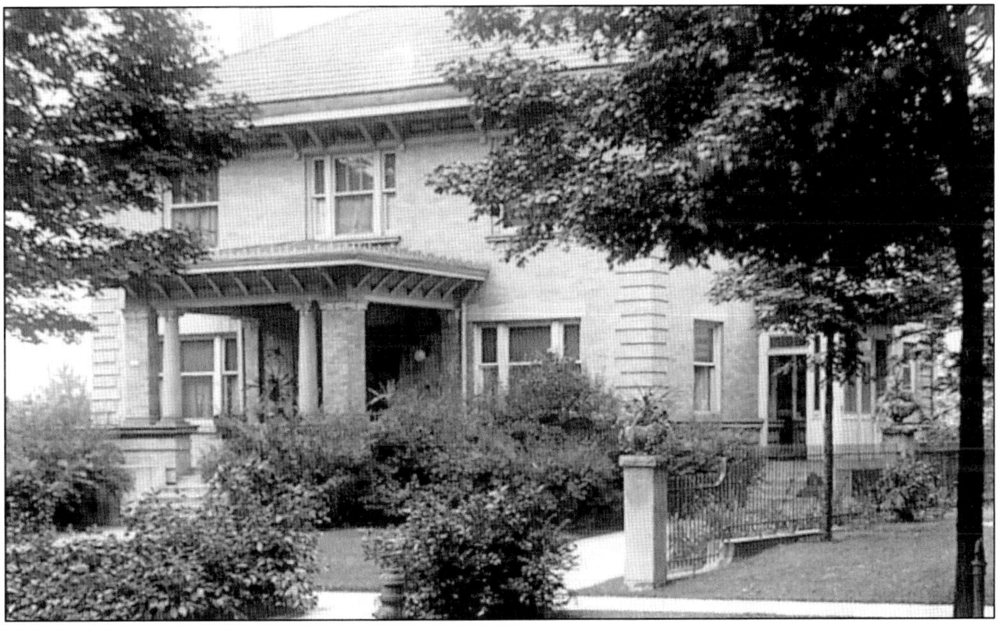

This real-photo view shows the home of Henry B. Herpolsheimer, a partner in the local dry goods firm, located at 99 Lafayette Avenue, just north of Fountain Street, from about 1910.

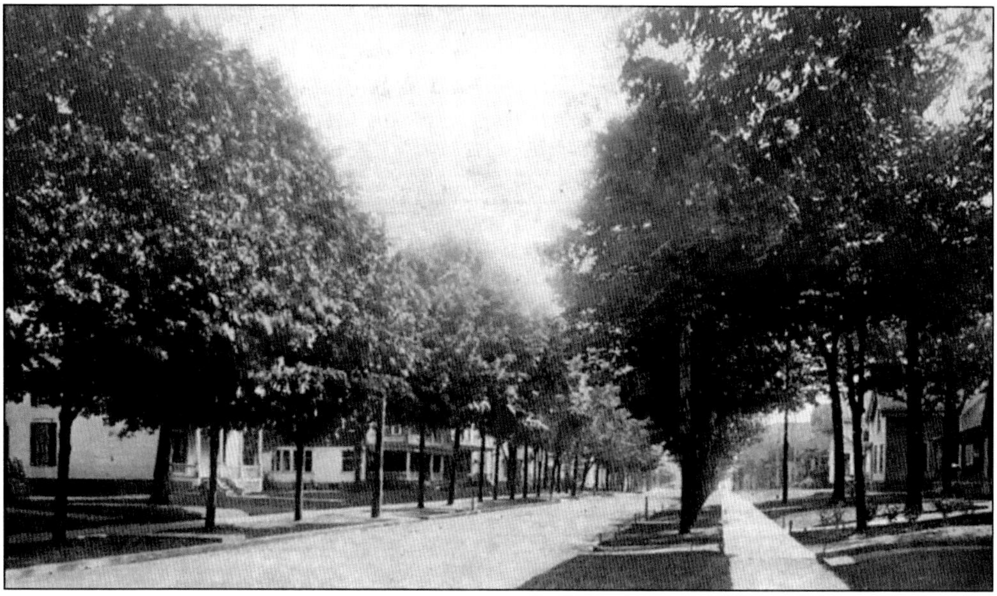

This is a picture of Crescent Street, looking west from College Avenue, from around 1910. As the comparatively small size of the trees lining the street would suggest, this part of the Hill District was newer and attracted fine but more modest homes than in other parts of the district.

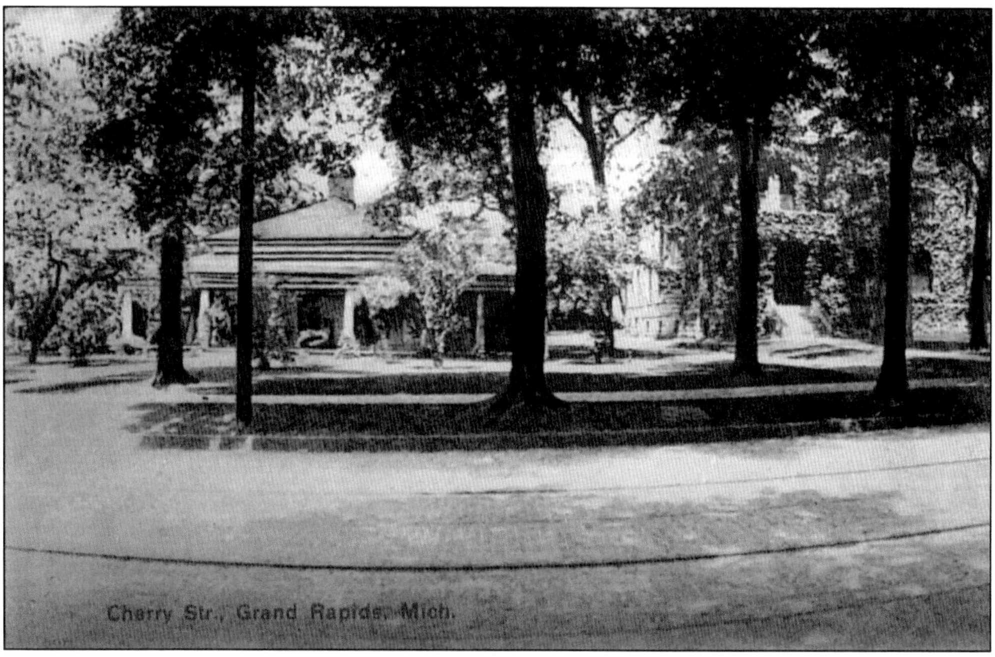

Several cards of individual homes in the Hill District were published in the early 1900s. This card, from 1907, shows the Damon Hatch House on the left and the Fox Castle at the right, located on Cherry Street, just west of College Avenue. The Hatch house, one of the first homes in the area, was built in 1845. The Fox home, built in 1888 of granite imported from Scotland, was owned by brothers Charles and E. Crofton Fox, successful local lumbermen.

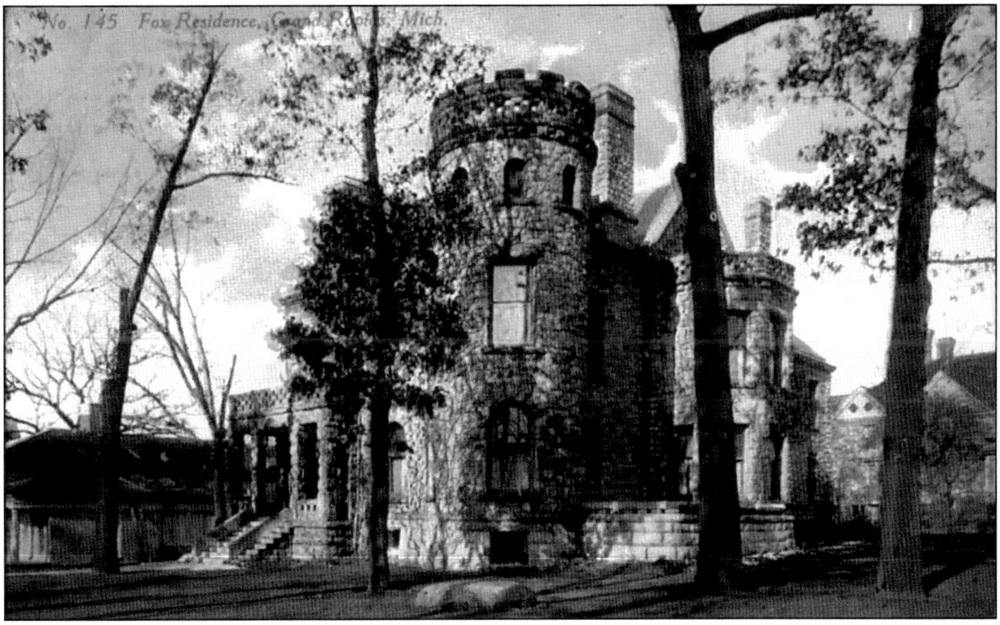

This is another view of the Fox Castle, a Norman castellated home at the corner of Cherry Street and College Avenue. Such elaborate structures were common among the wealthy in the late Victorian Age, when homes were built in a vast array of styles side by side, providing the fabulous variety of domestic architecture that characterizes the Hill District.

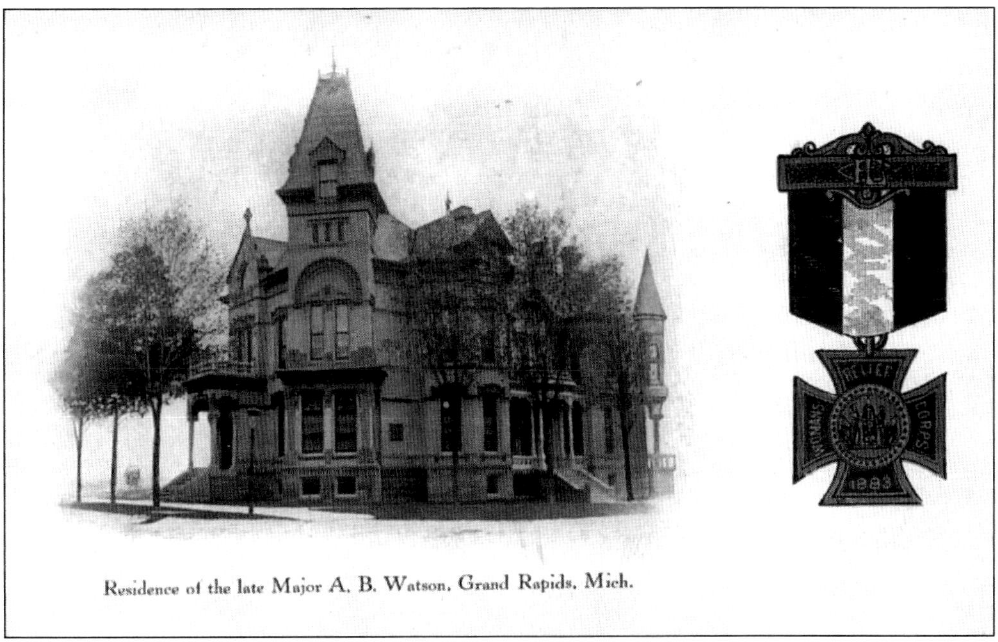

Though not actually within the Hill District proper, the home of Maj. Amasa B. Watson, at the corner of Sheldon Avenue and Fulton Street, is one of the many grand homes built in Grand Rapids at the eastern edge of the downtown area. This card was published by the Watson Company after the major's death in 1888. Major Watson was a decorated Civil War veteran and was held in high esteem in the city.

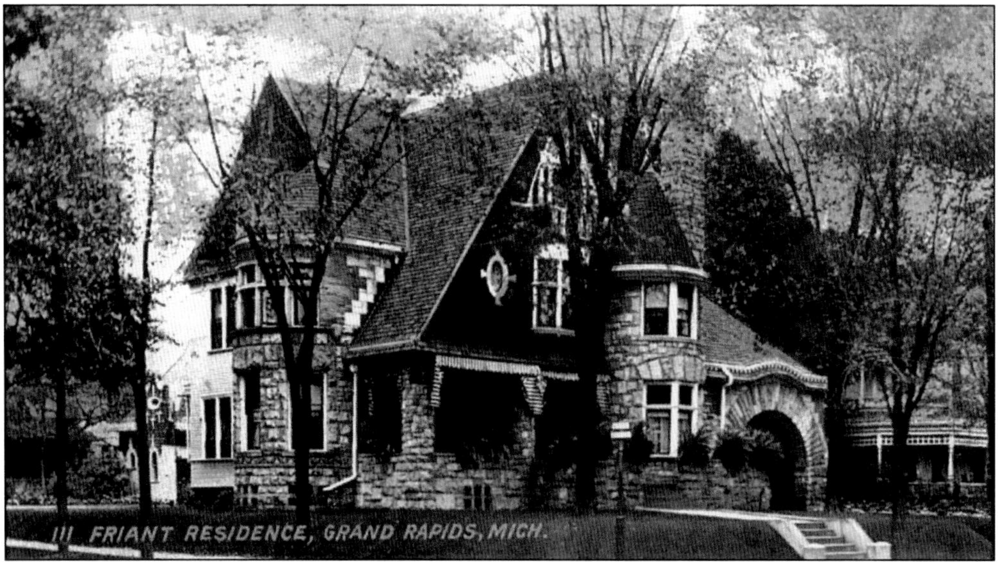

The Thomas Friant house, a beautiful example of the Queen Anne domestic style, appears at the corner of Cherry Street and Union Avenue in this postcard from 1910. This style of architecture is characterized by an often turreted, asymmetrical appearance and the use of many different building materials in construction. Friant was a successful and colorful lumberman, with lumber interests in Michigan and California. He was a business partner of local lumberman T. Steward White, whose home on Fulton Street later became the Grand Rapids Furniture Museum. White's son, novelist Stewart Edward White, modeled the hero in his very successful 1915 novel, *The Blazed Trail*, after Friant.

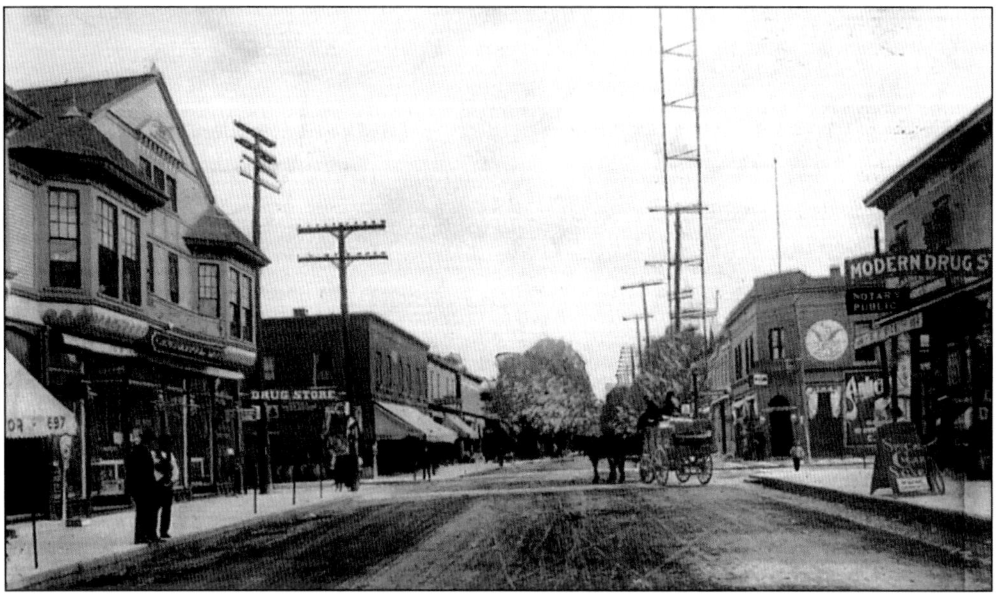

This view of the Madison Square business district, in the southeast end of Grand Rapids, is from 1910. Madison Square was the first suburban commercial area in Grand Rapids. The predominant mode of transportation at this time was horse drawn, and the street was still unpaved. The tower visible at the center is one of several dozen light towers erected at various points around the city between 1881 and 1885 in a curious early effort to light the city streets at night.

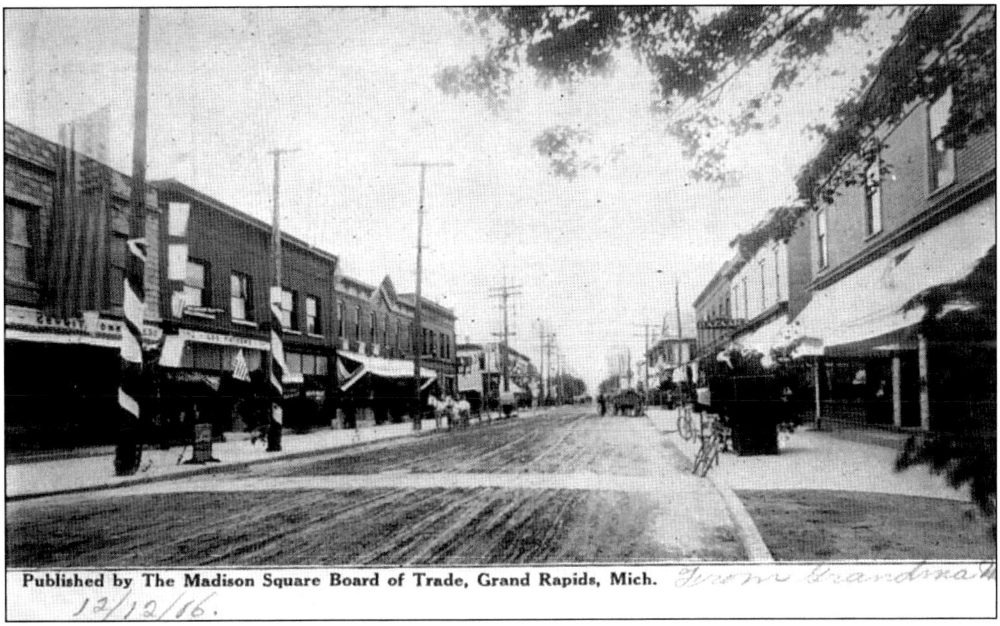

This postcard, published by the Madison Square Board of Trade in 1916, shows the prosperous and growing business district at the intersection of Madison Avenue and Hall Street. Horses still ran in the streets, which remained unpaved.

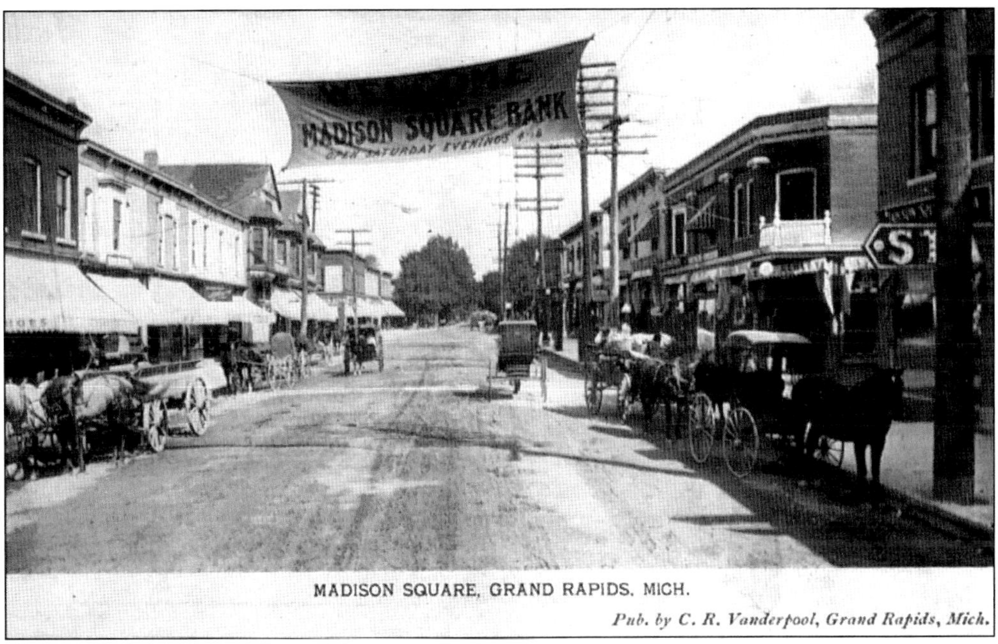

Another view of Madison Square, from about 1910, is seen here. The banner over the street announces the opening of the Madison Square Bank, at the right edge of the photograph, which was open for business on Saturdays (after payday) until 8:00 p.m., a concession to the many working-class people living in this neighborhood.

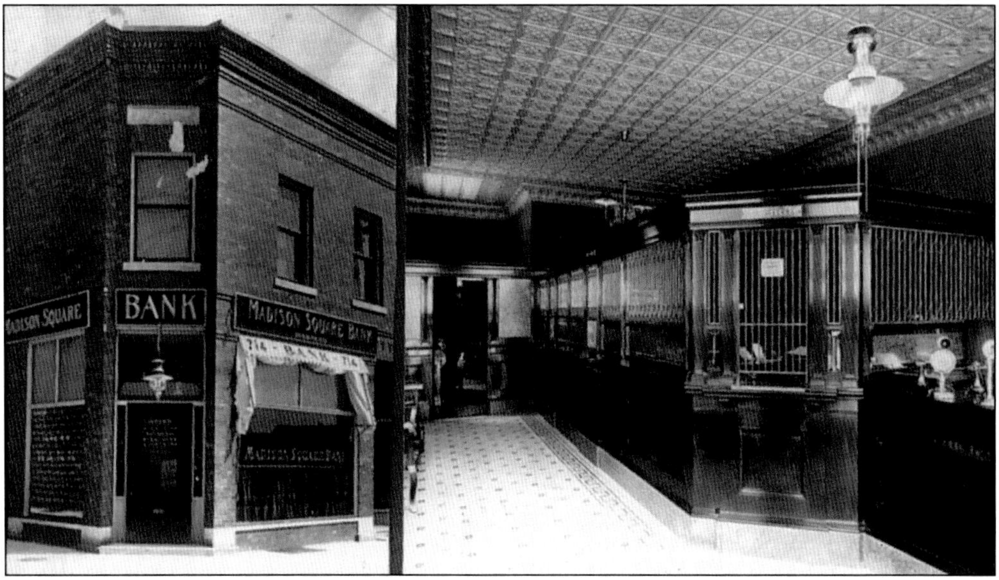

This is a real-photo postcard of the Madison Square Bank building and interior from 1910. The establishment of the bank in this neighborhood at this early date at the corner of Madison Avenue and Hall Street, well away from downtown, is an indication of the increasing economic prominence of the area.

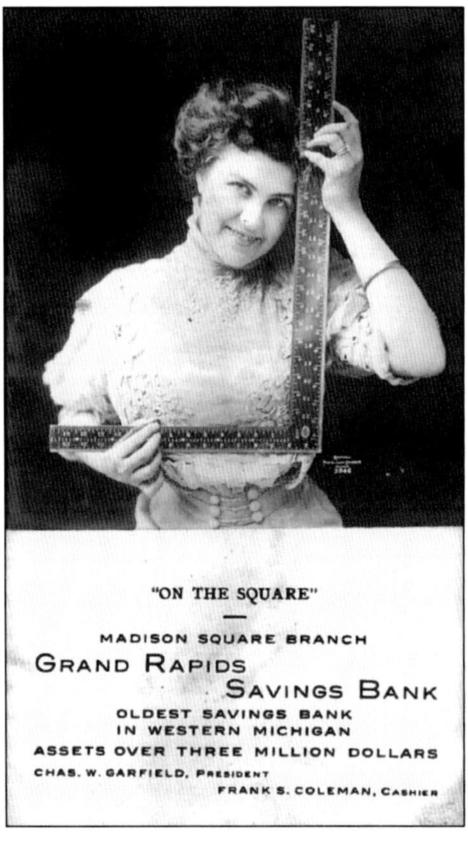

This postcard from 1915, actually a commercial announcement for the Grand Rapids Savings Bank, announces what is probably the first non-downtown "branch" of a downtown bank in the city, no doubt made necessary by the success of the "local" Madison Square Bank nearby.

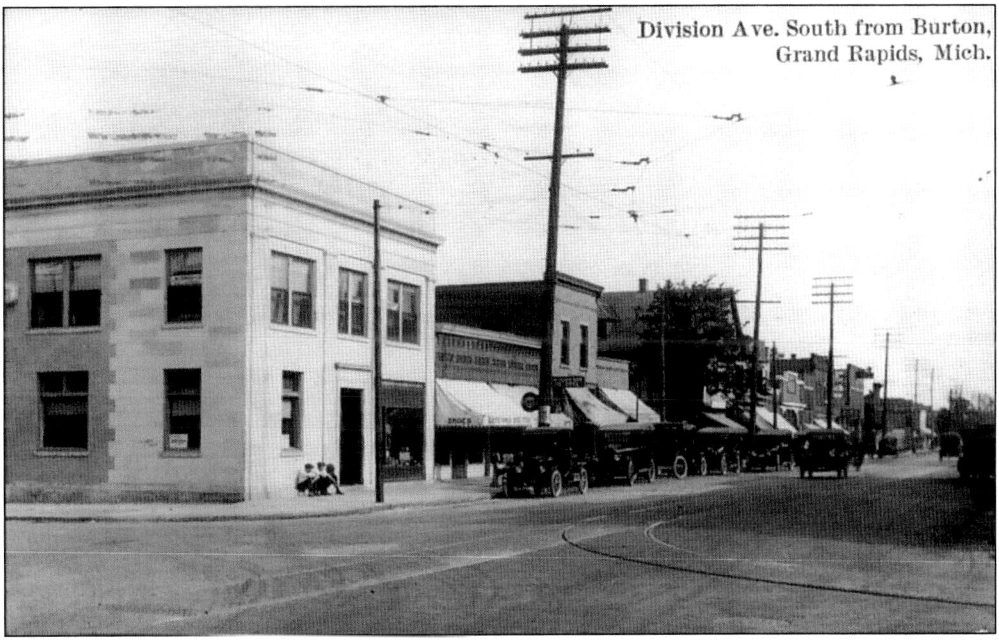

This real-photo postcard view features the intersection of Burton Street and South Division Avenue in 1922.

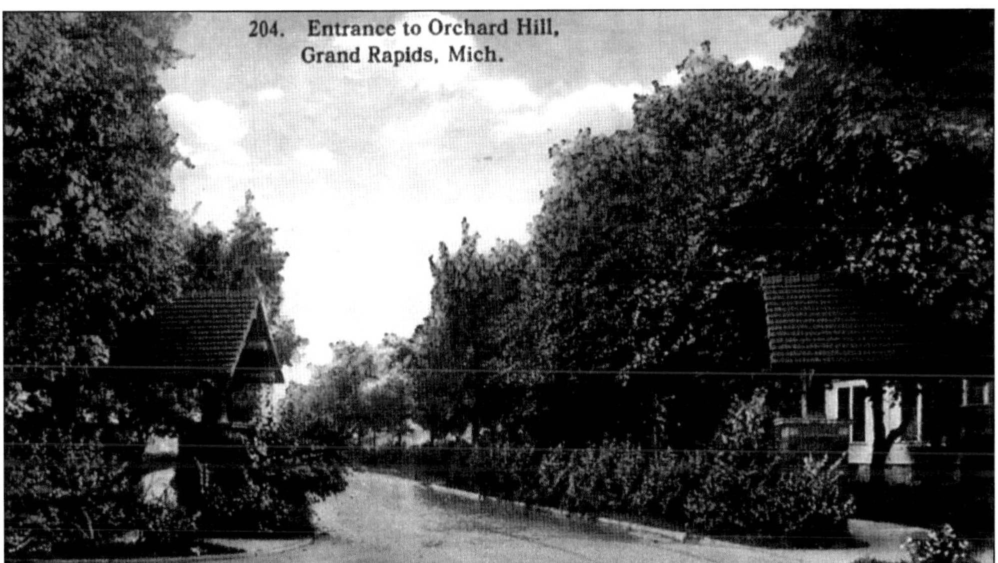

Farther to the east, near the corner of Lake Drive and Fuller Avenue, was this one-block residential area on Orchard Hill, a small, pleasant oasis of comfortable, closely packed homes in a busy neighborhood. The date is 1910.

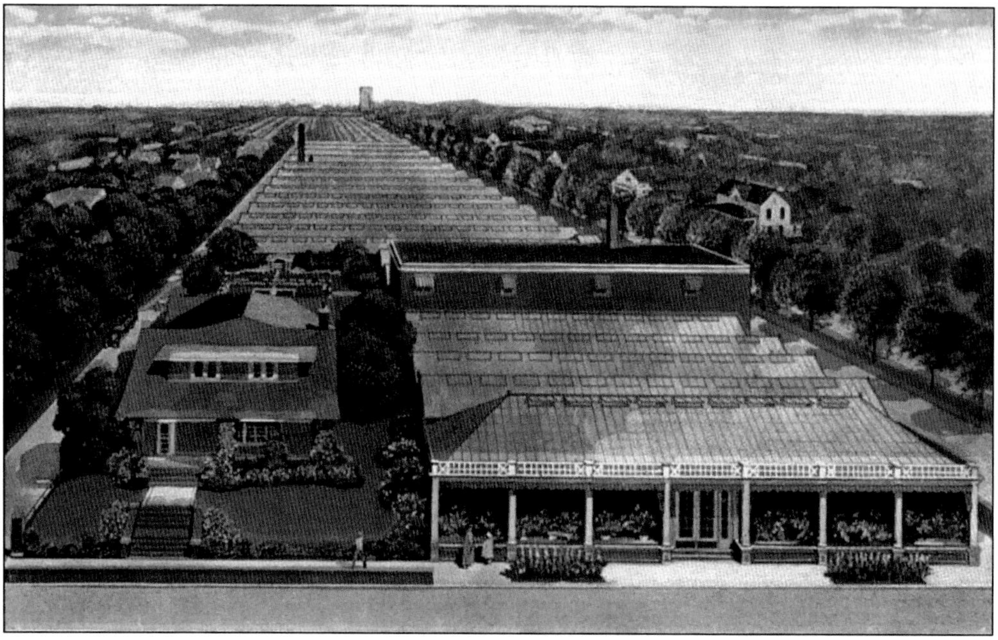

This is a promotional view of the Wealthy Street Floral Company, located on Wealthy Street just north of Fuller Avenue, from about 1925. The greenhouses of the company were not, in reality, as large as are shown here, but the artist of the card was exaggerating to demonstrate the prominence of his customer.

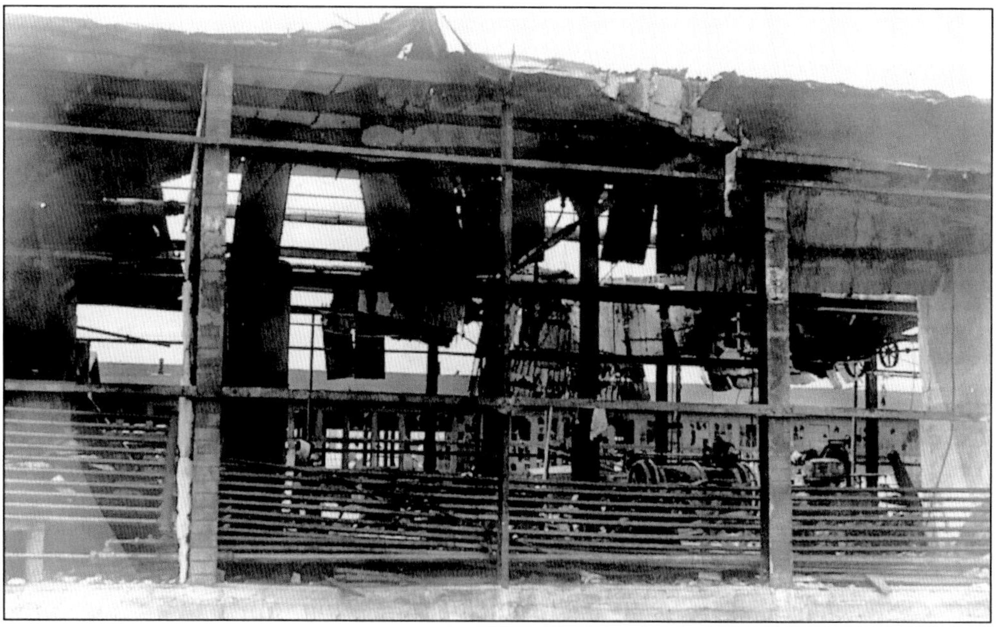

Another view of the Wealthy Street Floral Company shows the company after it suffered a disastrous fire in the early 1920s. The previous card was probably published to announce the reconstruction of the firm, which survived at this location for many years thereafter, until the property became too valuable for use as greenhouses and was developed.

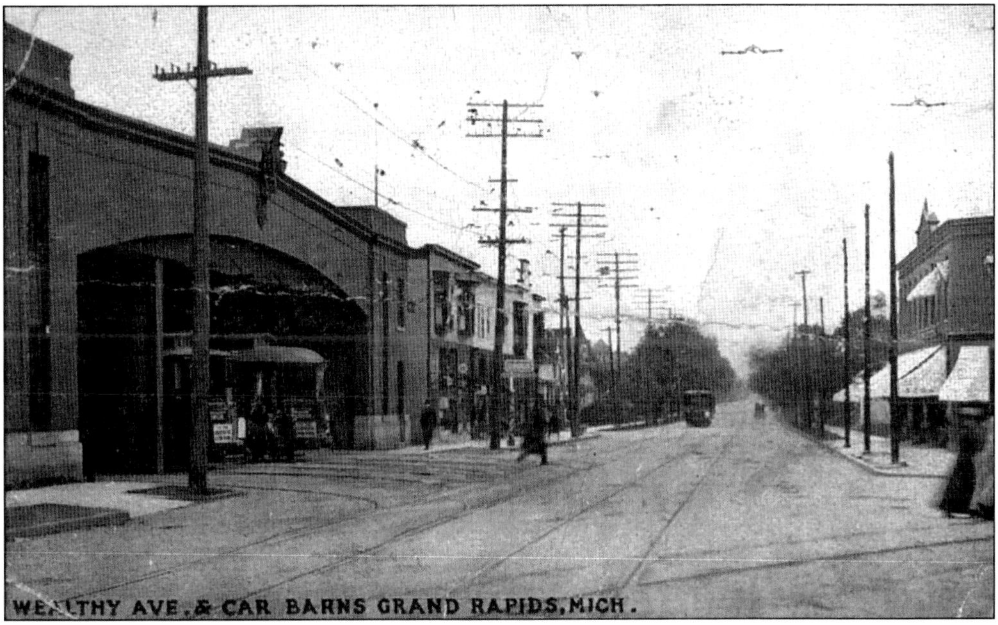

This 1915 view looks west on Wealthy Street from the intersection of Lake Drive in the heart of Easttown. At the left is one of the carbarns of the Grand Rapids Street Railway, now put to other uses. The establishment of the carbarn in this neighborhood was important, as it opened up streetcar transportation to the eastern suburbs, Ramona and East Grand Rapids, just east of this location.

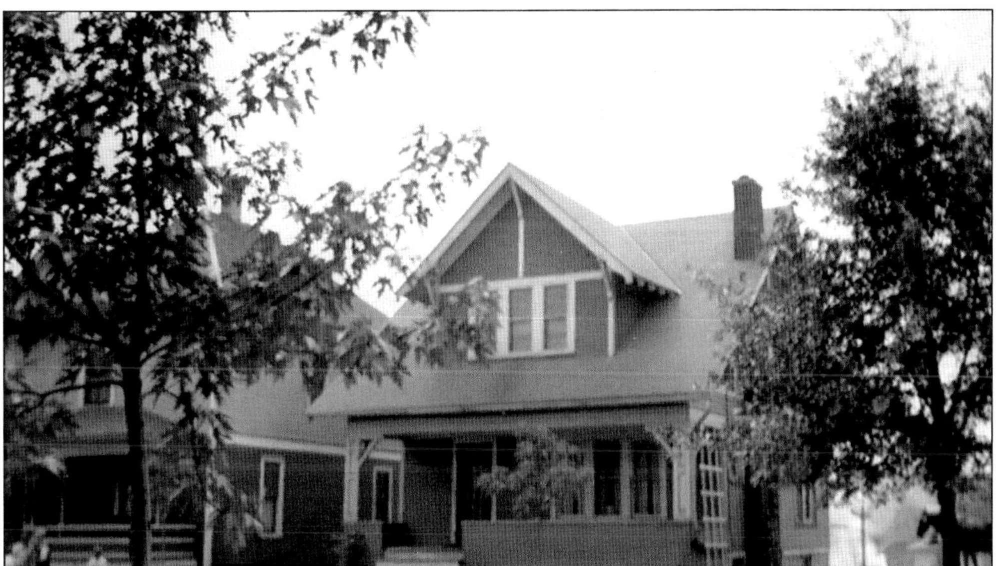

A real-photo view from around 1915 depicts a fairly typical house on an unidentified street in the rapidly developing southeast end of Grand Rapids. The most interesting feature of the photograph is the presence of a horse in the yard to the right of the house.

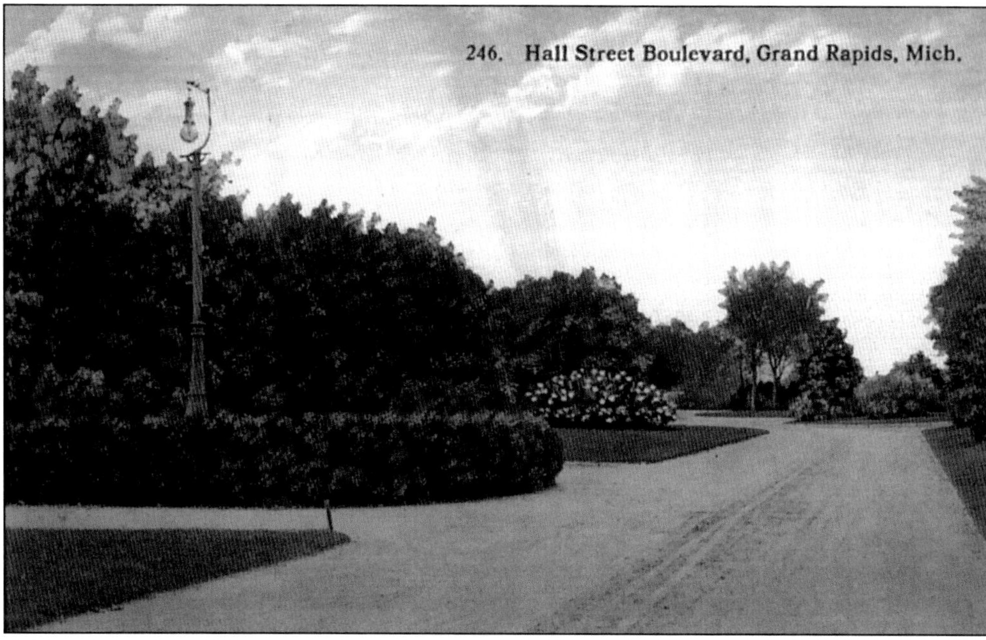

This postcard looks west down Hall Street from the corner of Eastern Avenue around 1914. Just ahead, where the street curves, is a boulevard section that once wound through Oak Hill Cemetery. The street still crosses the cemetery but has been straightened out in a concession to the needs of modern traffic.

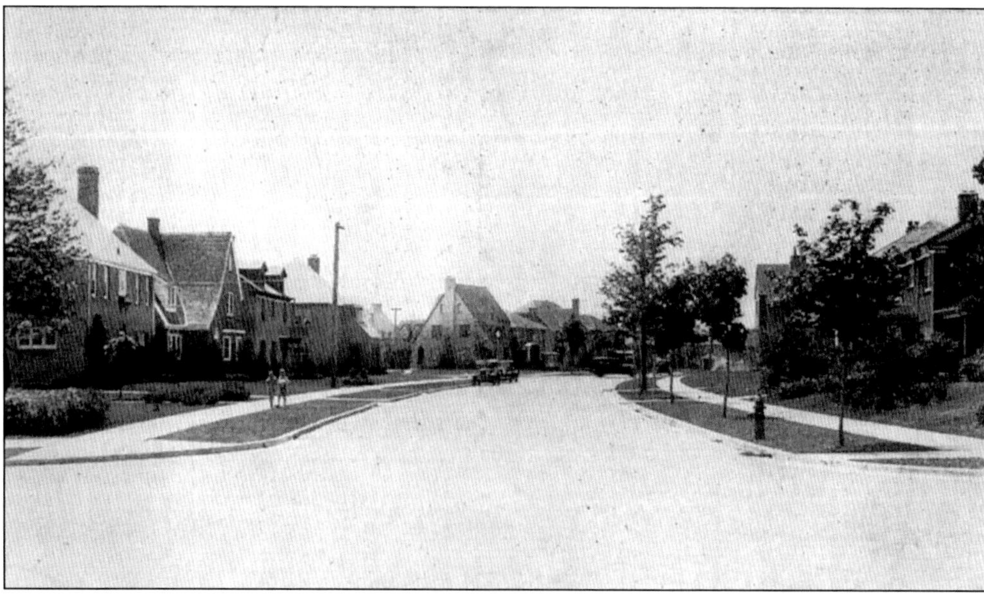

This view, from about 1930, looks west on Seminole Road in Ottawa Hills, in the southeast part of the city. This neighborhood, developed beginning in 1920 on the former Grand Rapids Golf Course, has many winding streets, actually the first such winding streets in the city, laid out along the former golf course fairways, all with American Indian names. The development was wildly successful in its day and soon attracted construction of a new high school a block north of this site in 1925.

Four

East Grand Rapids and Ramona

The city of East Grand Rapids, located immediately to the east of Grand Rapids, began as a small farming community in the early 1830s. Porter and Polly Reed, hailing from upstate New York like so many others, arrived in 1833 and established a farm on which most of central East Grand Rapids sits today. Thomas Reed, one of their three sons, bought out the interests of his two brothers after the deaths of their parents and, in 1876, purchased the Manhattan Beach area on the east side of the lake, which has since been known as Reeds Lake. For several generations, the Reeds were the dominant family in the area, owning and operating the successful resort at Manhattan Beach and later platting and selling lots along the lake, as well as on parts of the old family farm. John W. Fisk, another pioneer, lived at the intersection of the present Robinson Road and Lakeside Drive, overlooking the lake that bears his name and, in the early 1870s, cut the then navigable canal between Fisk and Reeds Lakes. The village prospered, largely as a recreation site, and was incorporated in 1891.

Beginning around 1880, small resort operations prospered on the western shore of the lake, visited by locals seeking a relaxed atmosphere and the cooling lake waters. In 1897, the Grand Rapids Street Railway Company began the development of the Ramona Park area on land at the western edge of the lake that was owned and developed by Benjamin Hanchett, the president of the company, as a picnic park. What began modestly developed in earnest after the beginning of the 20th century into an assemblage of boat liveries and amusement park rides and attractions, taverns, beer gardens, and occasionally unsavory operations, all located near Grand Rapids but outside of the jurisdiction of that city's constabulary. Most of the legitimate operation at Ramona, including the amusement park and rides and, later, the Ramona Theater, were owned and operated by the railway company, which benefited from the public use of its newly installed street railway lines running east from Grand Rapids. The seasonal attendance was tremendous, and eventually attracted big-name vaudeville performers to the area. Beginning in 1891, a series of steamships plied Reeds Lake: the *Major Watson*, measuring 130 feet in length and able to carry some 460 passengers, and the *Hazel A.*, a smaller, faster ship, operating on opposing excursion schedules until the early 1920s, when they were supplanted by the *Ramona*, which operated in the same excursion capacity until the park closed.

In 1972, local writer Tom LaBelle published a reminiscence of Ramona in the *Grand Rapids Press*.

> Gad, it was an ugly, tacky, exciting place! . . . Ramona Park on the shores of Reeds Lake was a hodge-podge of ill-matched buildings, wooden bracing and 16 shades of paint. There were two big, handsome buildings, one a dance hall and one a theater. The theater featured what someone described as "refined burlesque" in the form of a chorus line called the Marcus Girls. It also had some of the top names in vaudeville. . . . Groucho Marx in his memoirs said he and his brothers appeared at the old Ramona Theater in a musical act which also featured their mother. The boys got to horsing around with the material, he said, and the Marx Brothers were born. . . . Ramona was noise. . . . There was raucous music and the hollered come-ons of the concessionaires, the screams of girls on the Derby Racer. . . . Ramona must have been a terrible place to live next to. And it was an absolutely perfect place to take a girl that you liked or loved, or a visiting young rural relative, or a grandchild.

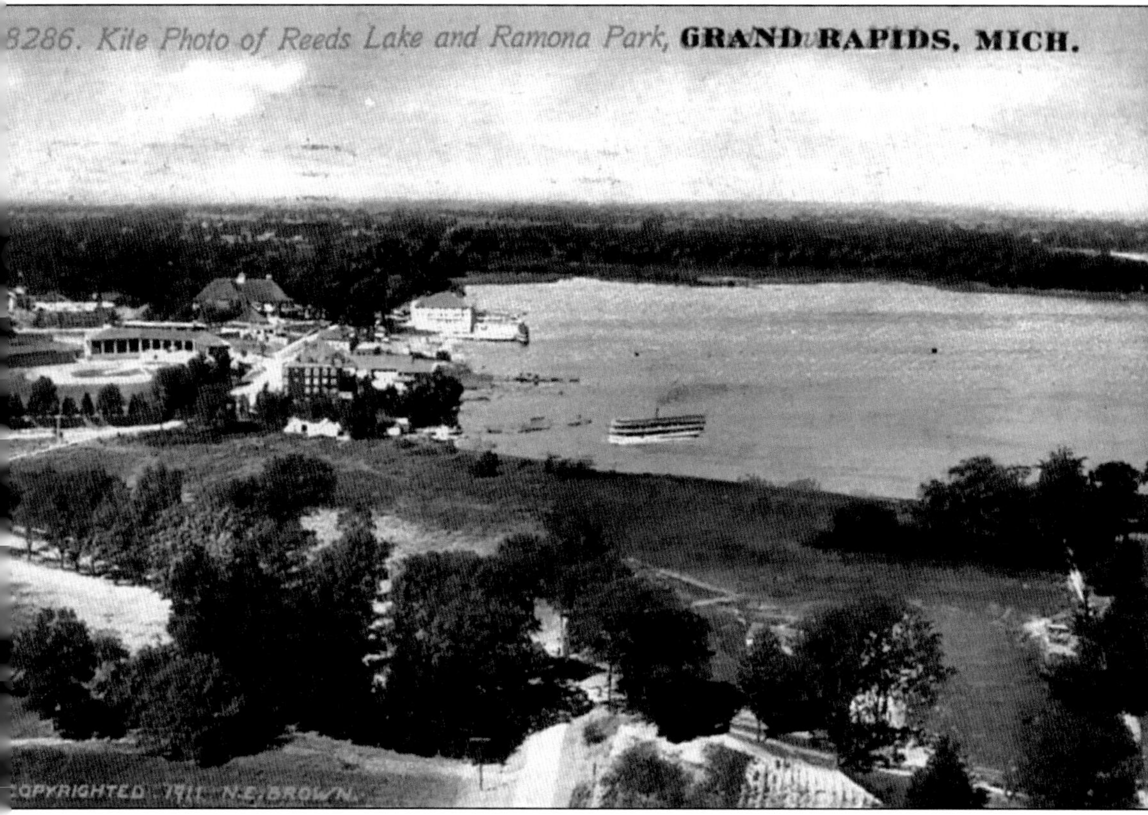

This is an early panoramic view of the Reeds Lake area in East Grand Rapids from 1912. The postcard image was published by N. E. Brown, a Grand Haven photographer, and was taken from a camera mounted on a kite, flown above the scene, with the shutter tripped by the photographer on the ground. In the foreground, an unpaved Lake Drive is visible. To the left is the baseball field, on the site of the present high school athletic field, and behind it the Ramona Theater. Behind and to the left of the theater is the Ramona amusement park. The square building at the center left is the Lakeside Club, a social club on the west shore of the lake. One of the two steamers that then plied the lake is visible as well. Tom La Belle lamented the changes to come:

> Ah, Ramona. It survived right up to the early 1950s - or about the same time when the country sank down exhausted in front of television sets and decided it was easier and safer to be a spectator. . . . I remember in its last days, when the place had lost considerable of its zip, including the vaudeville, and the big dance hall had been converted to a skating rink, the most melancholy walk in town was through Ramona Park in the rain. . . . The sodden old buildings seemed about to melt away. You could sense all this jazzy, ramshackle, 1930s splendor was doomed, that it hadn't a day to live, not another day. Nobody went in for this kind of stuff any more. Running a concession stand or a thrill ride was a marginal living at best and the dead hand of widespread affluence was on the place. The sleek people were about to inherit the earth.

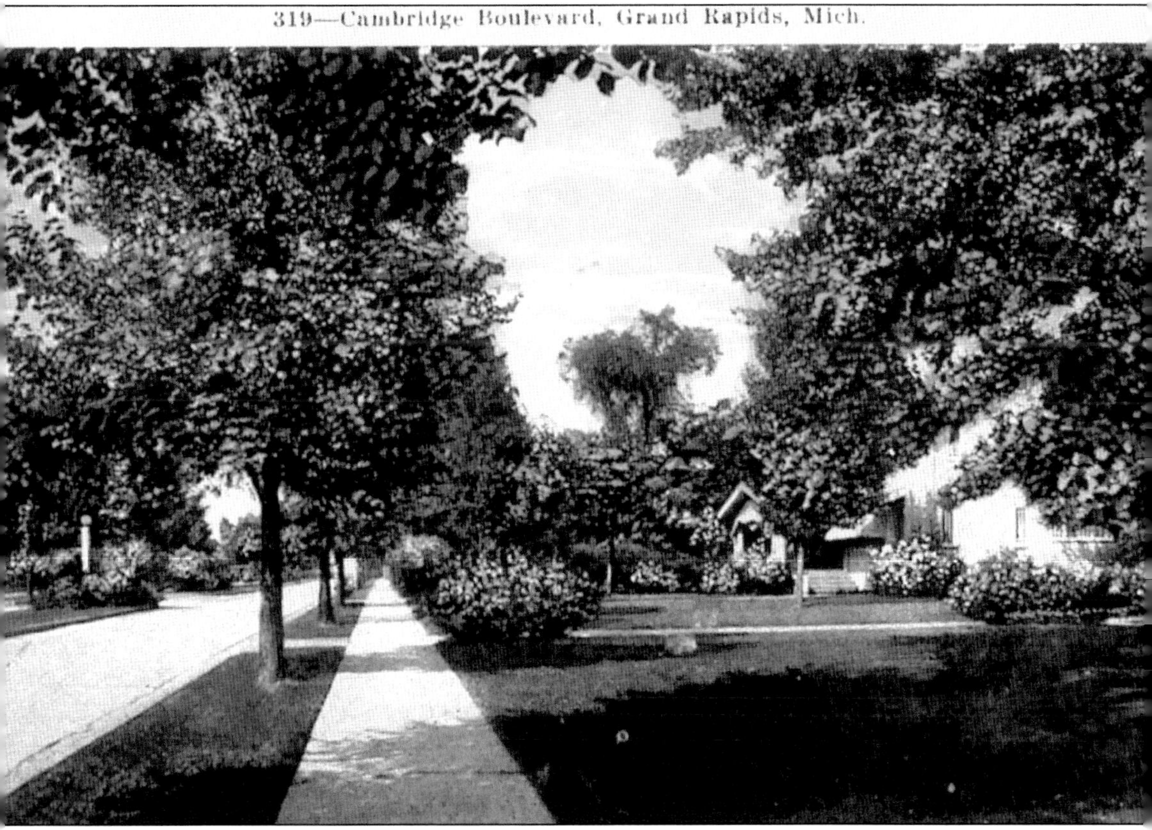

The developing neighborhood west of Reeds Lake is visible in this 1925 postcard of Cambridge Boulevard. In the 1920s and 1930s, the city of East Grand Rapids, incorporated in 1926, had attracted permanent, upscale residents. With this change in the character of the city, and the arrival of Prohibition, the unfettered "activity" of the resort area changed. The city constructed schools, sidewalks, and public works. The rise of the automobile sapped attendance at Ramona, and as attendance continued to flag into the 1950s, the park closed and was razed. According to LaBelle:

> They tore down the last of the buildings in the winter of 1955-56 to make way for the present Ramona Shopping Center. The whole 21 acres is now a neat, color-keyed and architecturally harmonious expression of Eisenhower bland. Stores and apartments have gaslight fripperies here and there, evoking, as they say, the 'gracious charm' of the 1890s. . . . You walk around in there now and you can't quite place where things were, where you mounted the platform to get on the Derby Racer, where that mechanized spook house stood, where the tracks were for the miniature train which carried passengers all around the park. . . . Most of the space is taken up with asphalt, spread like a black shroud over the buried bones of old Ramona.

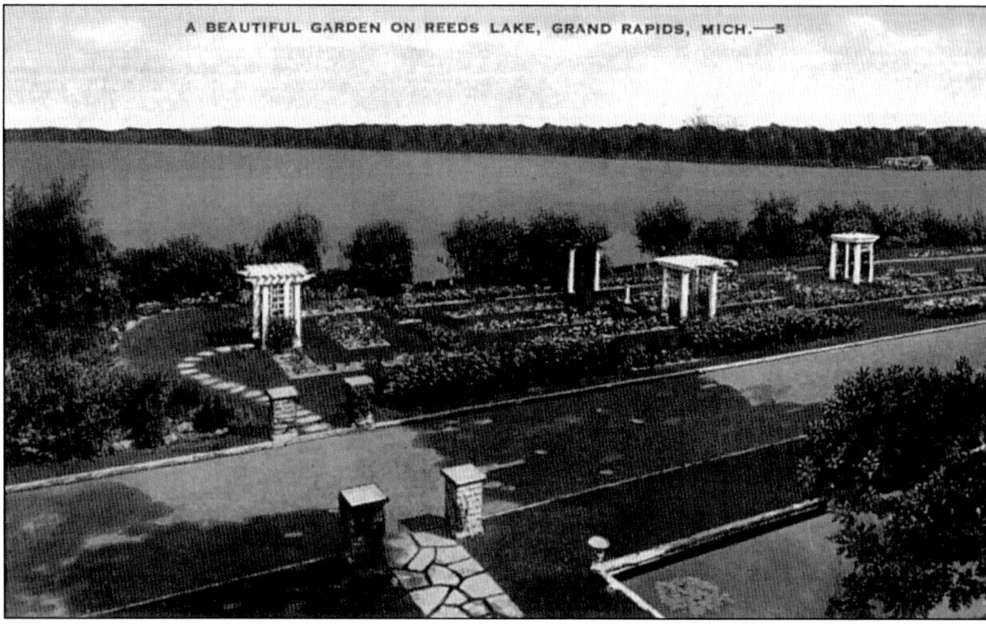

From early on, many of the early and grandest homes in East Grand Rapids were built on the south and east shores of Reeds Lake. Here is a view, from the late 1930s, of the shoreline garden front of one of the homes in this area.

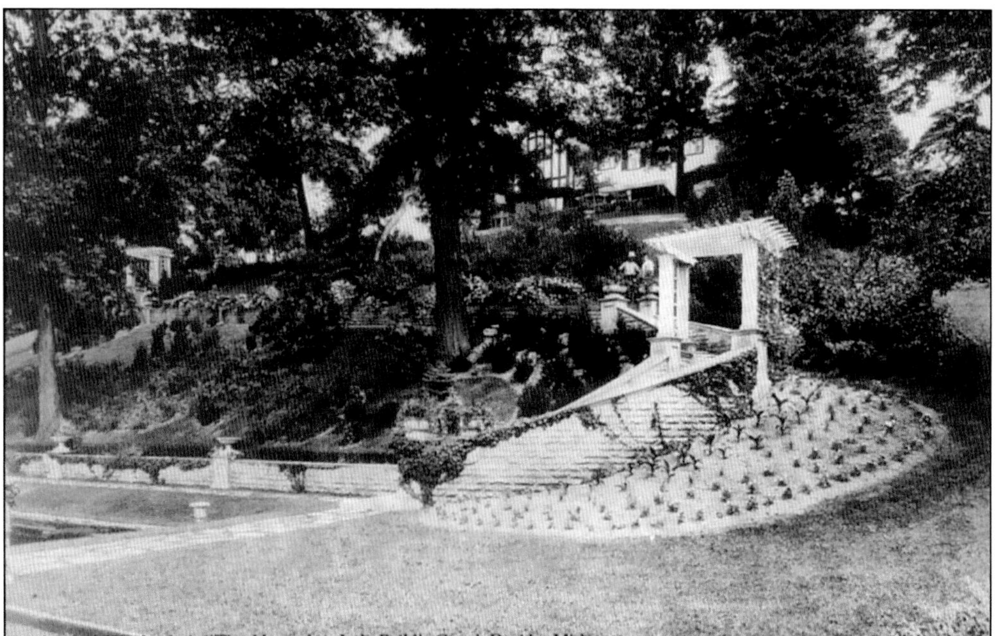

In this real-photo view from 1920, the elaborate garden and home of the William Jack family, located on Bonnell Drive on the southern side of the lake, is visible.

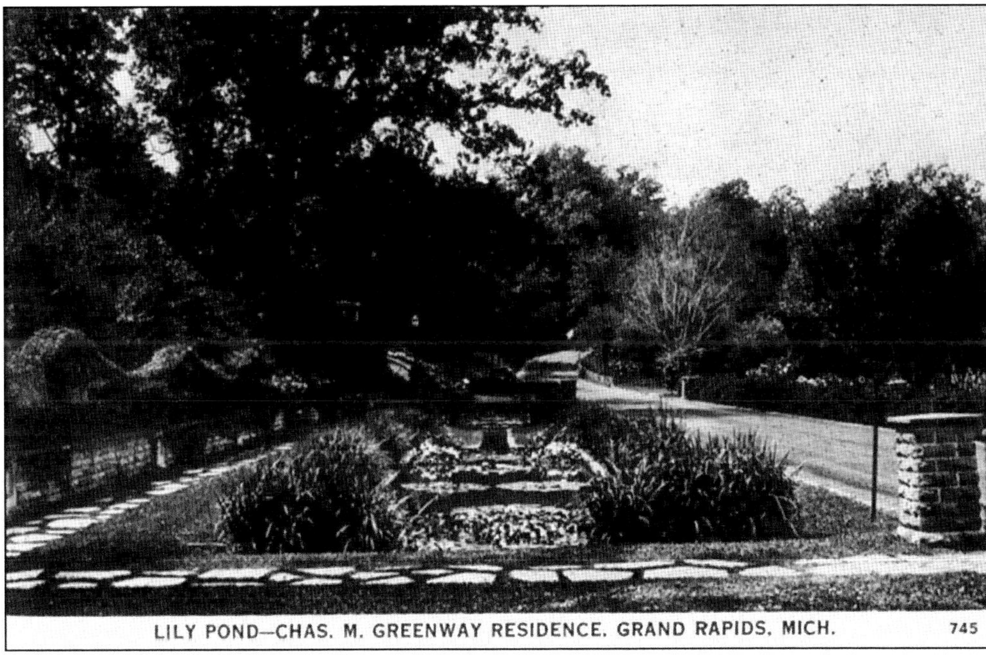

This view of the lily pond garden at the Charles W. Greenway home is from about 1928. The main house was high on the bluff off the left side of the photograph. Reeds Lake is off the right edge of the picture.

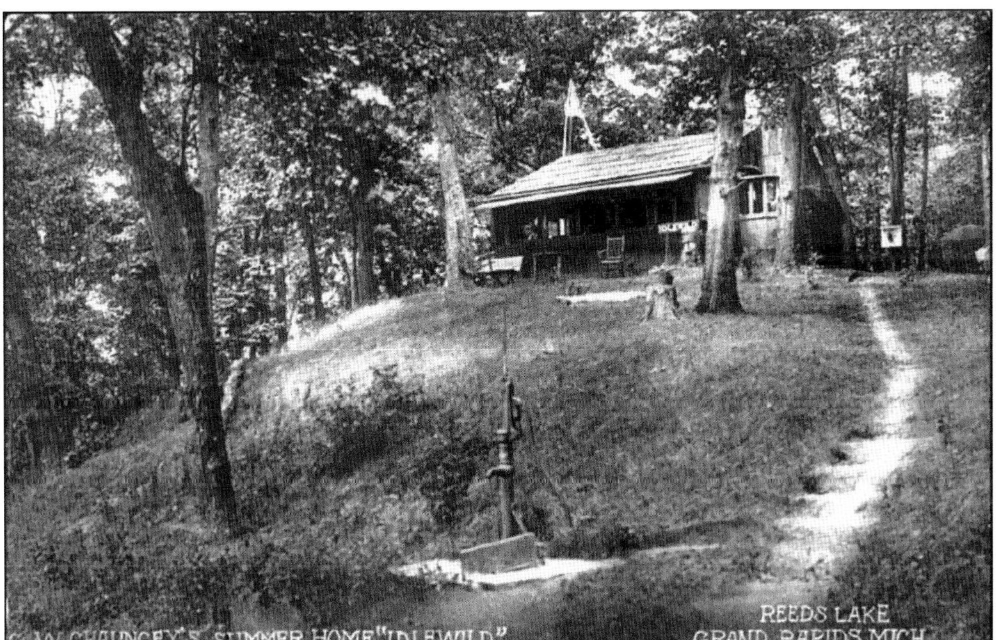

Not all of the homes around Reeds Lake were of the palatial type. This is the summer home of C. W. Chauncey, located on the southern shore of the lake, from about 1915.

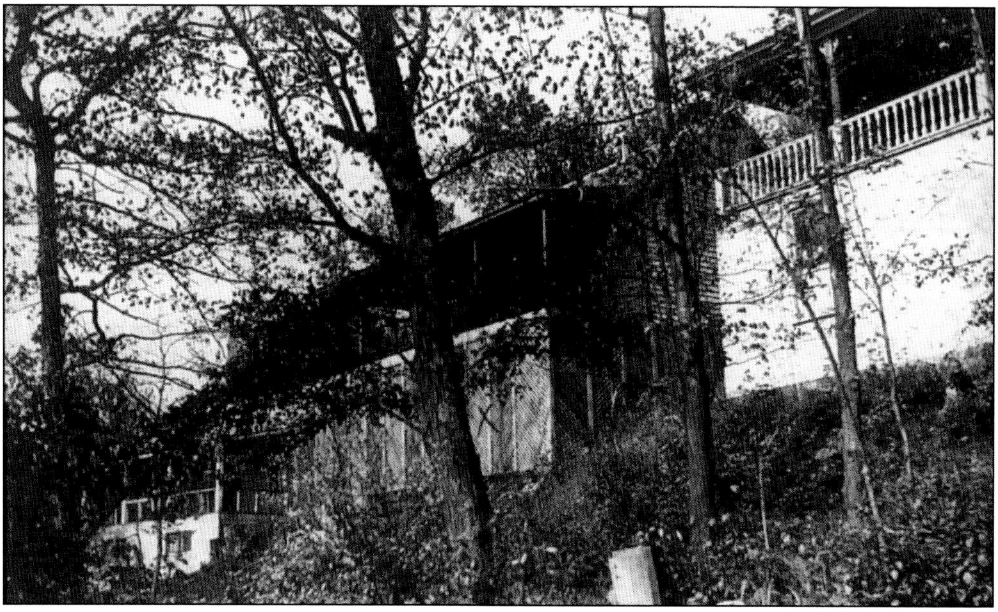

A real-photo view by the Innes Photo Shop is of some of the summer cottages found along the northeastern shore of Reeds Lake in the early 20th century.

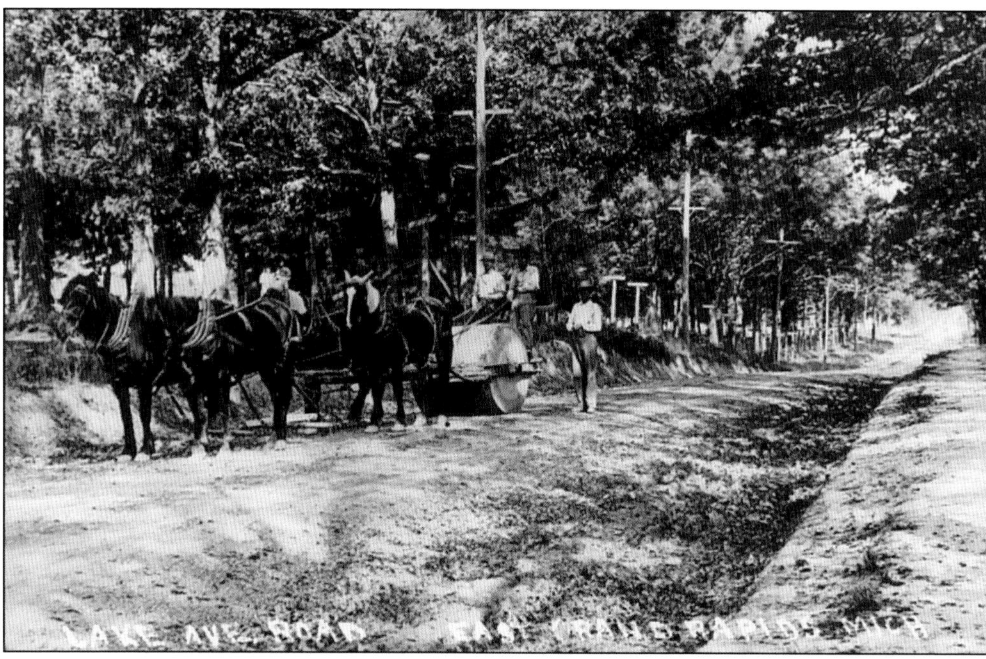

This is a real-photo postcard from the early 1920s, sent out by the Economy Road Roller Company, showing its road compacting equipment in operation. This scene is on Lake Drive at the present site of Wealthy School. Nearly all of the roads in the city were then unpaved and constructed either of dirt or cinders. These streets needed to be periodically compacted with heavy rollers to smooth out ruts and, in the summer, were watered to control the dust raised by traffic.

This bucolic scene from 1909 is Robinson Road, looking east, probably from the corner of Rosewood Avenue. This street began as a toll road, in 1873, the property of the Reeds Lake Gravel Road Company, and was later taken over by the City of East Grand Rapids, following its incorporation, as a public thoroughfare.

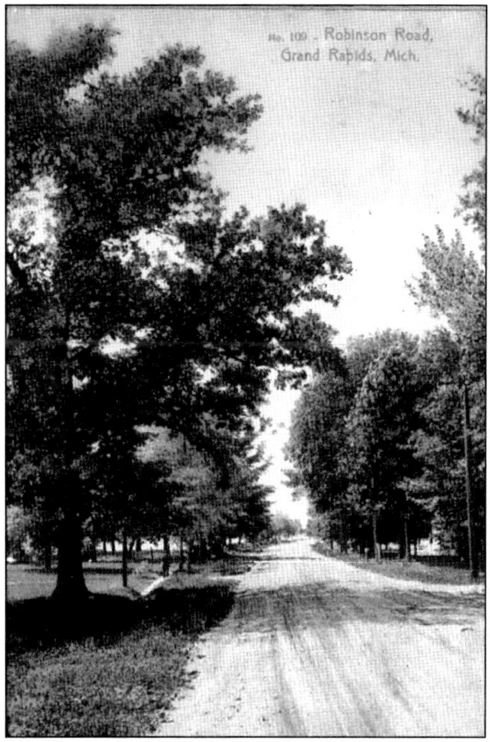

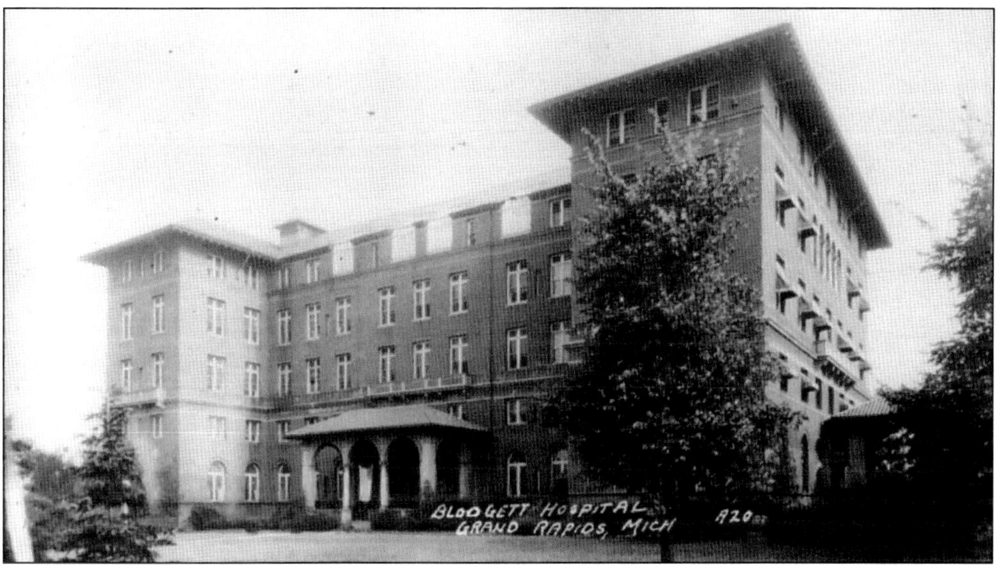

This real-photo postcard of the southern front of the newly completed Blodgett Memorial Hospital dates from 1916. The hospital was constructed to replace the former Union Benevolent Association Hospital on College Avenue downtown and was built and donated by John W. Blodgett as a memorial to his mother. The site upon which the hospital still stands was the original location of the Grand Rapids Golf Club, founded in 1895 as the first golf course in western Michigan. The club, renamed Kent Country Club to attract non–Grand Rapids members, relocated to a larger tract of land on the former Sweet farm, at the corner of Plainfield Avenue and Knapp Street, in 1901.

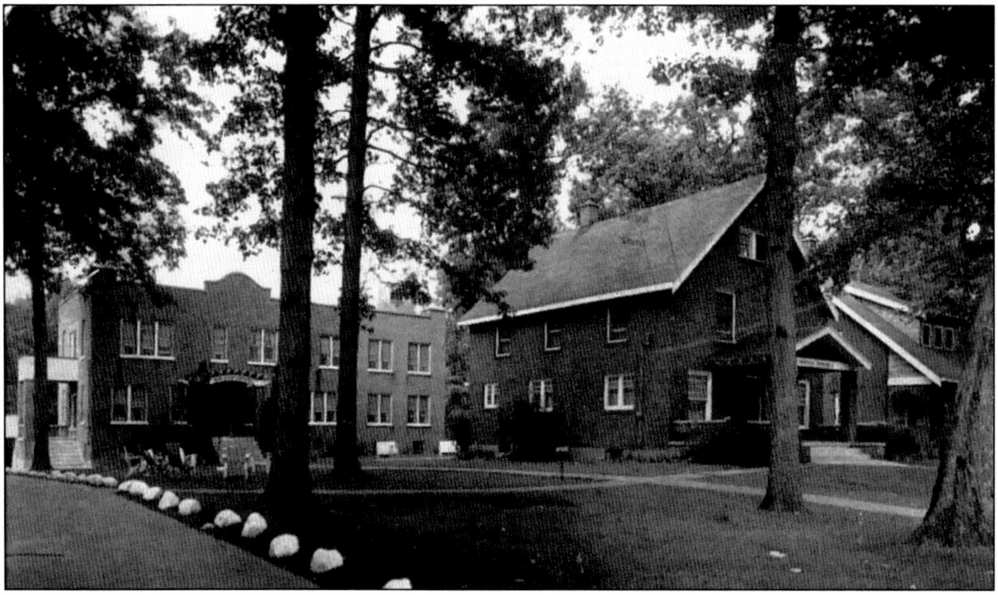

This is a postcard of the Burleson Hospital on Greenwood Avenue, west of Reeds Lake, from 1940. This is actually the third location of the private clinic specializing in the nonsurgical treatment of rectal and intestinal disorders, the clinic having originally been located near the corner of Fulton Street and Jefferson Avenue downtown and then later on the upper floors of the Morton House Hotel, before locating here in 1937. The buildings were later converted to residential use.

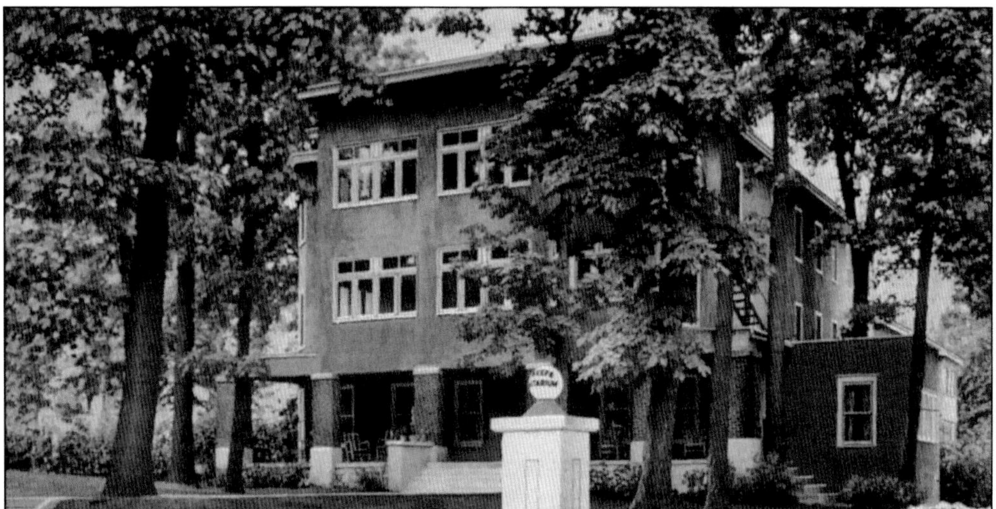

The O'Keefe Sanitarium was a private medical hospital, located next to the Burleson Hospital on Greenwood Street, beginning in 1911. The treatment offered was more general than at the Burleson Hospital and continued until 1923, when its founder and director, Dr. Thomas O'Keefe, died, and the buildings were converted to a convalescent facility. The buildings were later razed and replaced with another professional structure.

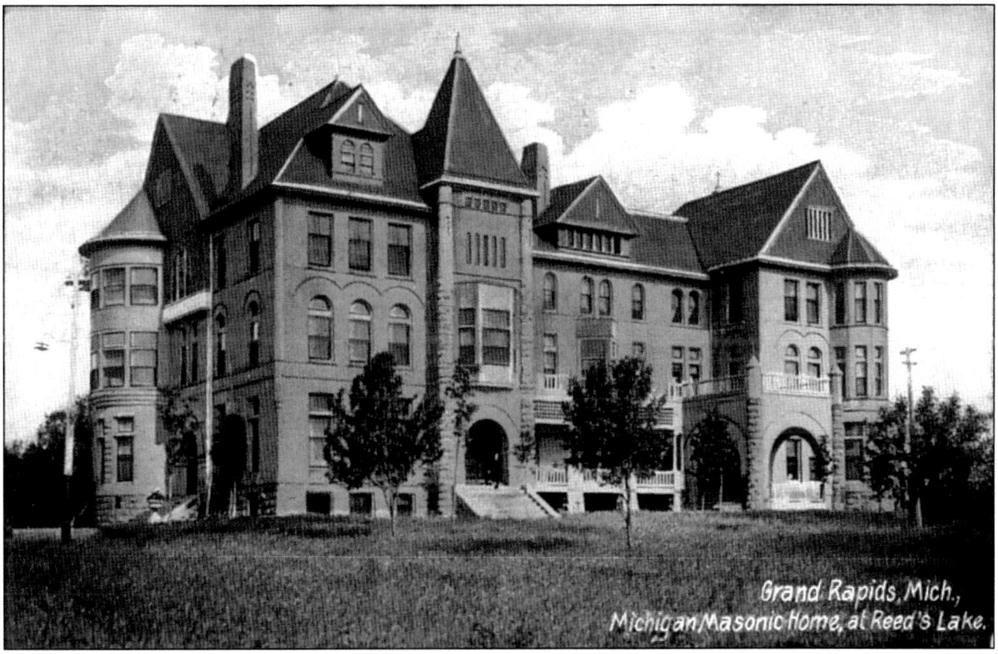

This is a view from 1908 of the Michigan Masonic Home, located on a large parcel of land south of Reeds Lake, between Breton Road and Argentina Avenue. The home was built as a convalescent facility in 1891 and housed 52 residents until it burned in 1910. The Masonic home was thereafter relocated to Alma, and the land on which it previously sat was developed for residential use.

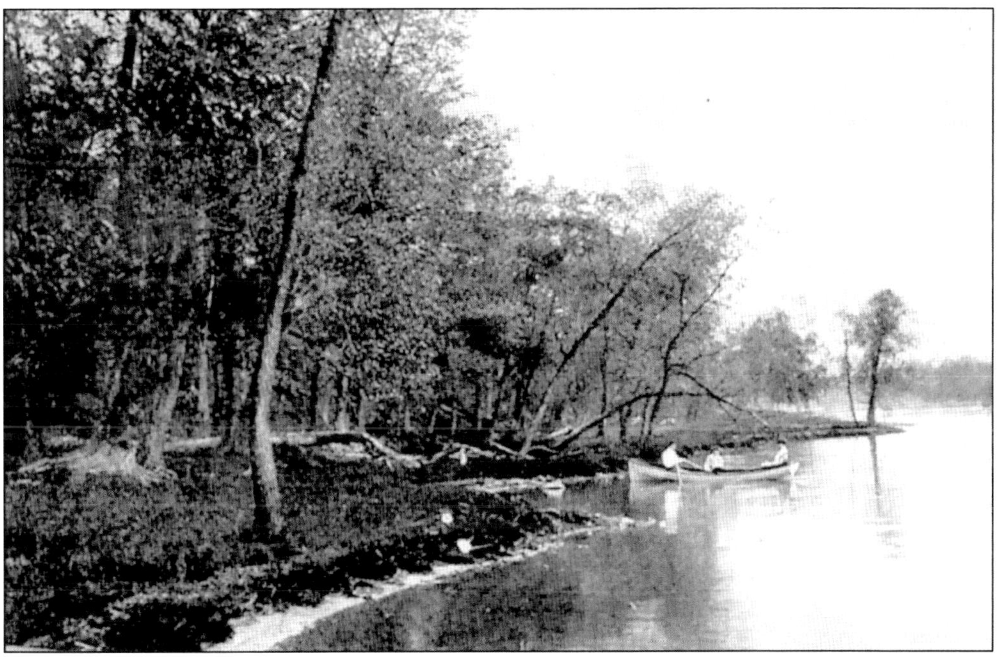

In this early postcard view of the south shore of Reeds Lake from 1907, much of the busy development of Ramona and related resort areas, which would come in the following decades, had yet to occur.

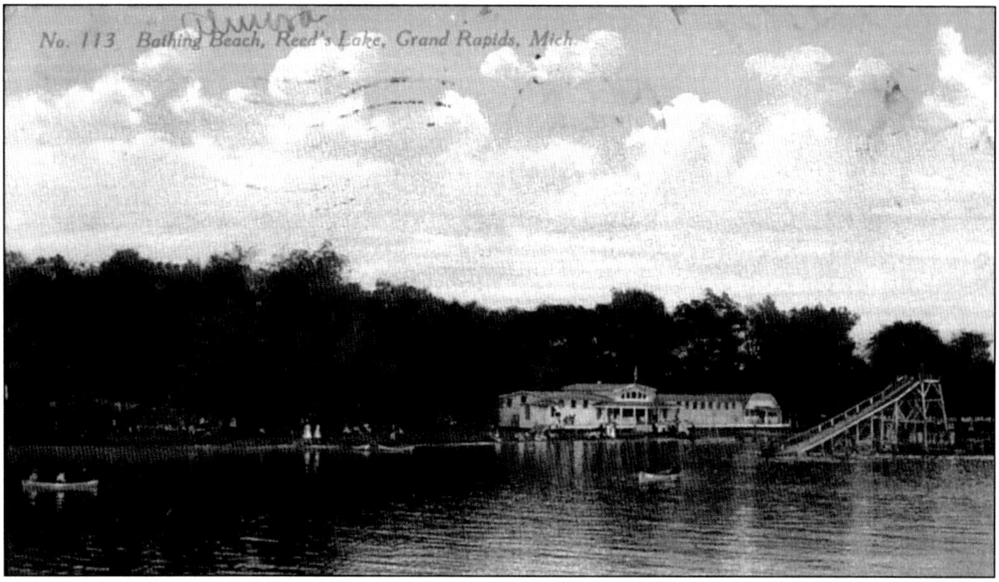

In this view from 1912, the Manhattan Beach resort area, on the north side of the lake near the present Manhattan Lane, is shown. The area was first identified and developed as a beach resort in 1884 by Charles S. Seidel, an employee of the O-Wash-Ta-Nong Club, located on the western shore. The boats operated by the Poisson family made regular stops at Manhattan Beach, and the resort was sold to the Thomas Reed family in 1905. The Reeds erected the buildings visible in the photograph, as well as the slide and other improvements. The beach resort continued to operate until it was sold for development of home sites in 1927.

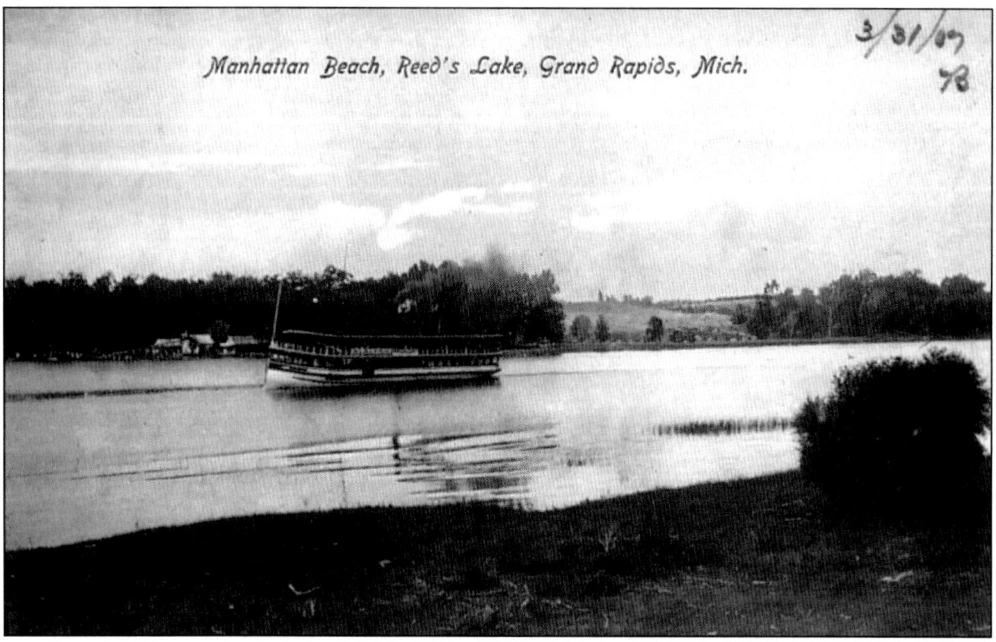

Another view of Manhattan Beach, dating from about 1906, shows the resort from across the lake. In the foreground, one of the several passenger ships that plied the lake is visible. These ships provided not only a pleasant and cooling ride for passengers on hot days and evenings but also brought passengers to several landings around the lake, including Manhattan Beach.

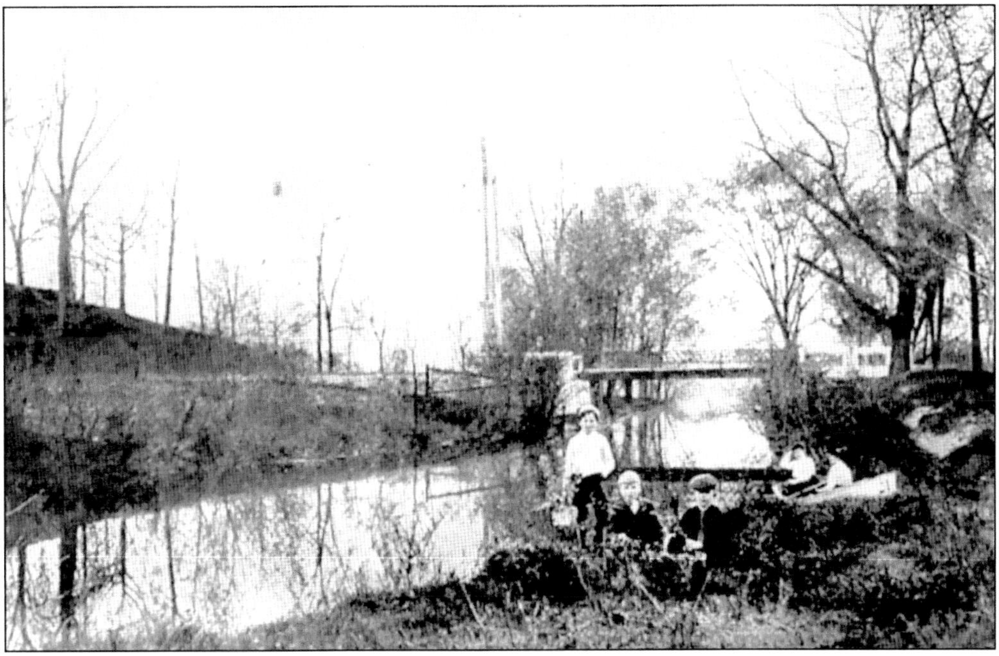

These young fishermen are seen on the northern shore of the canal, which was cut in about 1875 between Reeds and Fisk Lakes. This view looks west toward Fisk Lake. The bridge over the canal is still present, though now replaced as part of Lakeside Avenue.

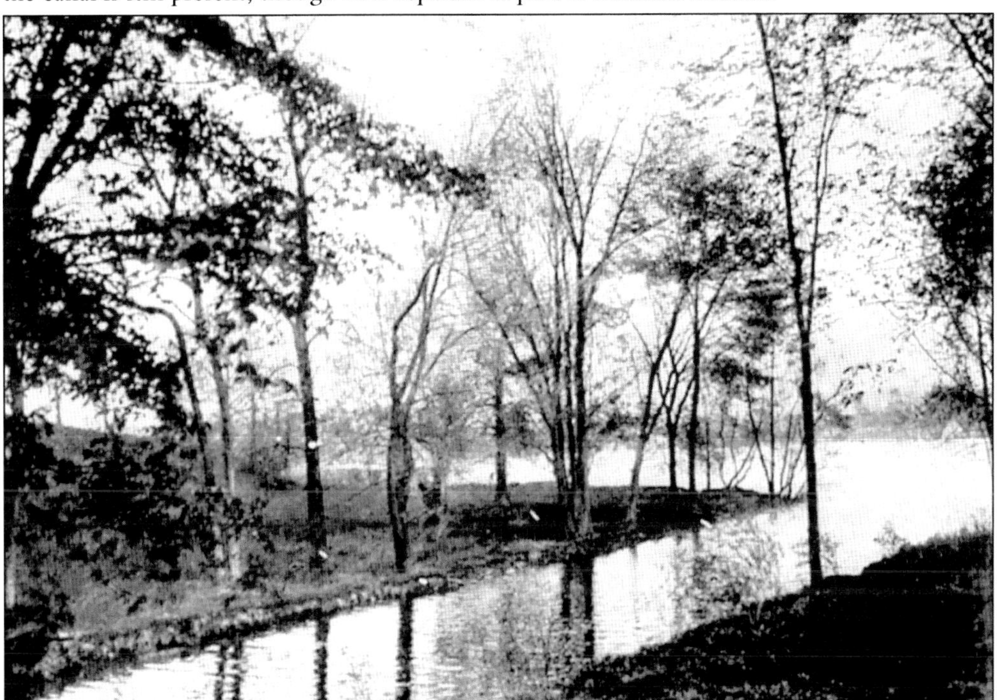

This is another view of the canal between Reeds and Fisk Lakes, this time at the terminus of the canal looking out onto Fisk Lake, just west of Lakeside Road. The canal, then deeper and better maintained than it is today, allowed small boat traffic to freely pass between the lakes.

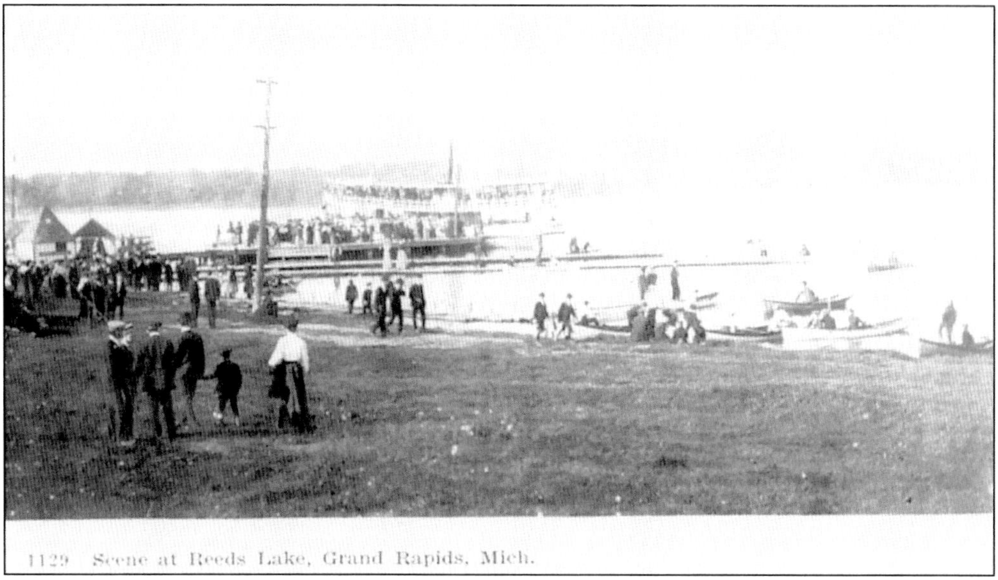

This scene from 1905 shows the activity along the western shore of the lake, including a boat livery and, in the distance, one of the two passenger ships that sailed on regular schedules. The crowd on the dock is likely waiting to board the ship when it arrives.

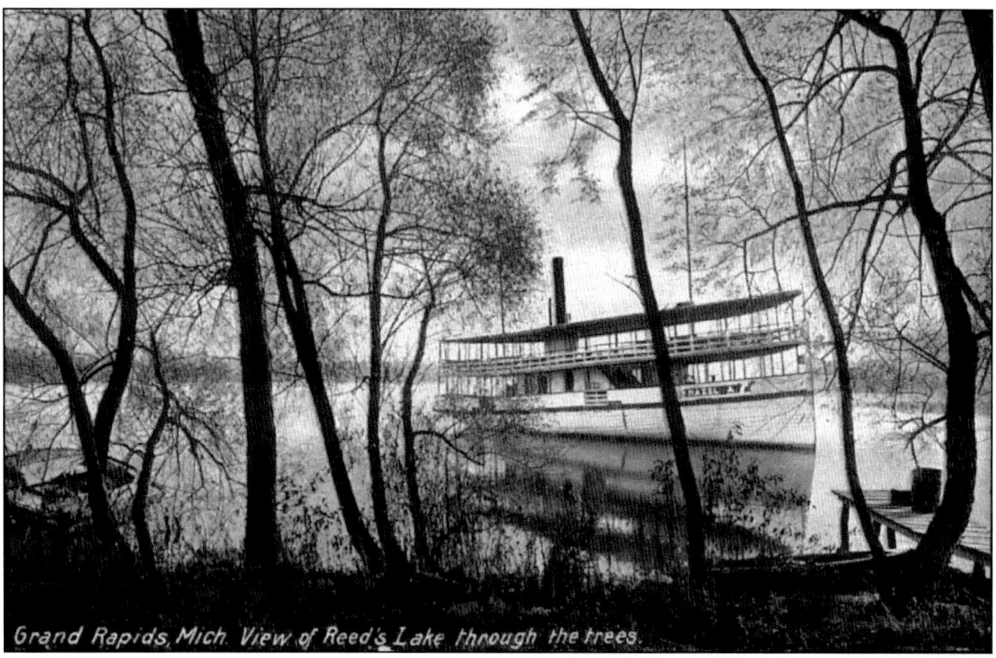

The *Hazel A.*, one of the boats that steamed around the lake between 1896 and 1923, is shown here making its rounds on Reeds Lake.

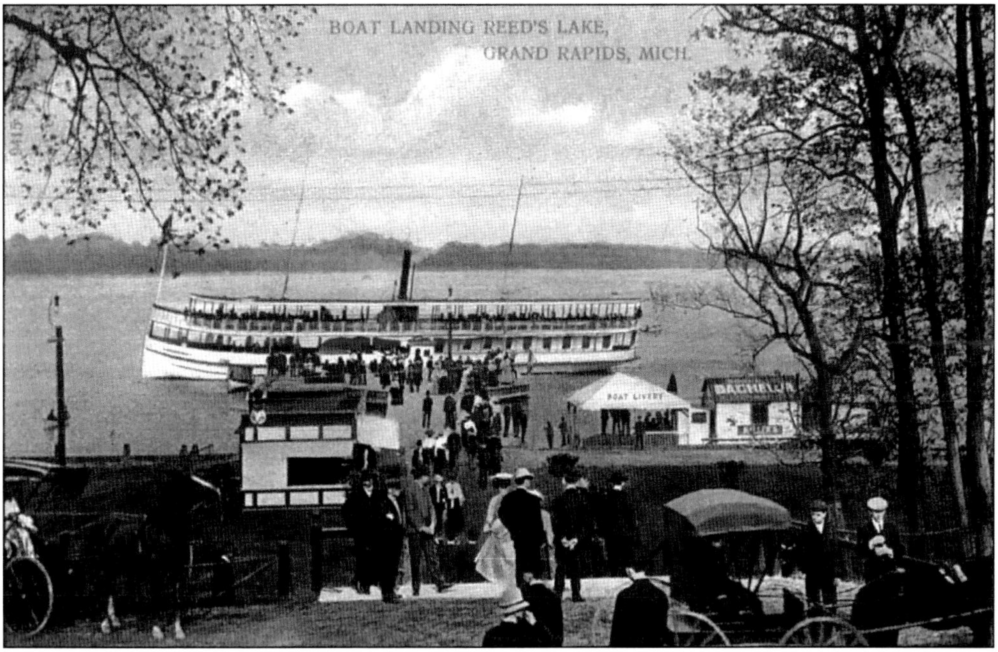

This card, from about 1915, presents a view of the Reeds Lake dock, on the present site of Collins Park, where the steamships docked and took on passengers during the entire life of the Ramona resort. To the right are several of the small boat liveries that were popular at the time.

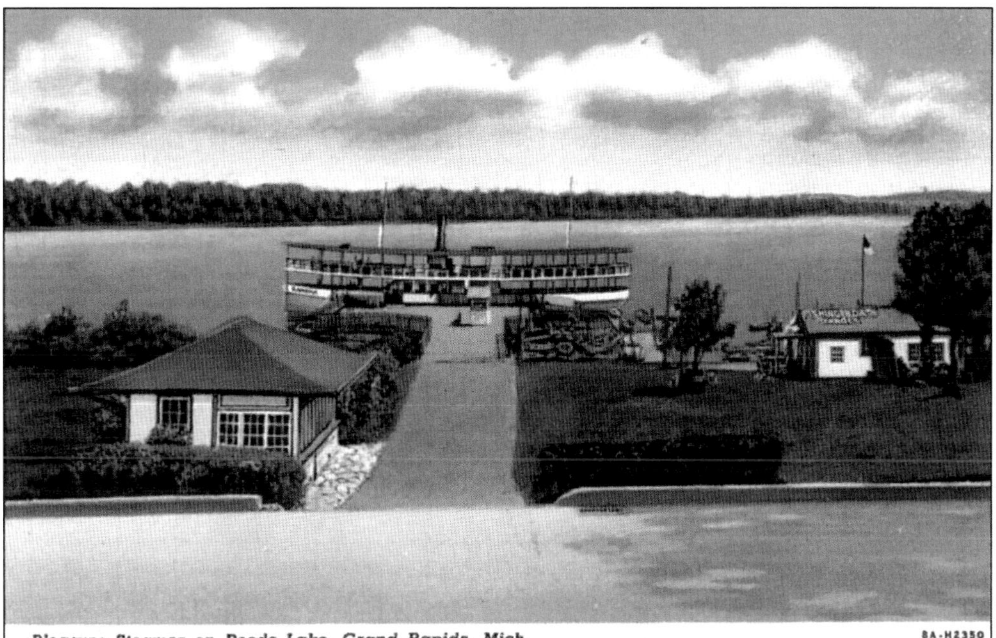

In a later view, a linen card from the 1940s features the same dock area. By this time, the steamship *Ramona* had replaced the earlier ships, the *Major Watson* and the *Hazel A.*, and was the sole ship still working the lake. The crowds still came, though not in this picture. The Miller boat livery is still there, too.

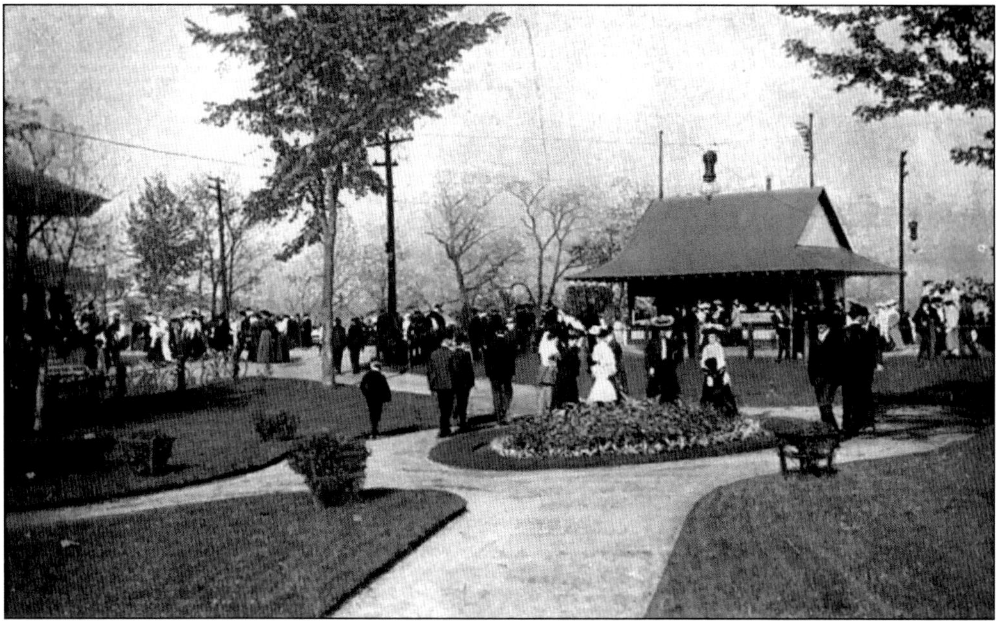

Farther up on the western bank of the lake, this park was developed by the owners of Ramona, the Grand Rapids Street Railway Company, to allow strolling and picnicking at about the location of the Lakeshore Club apartments today. Off the left edge of this photograph is where the Ramona amusement park, the primary attraction to the area when this photograph was taken in 1909, was located.

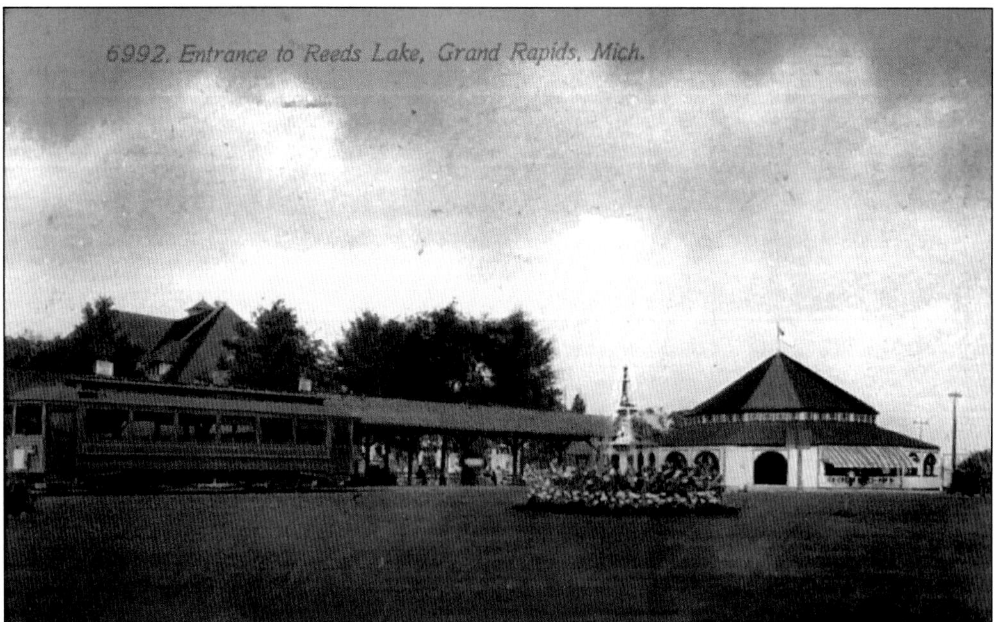

Taken in 1914, this view shows, in the foreground, the station where passengers from the Grand Rapids Street Railway streetcars disembarked. Above and behind the streetcar is the roof of the Ramona Theater.

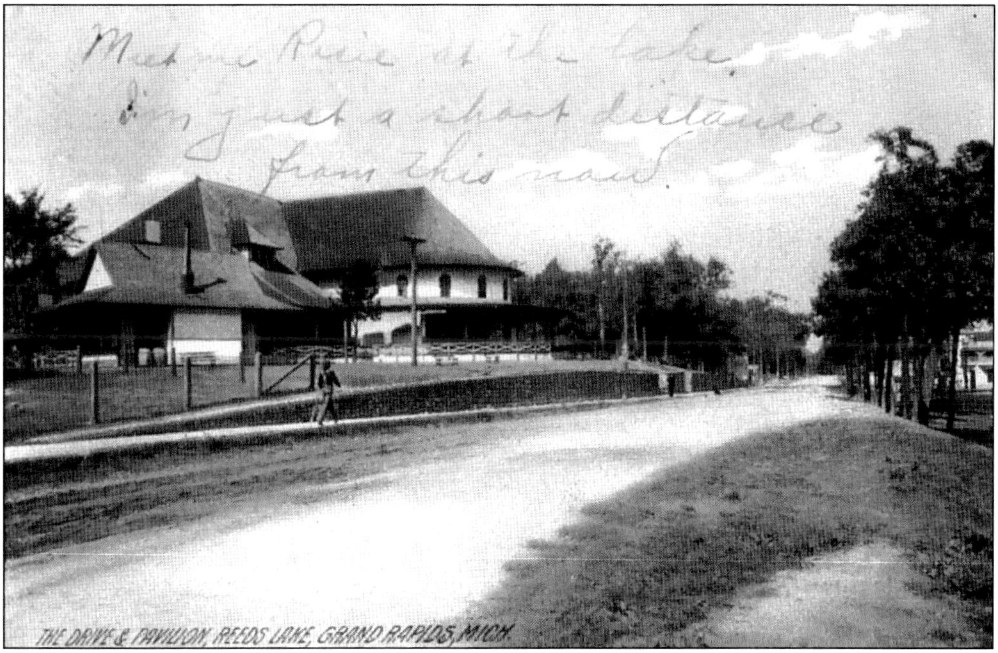

Looking northwest from the site of the present East Grand Rapids Public Library, this view from 1914 looks down an unpaved Lakeside Drive. Off the right edge of the photograph is the lake, and at the center is the Ramona Theater.

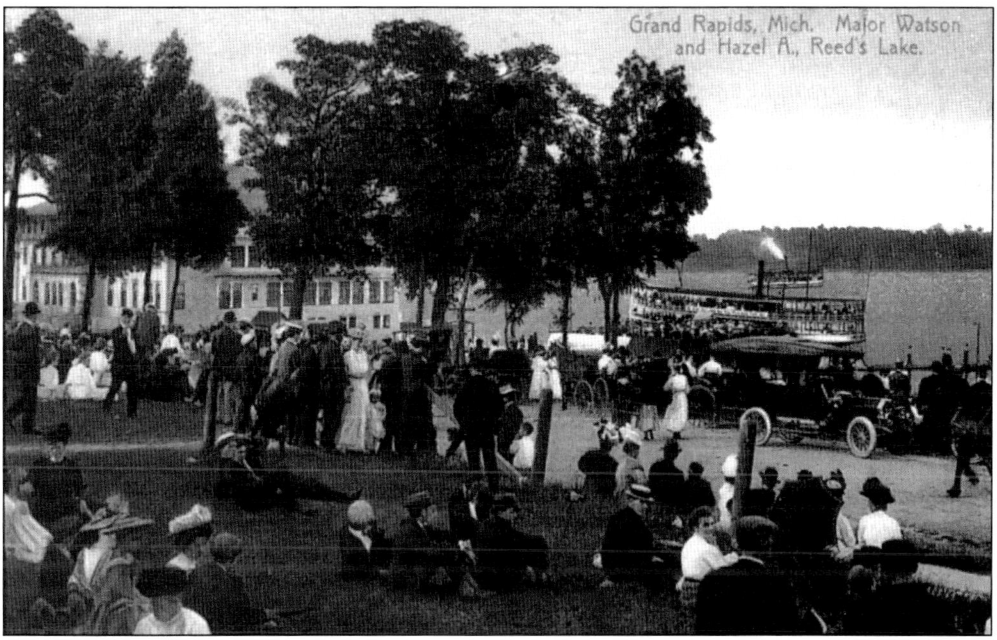

This view, from about 1910, shows the large and comfortable crowd that was usually found at the edge of Reeds Lake during the summer season at this time. At the right, the steamer *Hazel A.* is docked and taking on passengers. In the distance on the lake is the other of the pair of steamships on the lake at this time, the *Major Watson*. The banner on the *Hazel A.* reads, "Ride as long as you please for 10c." To the left, through the trees, is the clubhouse of the Lakeside Club.

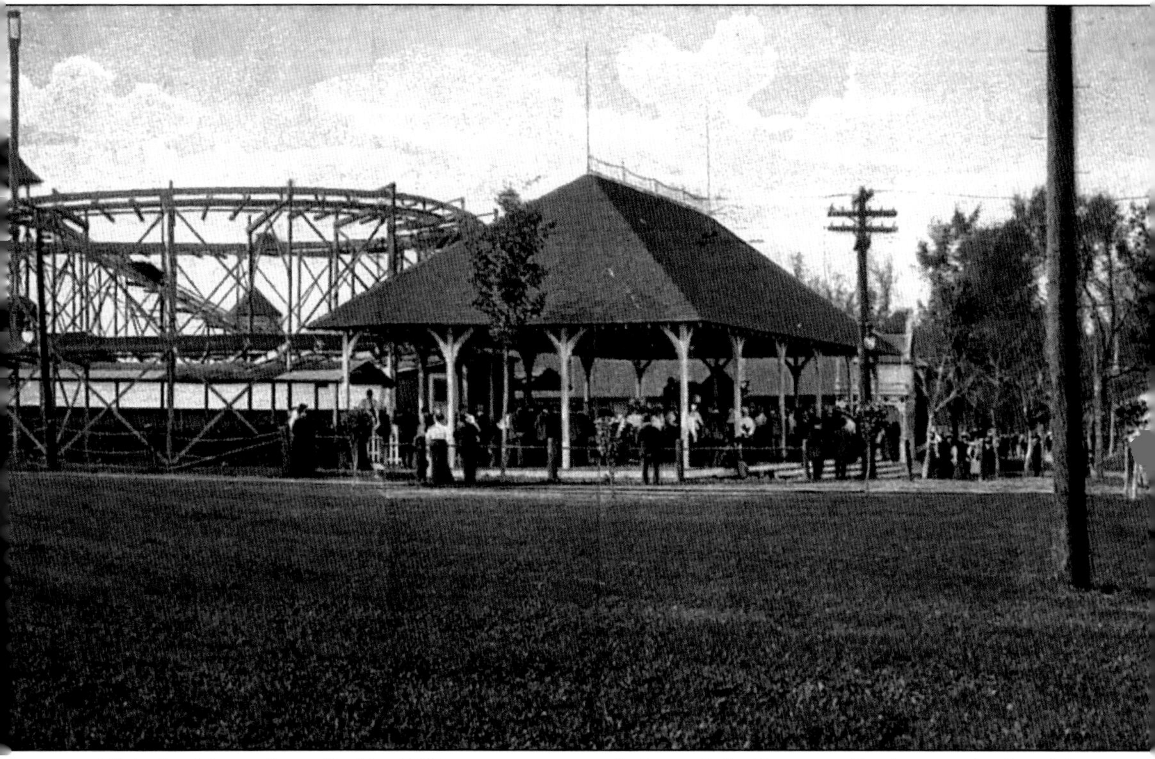

This double card, mailed in 1907, presents a good view of the Ramona Park area. At the right in the photograph is the edge of Reeds Lake, with the Lakeside Club visible. At the center right

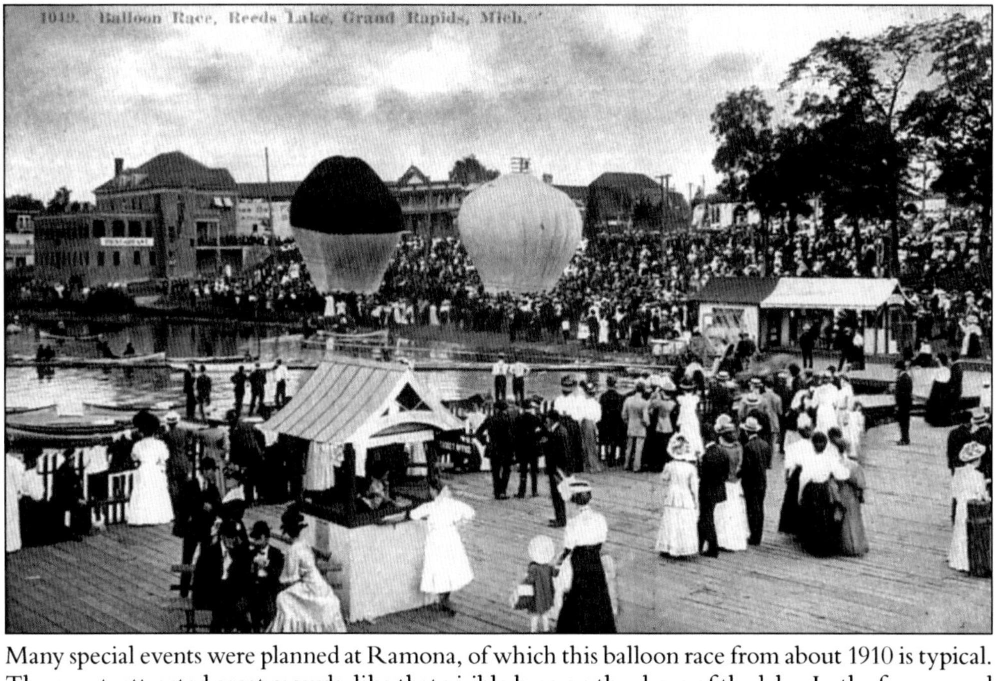

Many special events were planned at Ramona, of which this balloon race from about 1910 is typical. The events attracted great crowds, like that visible here on the shore of the lake. In the foreground is the steamship dock, and at the left is the rear of the restaurant of the Phoenix Club.

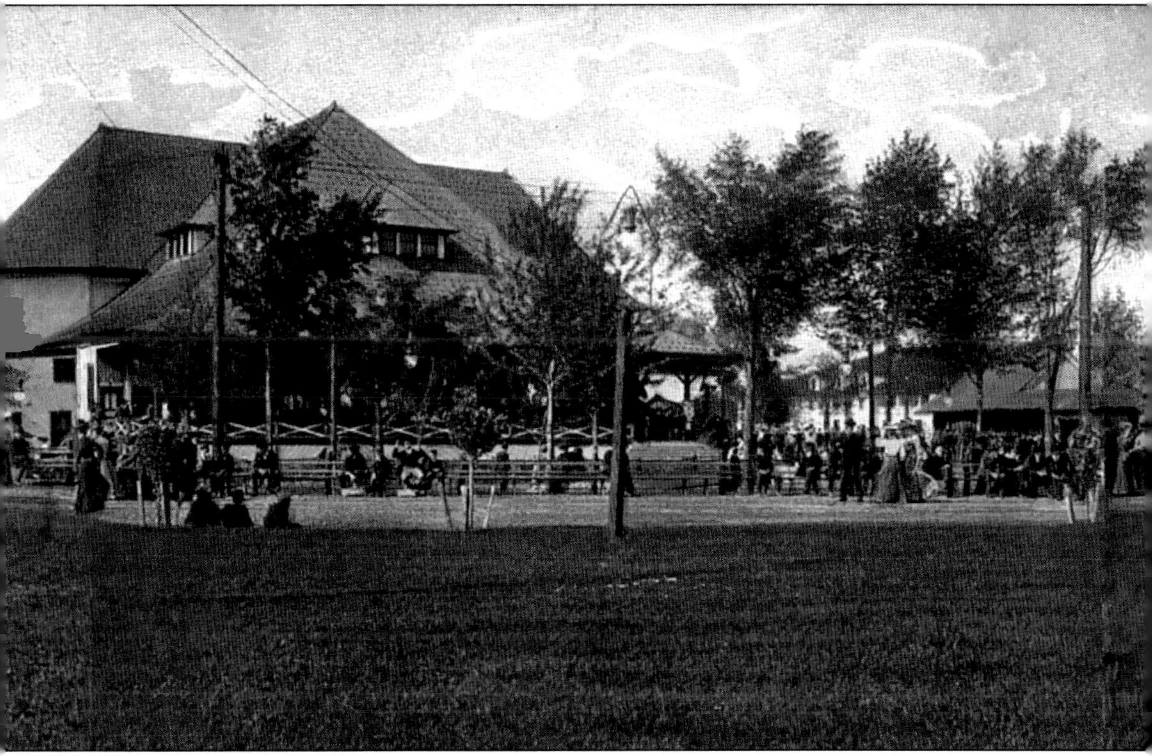

is the red roof of the Ramona Theater. To the left is the Ramona Amusement Park.

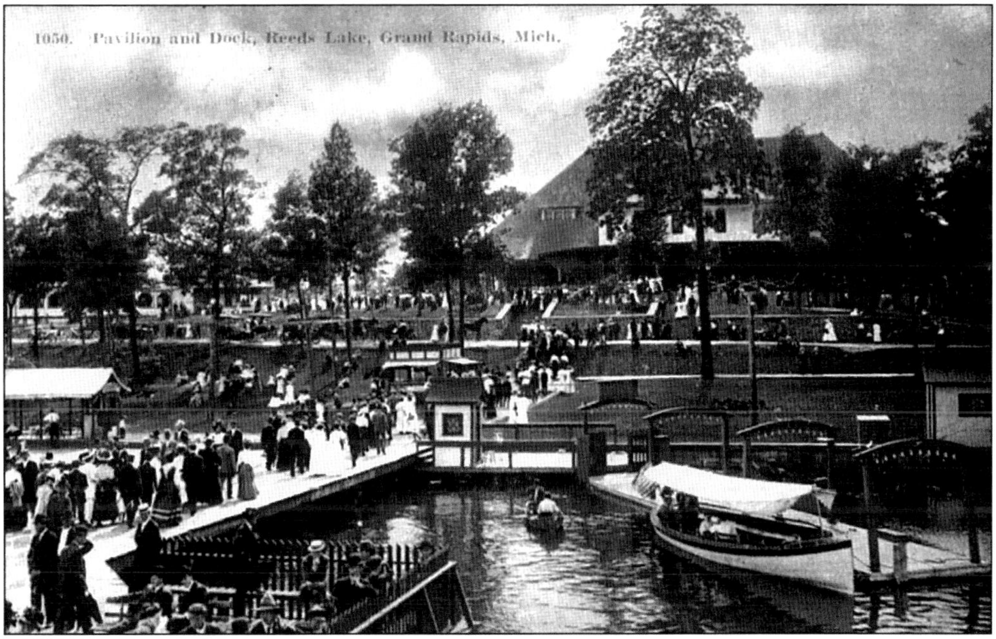

Another view of a similar crowd, on another day, was also taken in 1910 from the end of the steamship dock on Reeds Lake. In the foreground is one of the many boats available for rent. In the center is the large Ramona Theater, on the site of the present Lakeshore Club apartments.

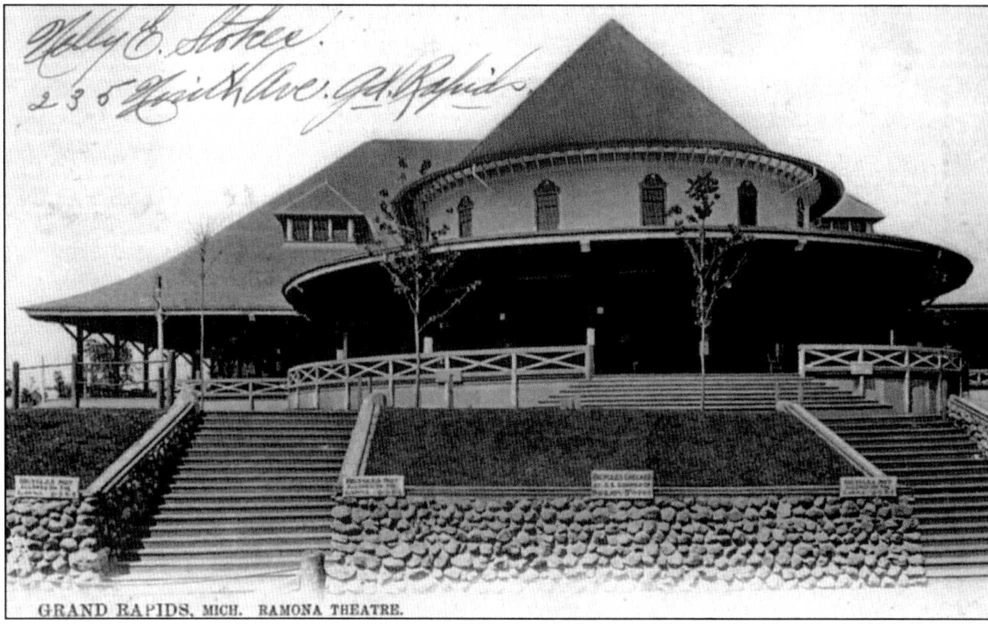

A view from 1905, this postcard shows the lakefront of the Ramona Theater. Reeds Lake would have been directly behind the photographer. This theater, active between about 1905 and 1940, attracted performers from far and wide, including the Marx Brothers, Jimmy Durante, and Edgar Bergen. This card was produced by the famous English publisher Raphael Tuck, who carried a royal warrant from the King and Queen of England.

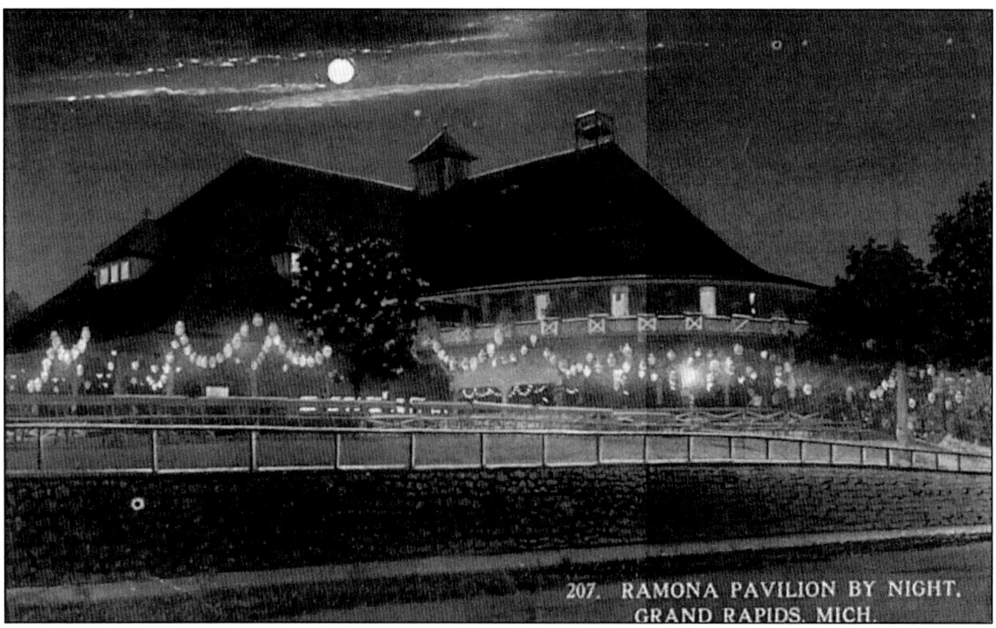

A night view of the Ramona Theater from 1913 depicts when hundreds of lighted lanterns decorated the area for visitors.

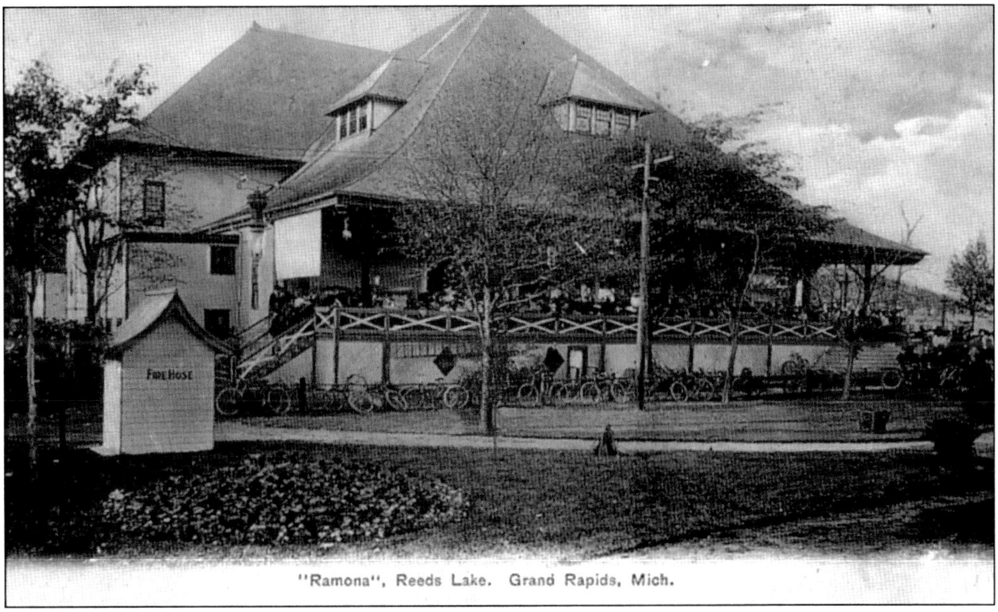

Another view of the Ramona Theater, from 1906, shows the land front of the structure. Note the large number of bicycles parked outside the theater. Bicycles provided a popular alternative means of transportation from the city out to Reeds Lake.

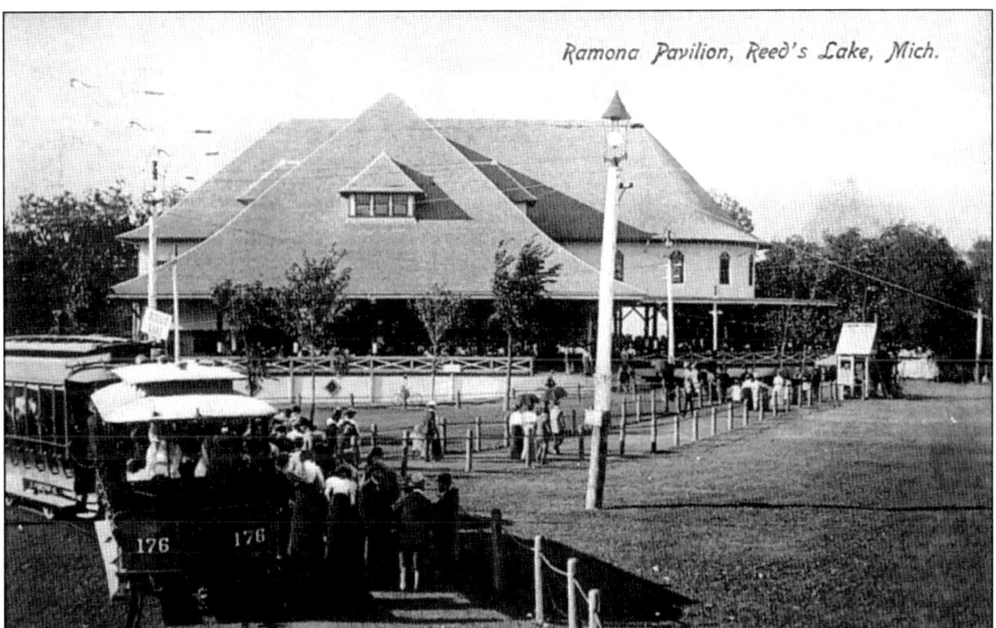

Streetcar passengers disembark in the late afternoon for a performance at the Ramona Theater.

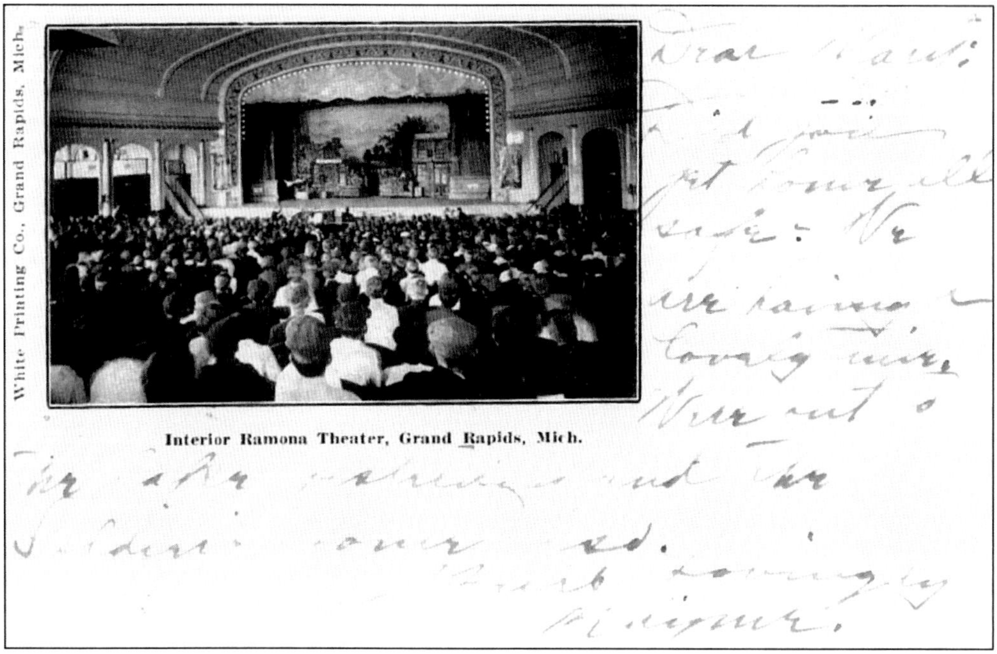

A rare view, from 1907, of the inside of the Ramona Theater shows a large crowd enjoying an actual stage performance.

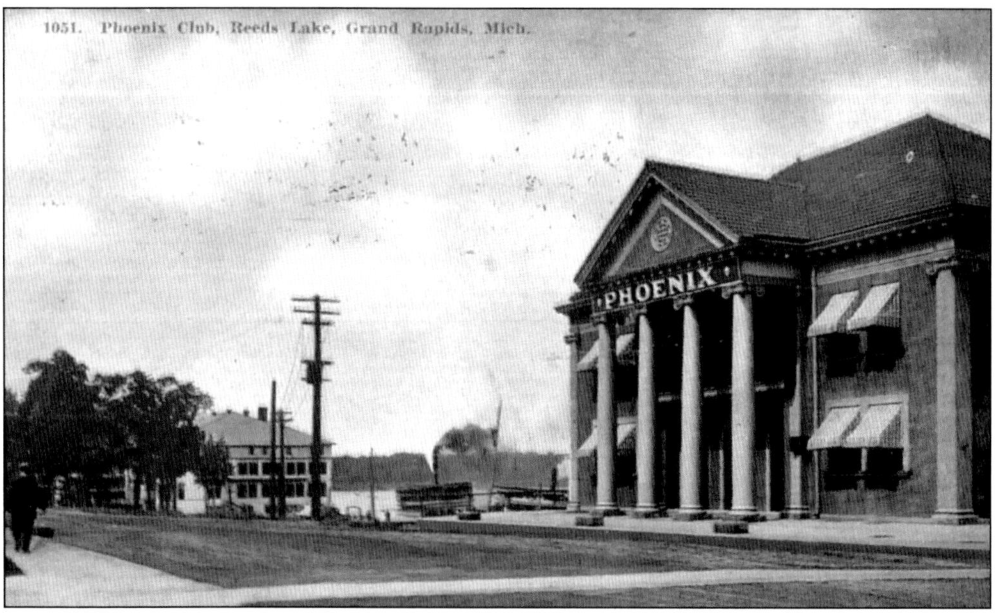

This is a view looking north along Lakeside Avenue from 1910. At the right is the Phoenix Club, a club and restaurant boasting an elaborate soda fountain, on the edge of the lake. On the left is the clubhouse of the Lakeside Club. Between the buildings, the lake is visible, along with both of the steamships out on the lake.

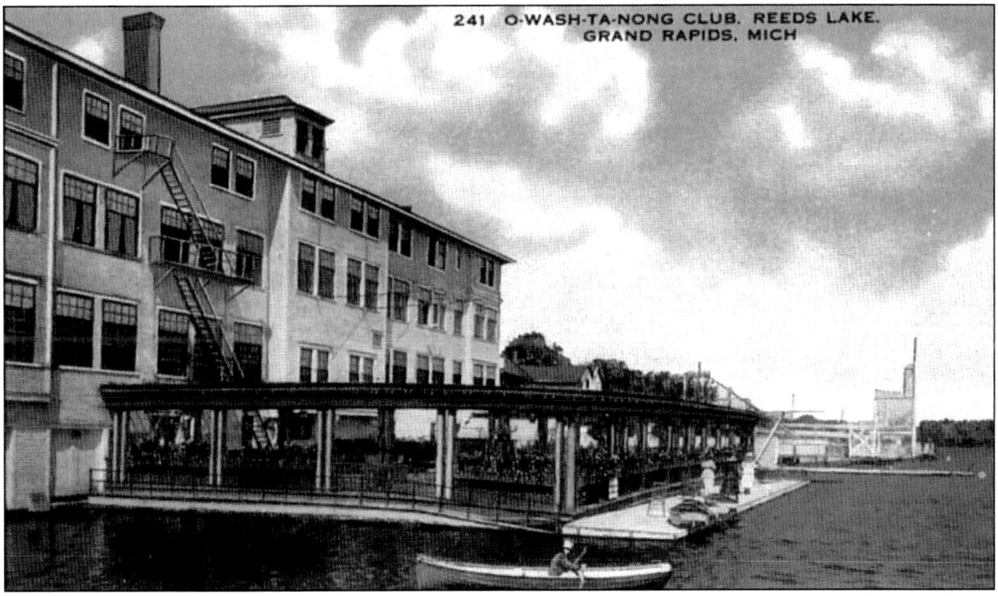

The O-Wash-Ta-Nong Club, located literally at the water's edge, sat approximately where Collins Park is today. This clubhouse went through several manifestations over the years. The original club, its name taken from the Ottawa name for the rapids on the Grand River where the city of Grand Rapids was founded, came into being in 1886. Its 500 members used this building only in the summer season, having use of club rooms downtown during the rest of the year. The original club failed in 1892, and the clubhouse on this site was demolished. The club was briefly revived in 1914 in an effort to rekindle happier days, and the building pictured was built but once again failed a few years later. While it stood empty, it burned to the ground in 1918.

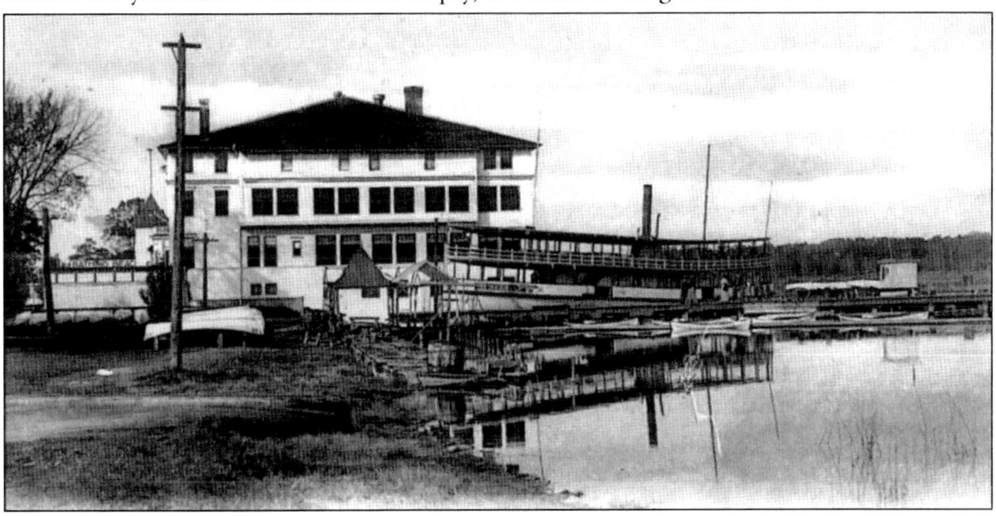

This is a view of the Lakeside Clubhouse, built on the same site as its predecessor, O-Wash-Ta-Nong, in 1895. The original Lakeside Clubhouse on this site burned in 1904 and was rebuilt the following year. The club continued only for another four years thereafter and then disbanded. When the Masonic home, located a couple of blocks south of this site, burned in 1910, many of the residents of that facility were temporarily housed in the former clubhouse. The last use of the building was the brief reappearance of the original O-Wash-Ta-Nong Club between 1914 and 1918, when the building burned for the last time.

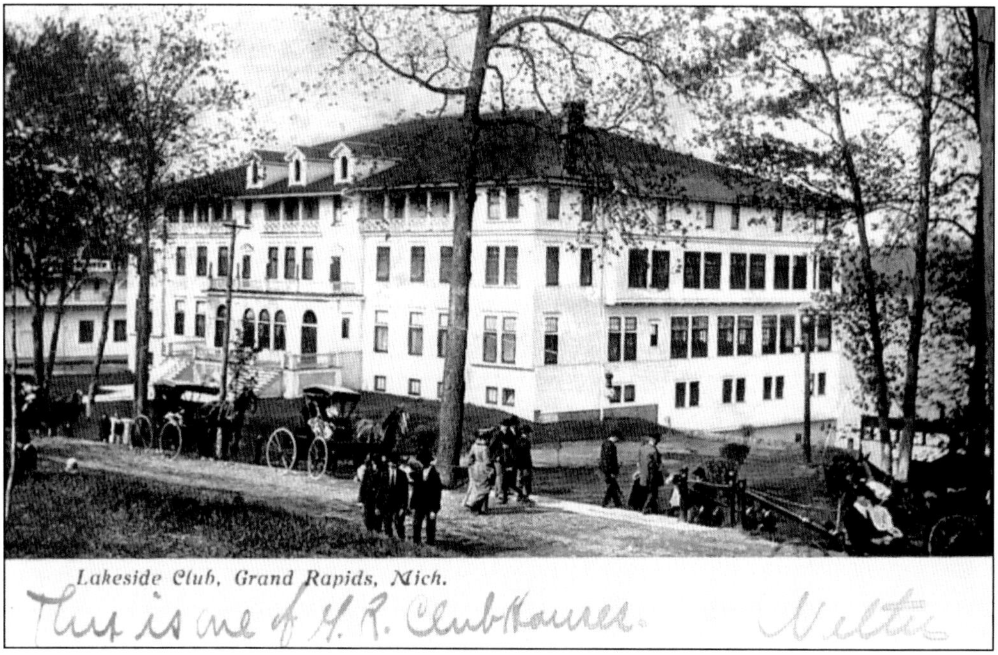

Another view of the Lakeside Club building, taken in 1907, shows the facility the year before it closed.

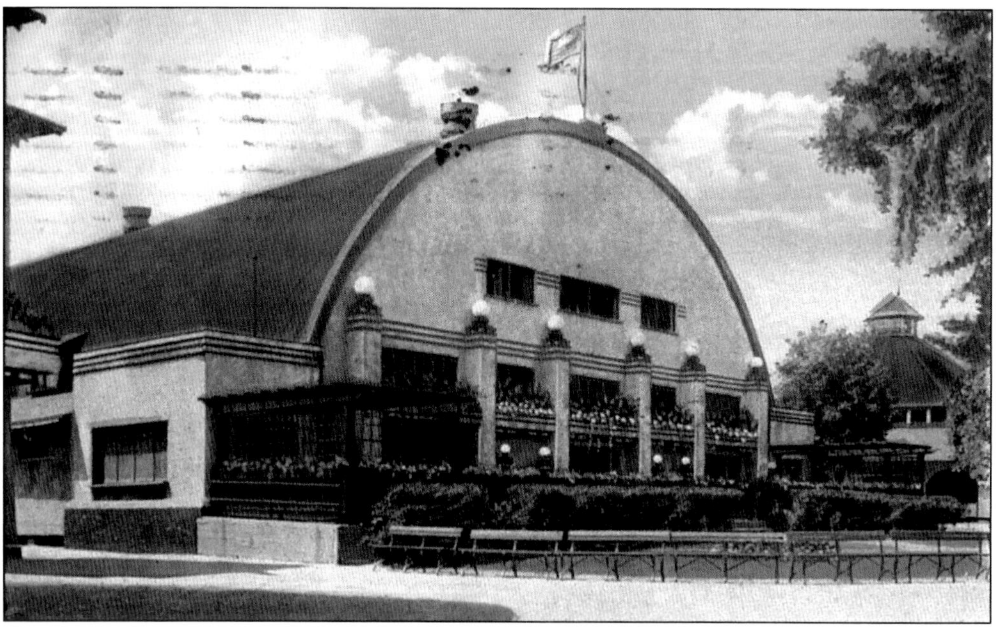

The Dance Pavilion at Ramona, built in the 1920s, played host to many of the greatest bands of the 1930s and 1940s, including Tommy Dorsey, Glenn Miller, and Bob Crosby. Later used as a roller-skating rink, the structure was moved, in sections, when Ramona closed down in the 1950s to a location on Plymouth Avenue, north of Michigan Street. There it was finally razed in the 1970s.

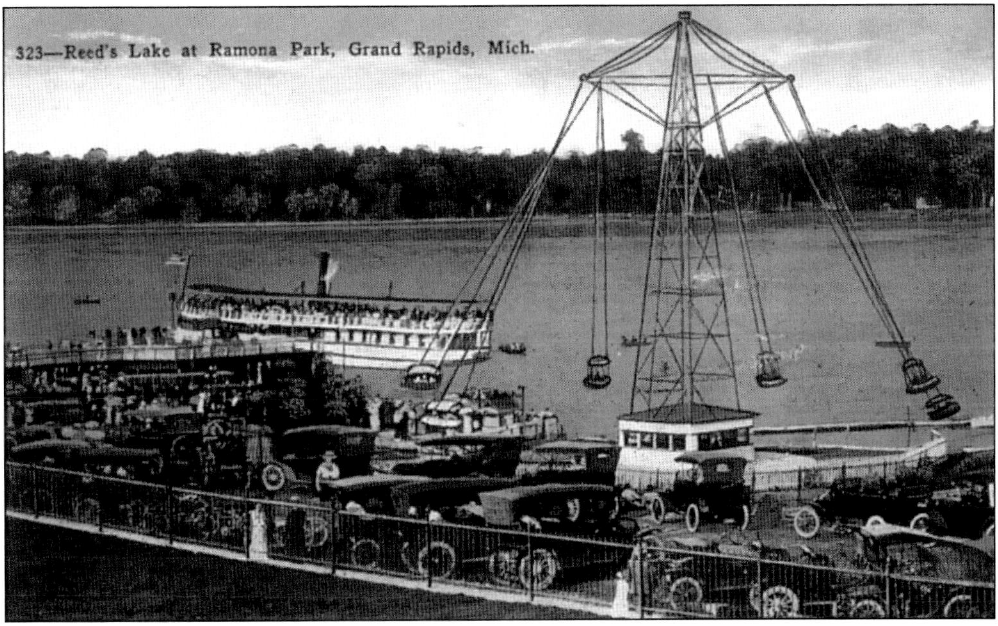

A view from 1917 shows one of the many rides located at the Ramona Park on the edge of Reeds Lake.

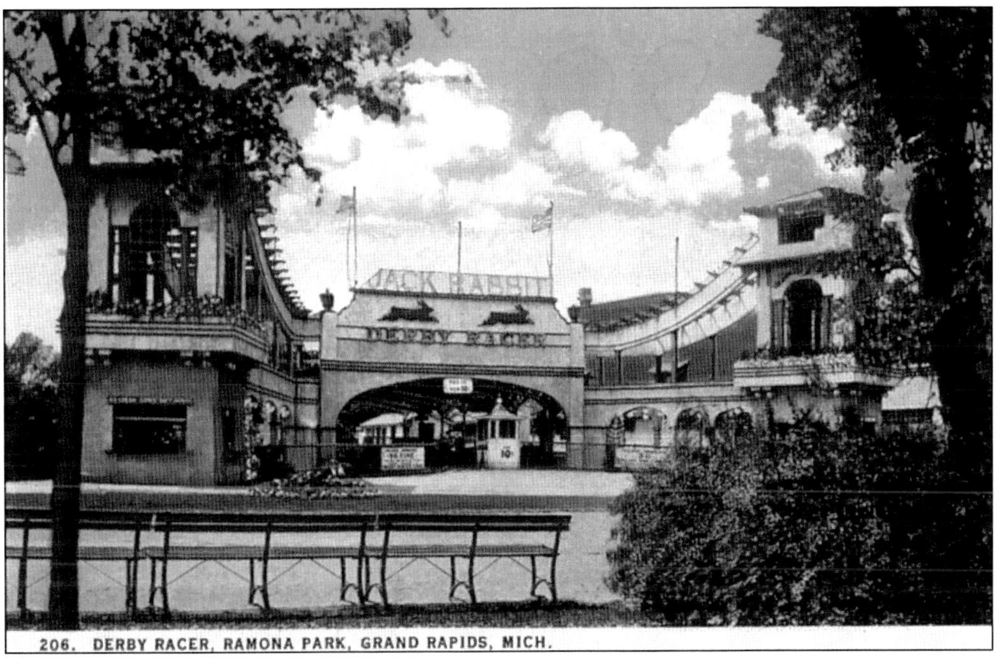

This is a view from 1923 of the most famous and popular amusement attraction at Ramona, the Derby Racer roller coaster. Built in 1914 of 75,000 board feet of lumber, the Derby Racer operated continuously, in season, for the next 42 years. Described as "a sure cure for the blues," where "you can't buy more fun for a dime," the Derby Racer was thought to be the largest amusement ride in the country at the time of its construction.

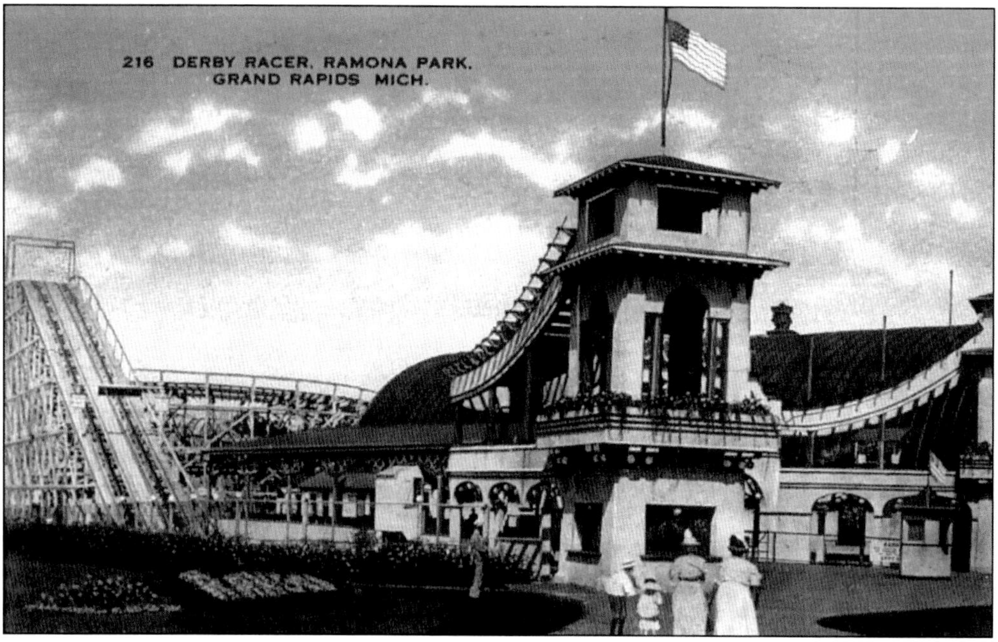

In this view of the Derby Racer, from 1917, the unusual "double track" is visible. The roller coaster was built in this way to allow two trains of cars, loaded with screaming riders, to actually race one another side by side.

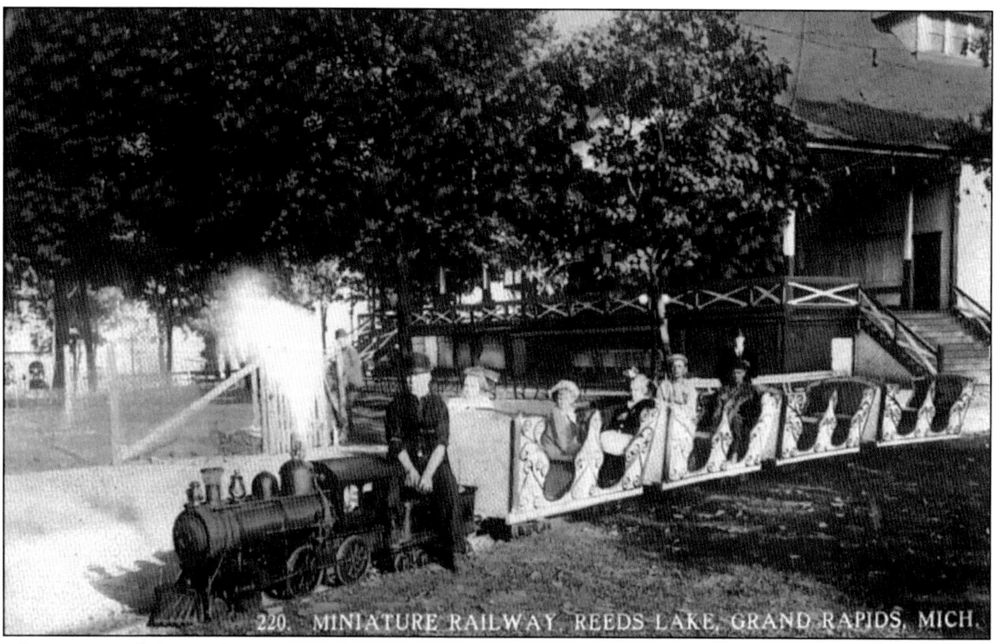

This postcard from about 1925 shows the built-to-scale railroad that ran through and around the Ramona Park area. The train was owned and operated by Harry Glidden, pictured here sitting on the engine. Glidden was actually a Rock Island Railroad engineer who worked his real railroad job during the off-seasons.

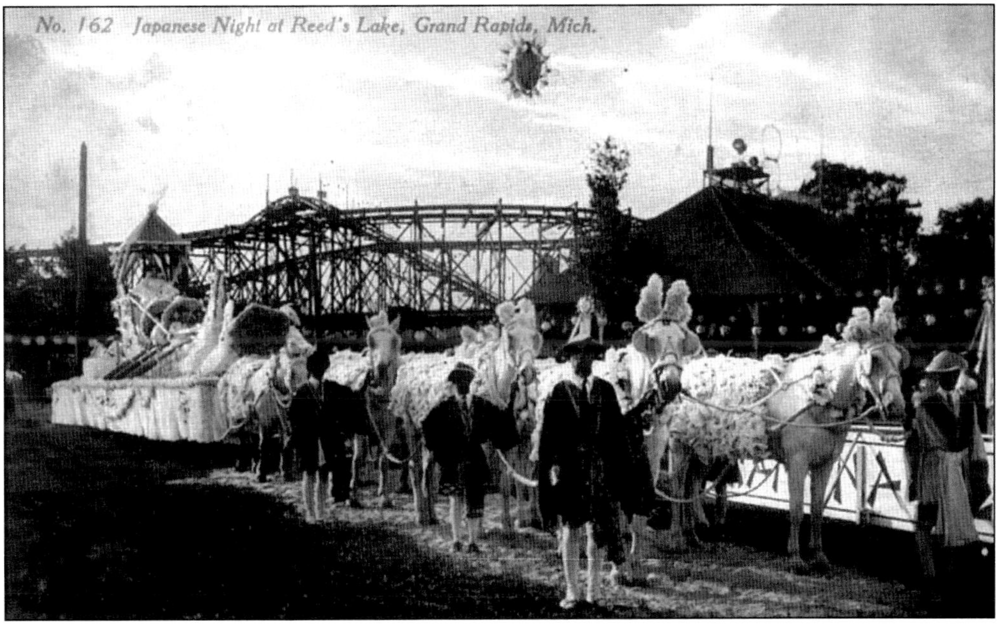

In 1915, "Japanese Night" at Ramona, described in the local press as an "event of surprising grandeur," was typical of the many such events that were created by the management to boost the attendance of local crowds. In the background, the Ramona Theater is visible, as are the tracks of the Derby Racer.

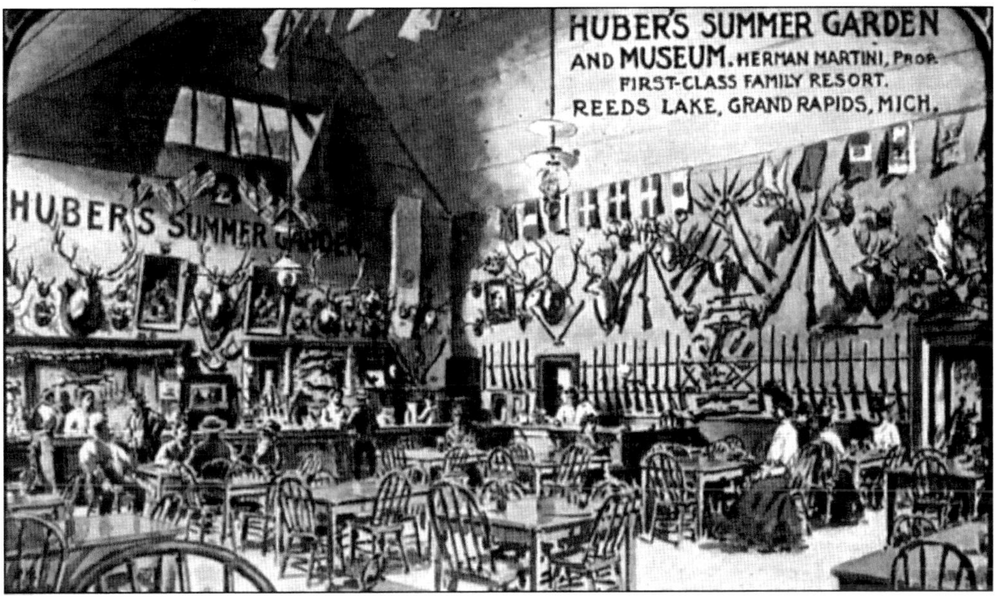

This rare commercial card from 1907 was produced for Huber's Summer Garden, a restaurant and beer garden located literally at the intersection of Lovett and Greenwood Streets. The building was built immediately north of the Ramona Park property in 1889 by Henry Huber and was thereafter operated quite successfully as a restaurant and beer garden by the Huber family until the passage of Prohibition in 1919, which ultimately brought it, and others in the area like it, to ruin. Huber's was noted for a fine collection of war relics and hunting trophies, which were presented to the Kent Scientific Museum when the restaurant closed in 1921.

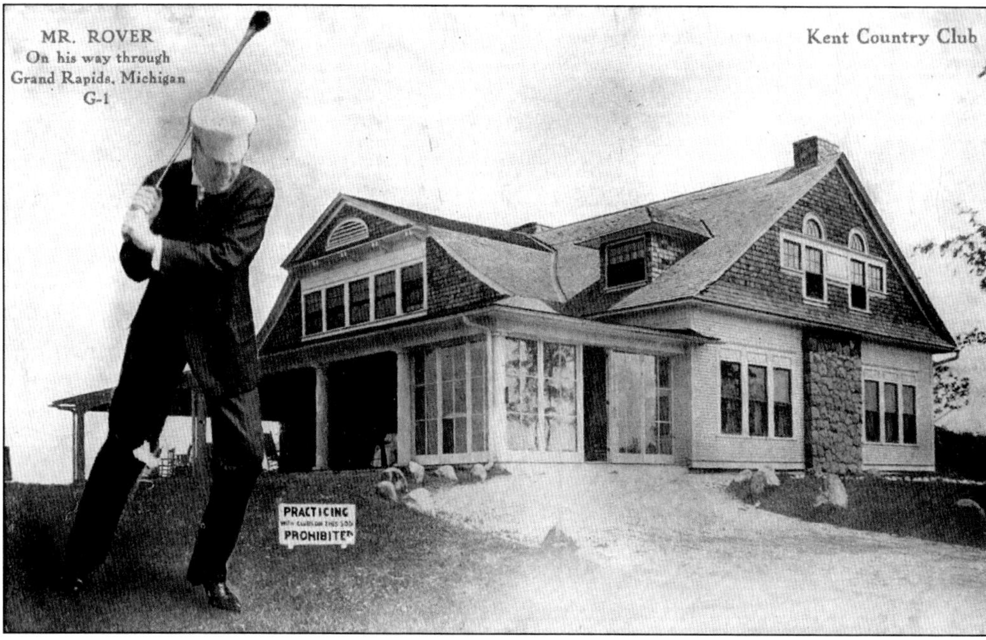

This, the first card in the Mr. Rover series, pictures the front lawn of the Kent Country Club in northeast Grand Rapids.

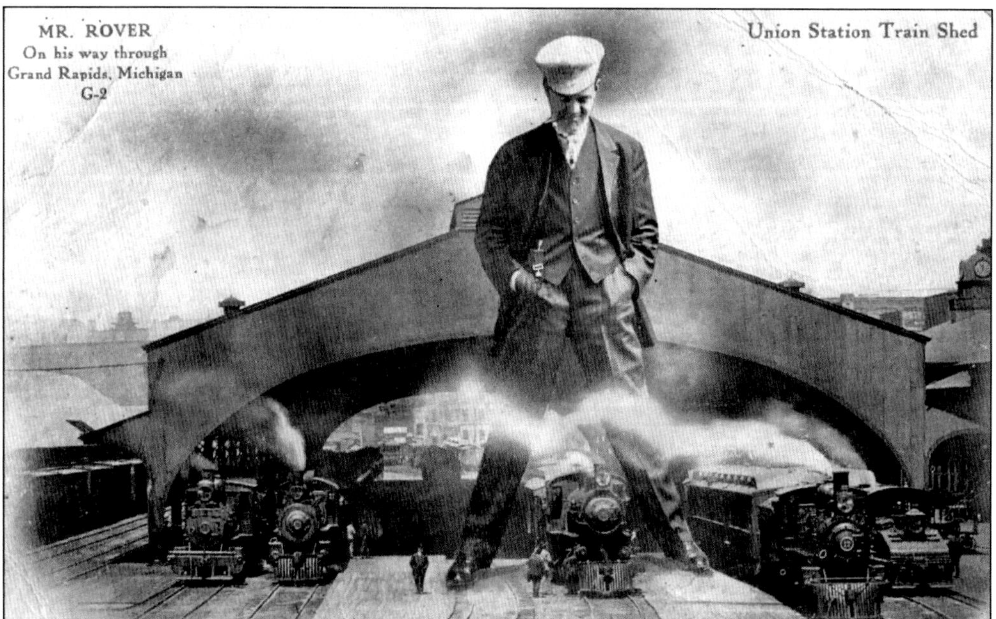

In the second card in the series, Mr. Rover is standing above the trains departing from the train shed at the union station, then located on South Ionia Avenue, behind the present location of the Van Andel Arena.

Five

The Mr. Rover Cards

Beginning around 1907, a series of privately printed "exaggeration" postcards was published in Grand Rapids by the Reed-Tandler Company. Titled as "Mr. Rover on his way through Grand Rapids," the cards number approximately 28, though the exact number of original images is not known. These comic cards were quite popular when first published, described in a 1911 newspaper account as "famous," and went through several printings, each slightly different from the others. They remain among the most highly sought after trophies for local postcard collectors. Believed to be the most complete set of these cards ever assembled, all but one of the known cards in the series are pictured here. The author is grateful to Ron Carowitz, and the late Justin Tieri for their assistance in providing images of some of the rare cards presented.

The history of the series and the identity of "Mr. Rover," depicted on each card as an oversized presence and participant in each card's scene, is the subject of some controversy. For many years after the appearance of the series, Mr. Rover's identity remained obscure, not because it had been hidden but as a result of the conduct of the model himself. In January 1911, a young, married local insurance executive suddenly, and without apparent explanation, disappeared from Grand Rapids, taking with him the cash assets of his business, along with his female stenographer. The couple also took the bulk of the assets of the executive's wife. Harry H. Wykom, identified in the local press as both the absconding executive and as the model for the Mr. Rover postcard series, was described by his friends and business associates as a "hail fellow, well met," active in business and social circles. His stenographer was Mamie Lynch. No one knew where the pair had gone except for the mother of the stenographer, who reported that her daughter had "gone away for a vacation," but refused to disclose just where she had gone. A desk clerk at a hotel in Detroit claimed to have seen the couple and reported that they had checked out of the hotel, "going east." Neither Wykom or Lynch were ever seen in Grand Rapids again. They left behind a shattered business, soon set upon by the insurance inspectors and the companies whose stolen premiums had financed the departure, and many questions, which remain to this day unanswered.

Knowing the events of 1911, it is hard to say whether Wykom's plans were part of the Mr. Rover image. All of the postcards predate Wykom's sudden departure, and at least one image, of the Grand Rapids Police Department headquarters, depicting Mr. Rover running away, tantalizingly suggests his future plan.

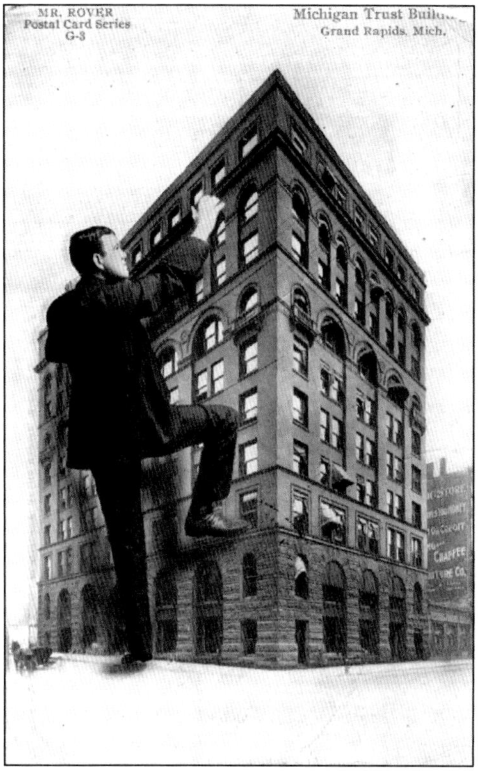

Here Mr. Rover is seen scaling the side of the Michigan Trust Building at Ottawa Avenue and Pearl Street, then the tallest building in the city. This is the third card in the series.

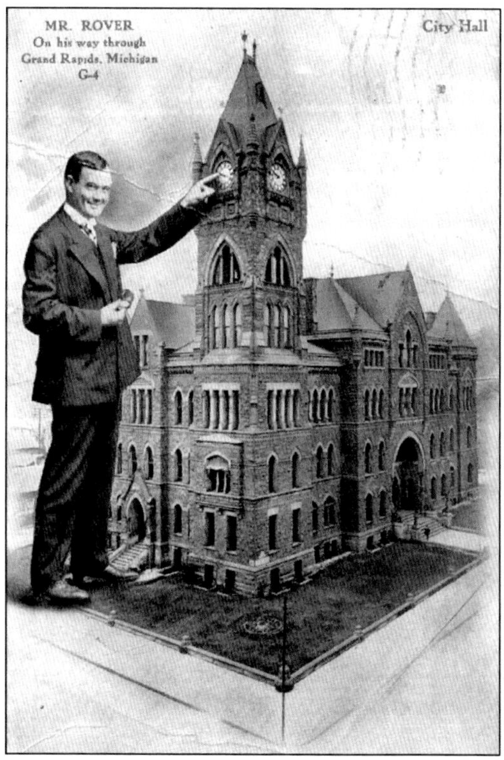

The fourth card in the series shows Mr. Rover correcting the hands on the clock of the Grand Rapids City Hall. (Collection of Justin Tieri.)

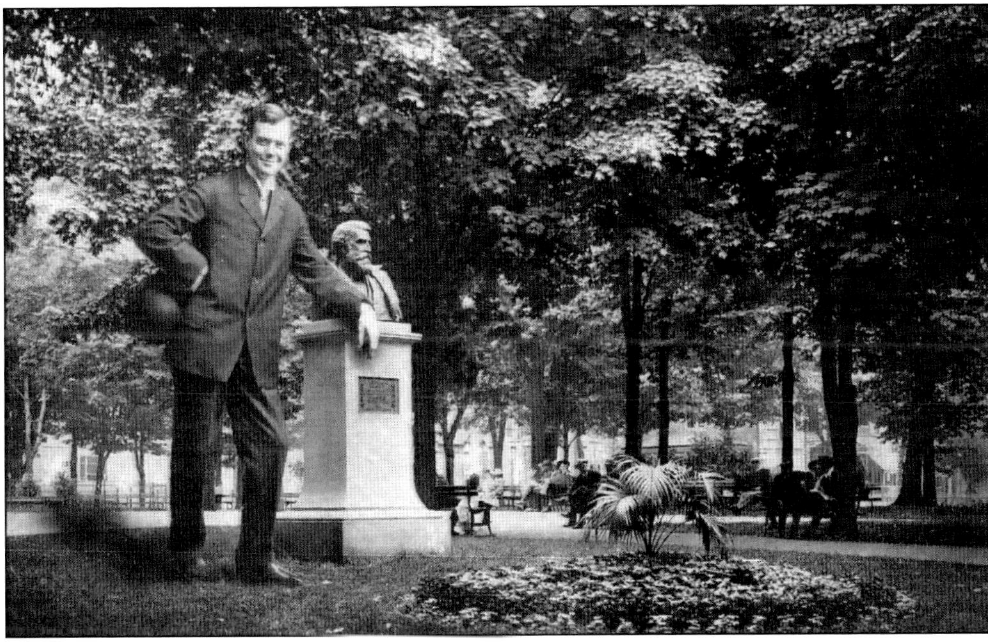

Mr. Rover here stands in Fulton Street Park, now known as Veteran's Memorial Park, leaning on the Thomas Gilbert Memorial. This is card No. 5.

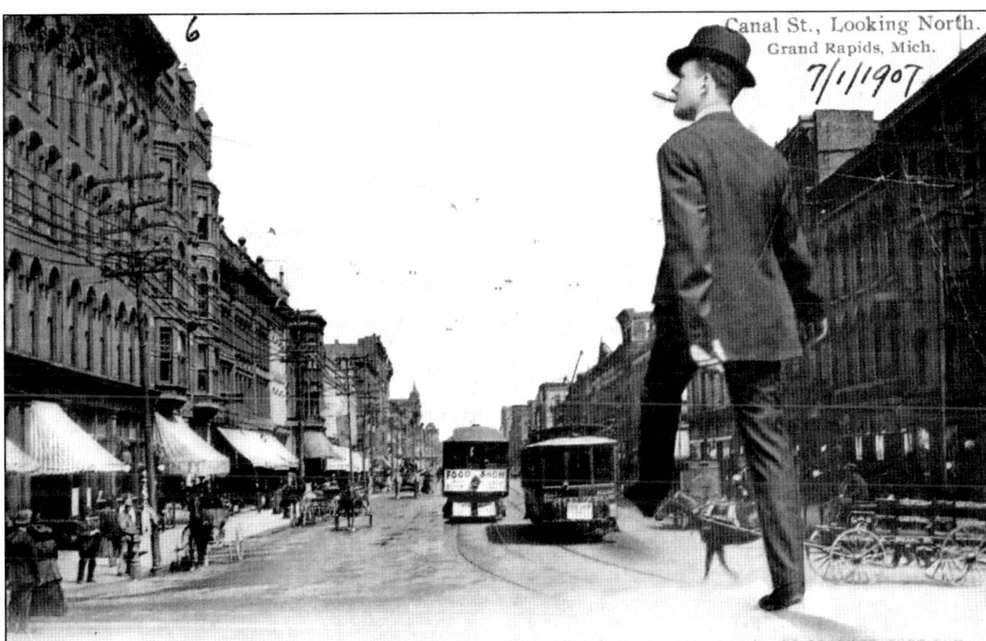

The sixth card in the series shows Mr. Rover strolling north on Canal Street (now Monroe Avenue) toward Michigan Street. This card was mailed on July 1, 1907. (Collection of Justin Tieri.)

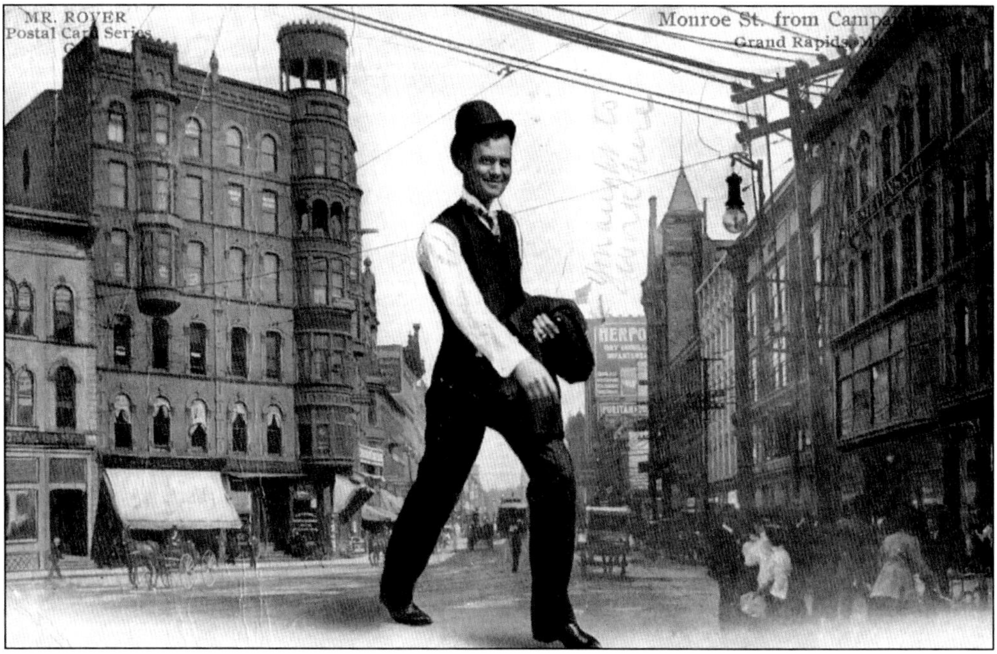

Mr. Rover is here walking across Campau Square. Behind him Monroe Avenue stretches to the southeast. This is No. 7 in the series.

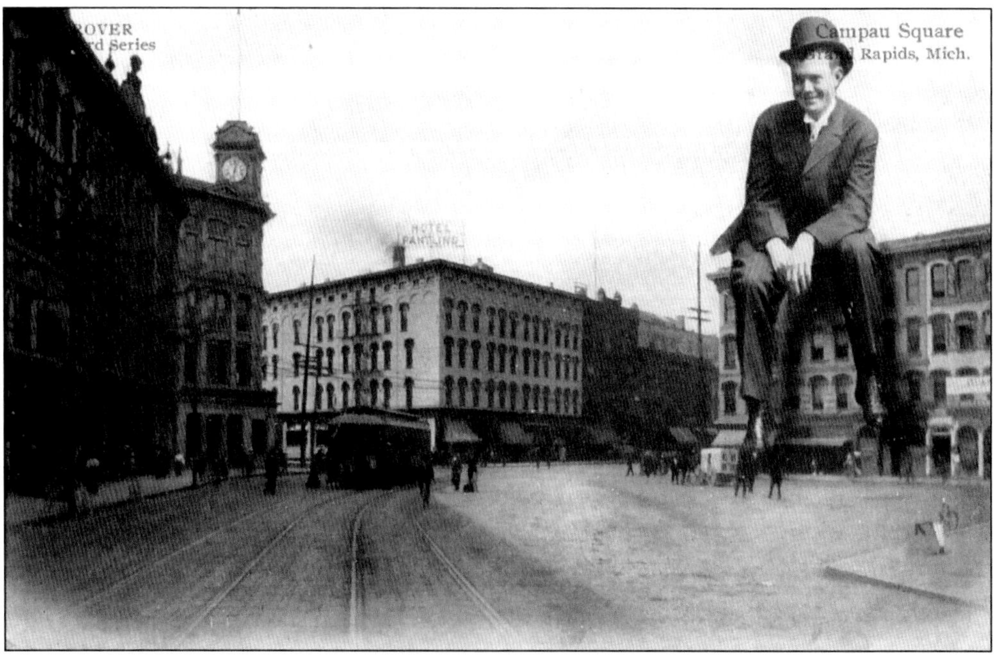

In another view of Campau Square, this time Mr. Rover is seated to the right, watching people boarding a streetcar. This is No. 8 in the series.

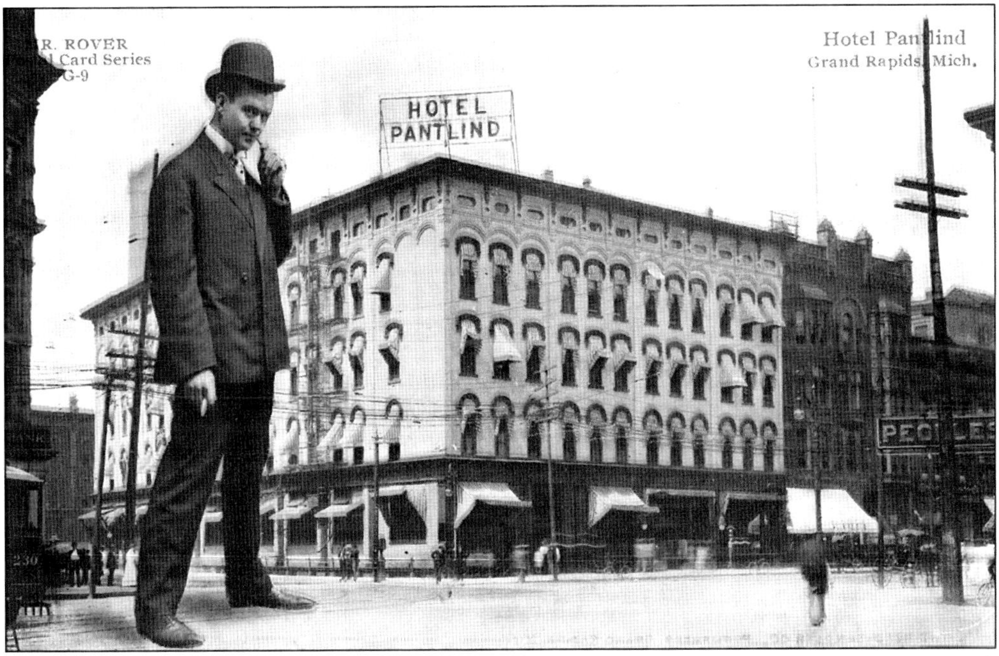

In the ninth card in the series, Mr. Rover stands on the western edge of Campau Square, with the old Pantlind Hotel at the center. (Collection of Justin Tieri.)

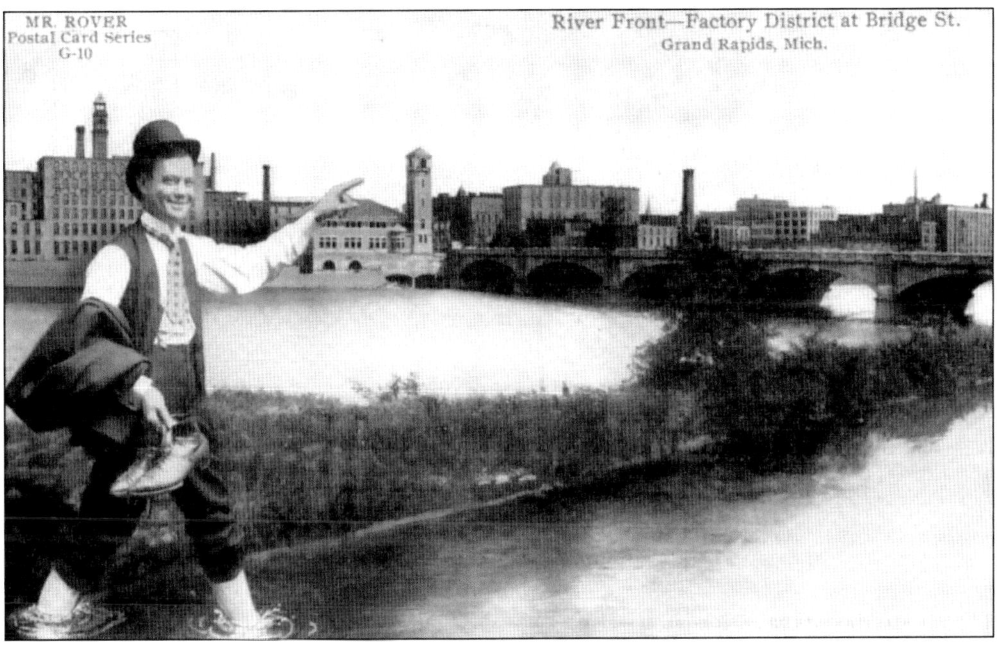

The tenth card in the series shows Mr. Rover wading in the west side canal, which then ran parallel to the west bank of the Grand River. In the background is the Bridge Street Bridge, and at the center is the then newly constructed Grand Trunk Railway Station. (Collection of Justin Tieri.)

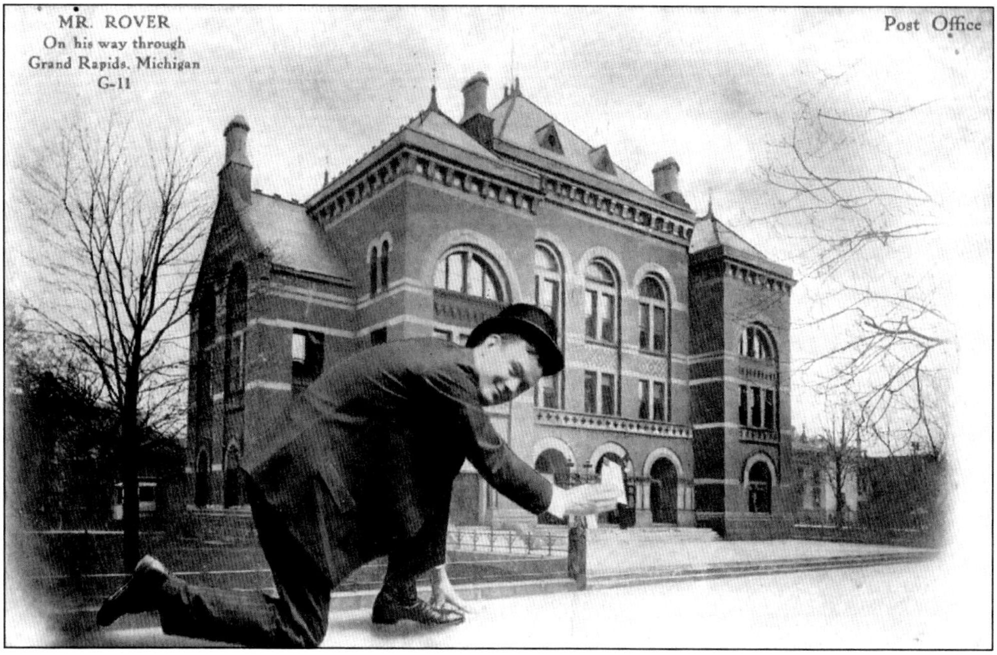

Here Mr. Rover is seen mailing a letter at the old U.S. post office and courthouse, replaced just a couple of years after this card was published in 1907. This card is No. 11 in the series.

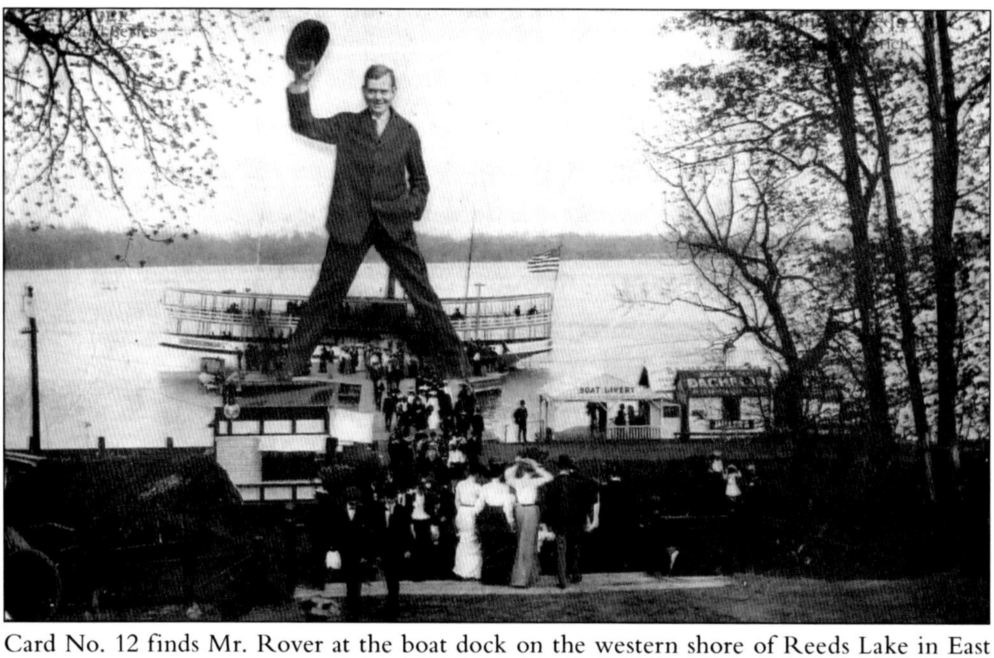

Card No. 12 finds Mr. Rover at the boat dock on the western shore of Reeds Lake in East Grand Rapids.

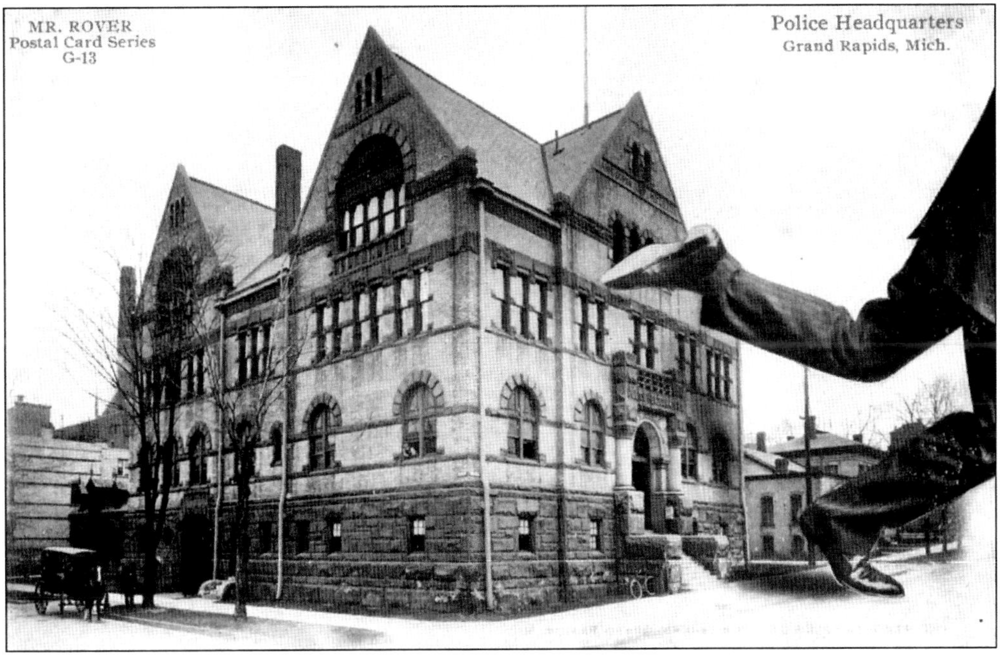

In perhaps the most interesting card in the series, given the private history of Harry Wykom, Mr. Rover is here seen running away from the Grand Rapids Police headquarters, then located on Ionia Avenue, just south of Michigan Street. This is card No. 13. (Collection of Justin Tieri.)

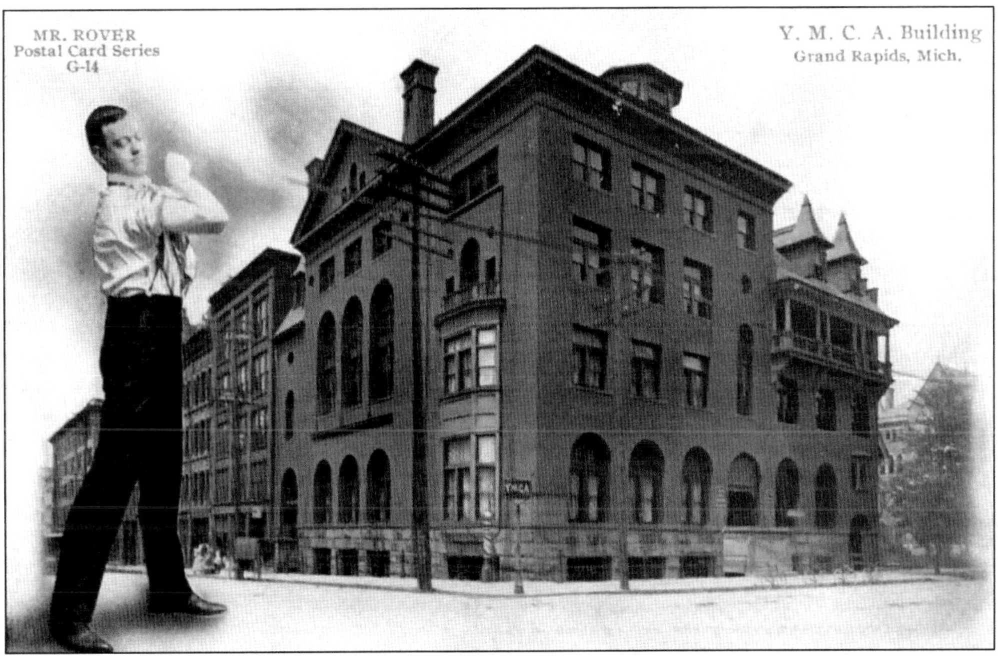

Card No. 14 shows Mr. Rover flexing his muscles outside the YMCA building, then located at the corner of Ionia Avenue and Pearl Street. The building is now used for office space, as the Federal Square Building. The date is 1907. (Collection of Justin Tieri.)

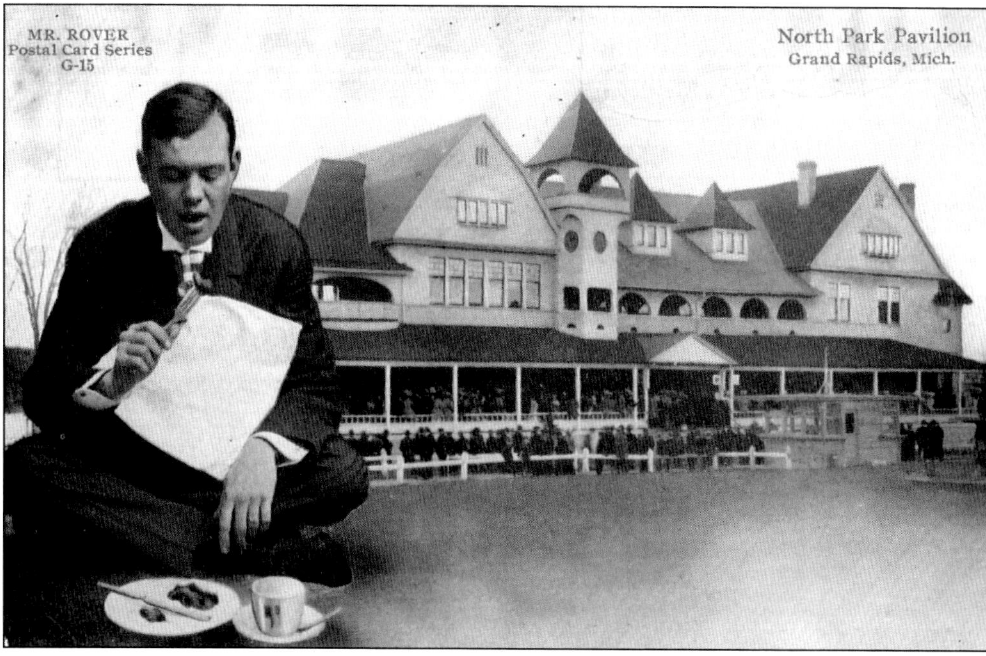

In card No. 15, Mr. Rover pauses for a picnic lunch at the North Park Pavilion, then located on the river north of town. (Collection of Justin Tieri.)

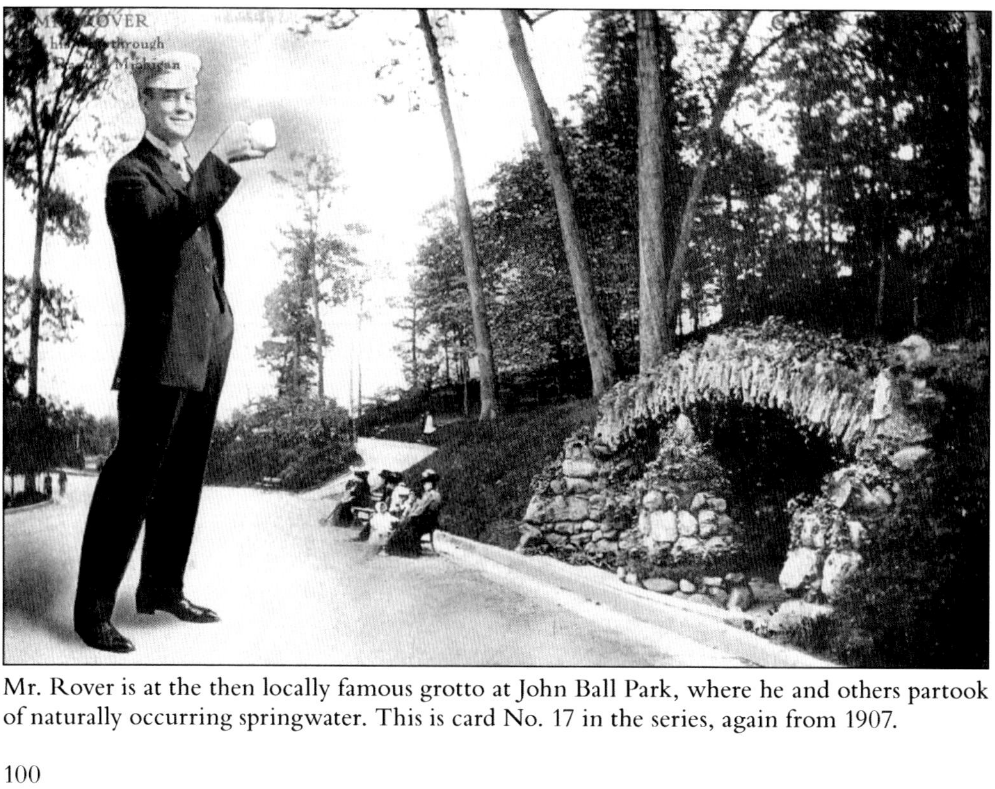

Mr. Rover is at the then locally famous grotto at John Ball Park, where he and others partook of naturally occurring springwater. This is card No. 17 in the series, again from 1907.

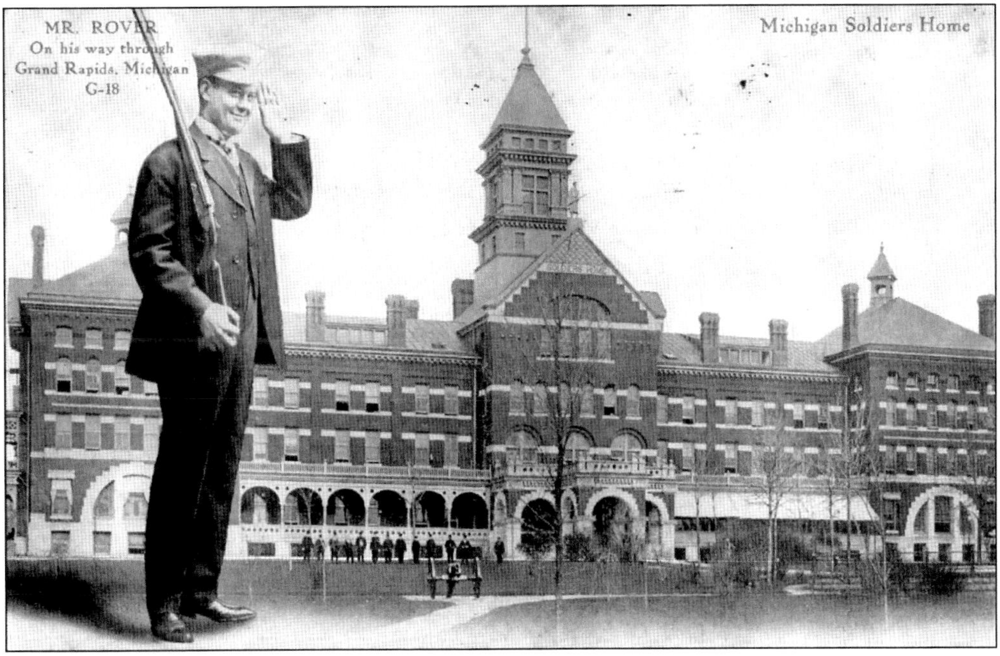

Mr. Rover stands at attention before the main building of the Michigan Soldier's Home on Monroe Avenue in the North Park area, north of Grand Rapids. This is No. 18 in the series. (Collection of Justin Tieri.)

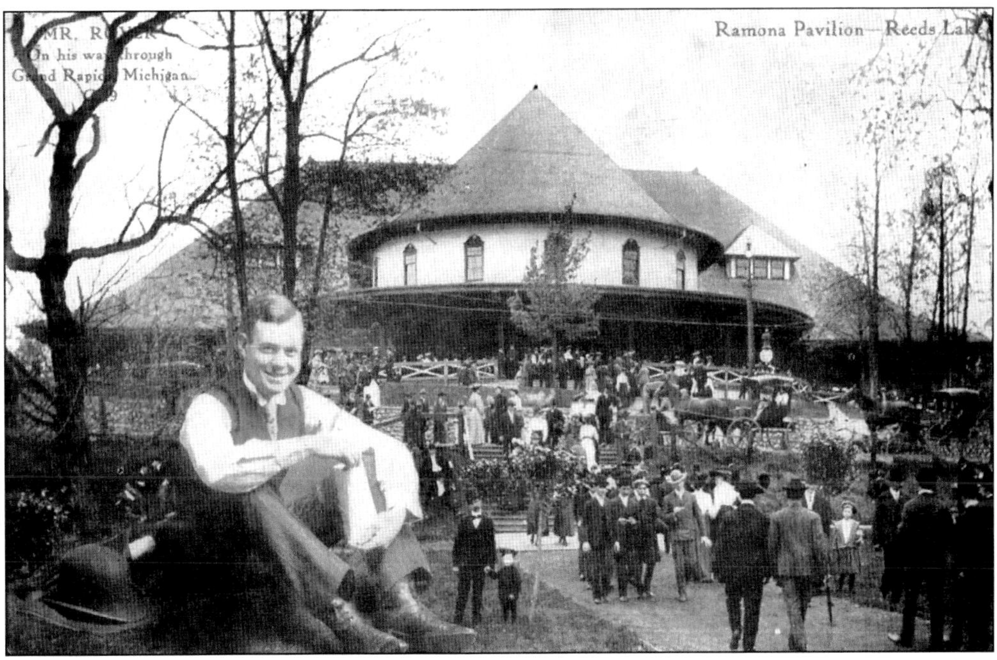

Card No. 19 finds Mr. Rover seated on the western shore of Reeds Lake, just outside of the Ramona Theater.

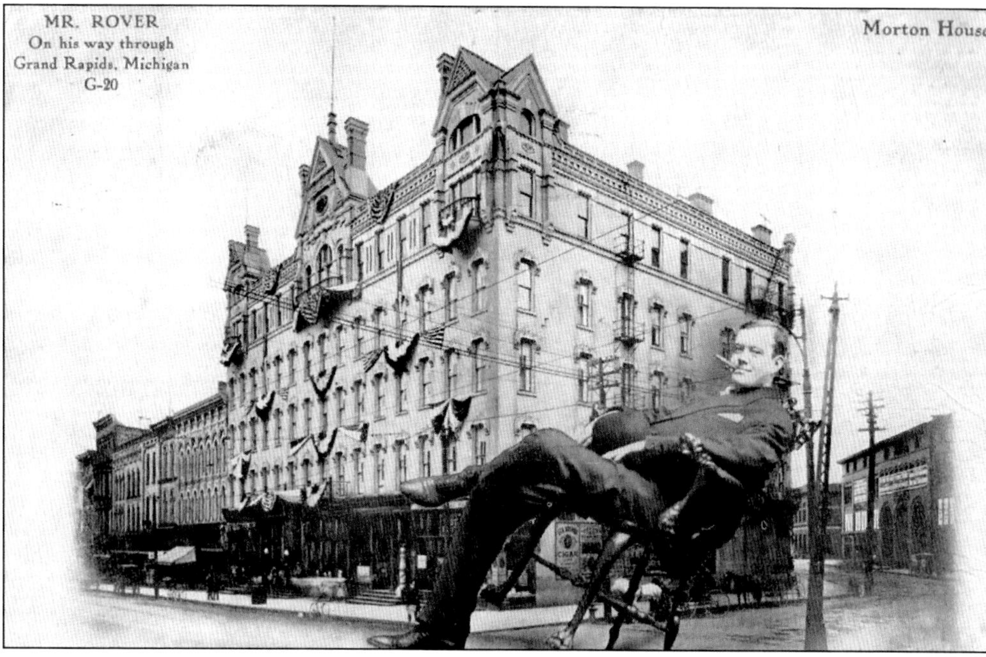

The old Morton House Hotel, later replaced with the present structure in 1923, is in the background of card No. 20, showing Mr. Rover seated at the corner of Monroe and Ionia Avenues. (Collection of Justin Tieri.)

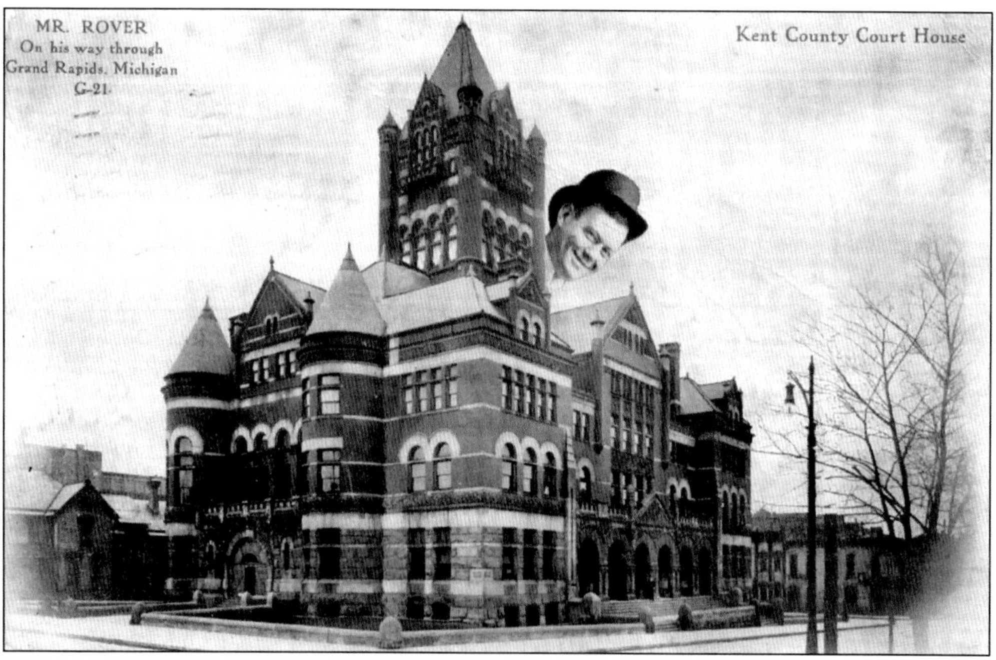

Here Mr. Rover peeks out from behind the tower of the Kent County Court House, then located on Ottawa Avenue, south of Pearl Street. This is card No. 21 in the series.

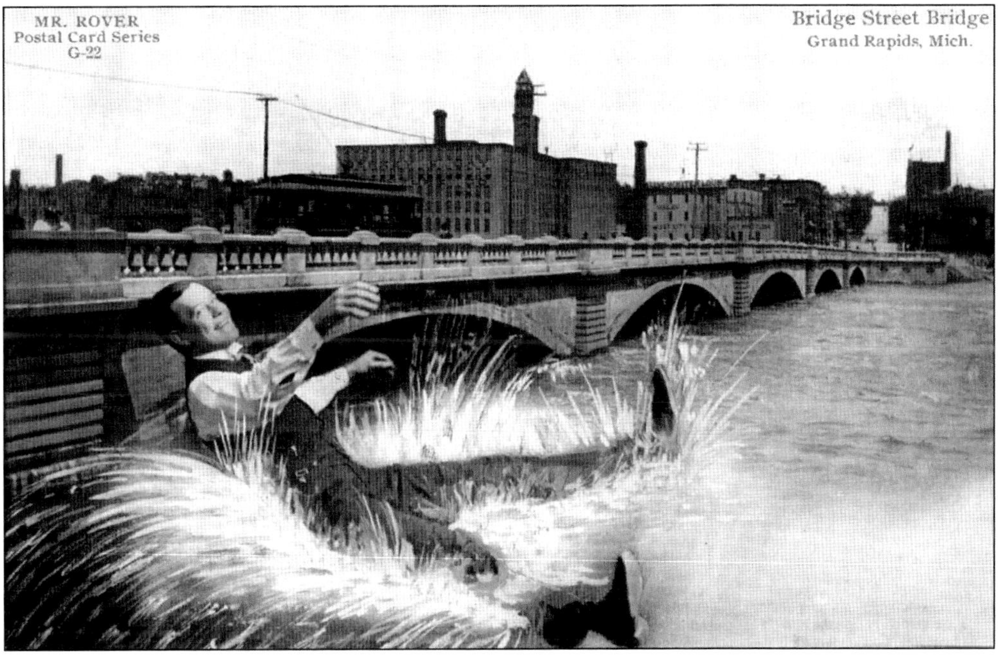

Card No. 22 shows Mr. Rover making a splash in the Grand River off of the Bridge Street Bridge. (Collection of Justin Tieri.)

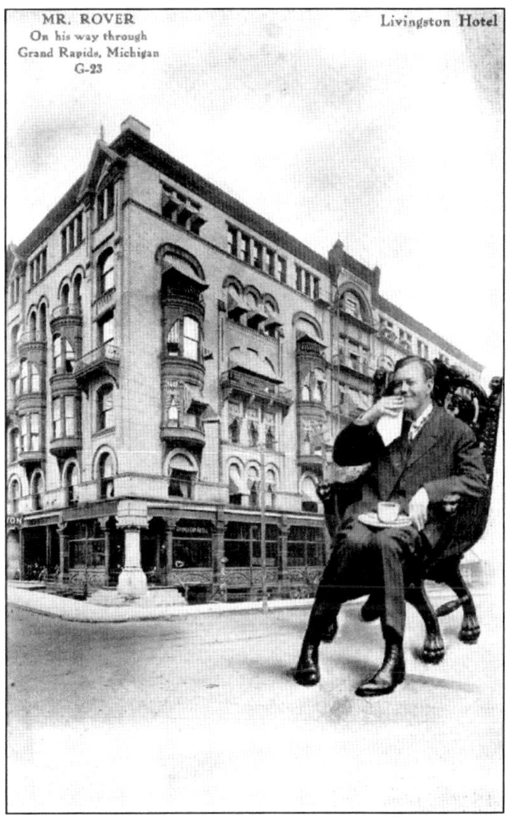

Mr. Rover eats lunch at the Livingston Hotel, then located at the southeast corner of Fulton Street and Division Avenue. This is card No. 23.

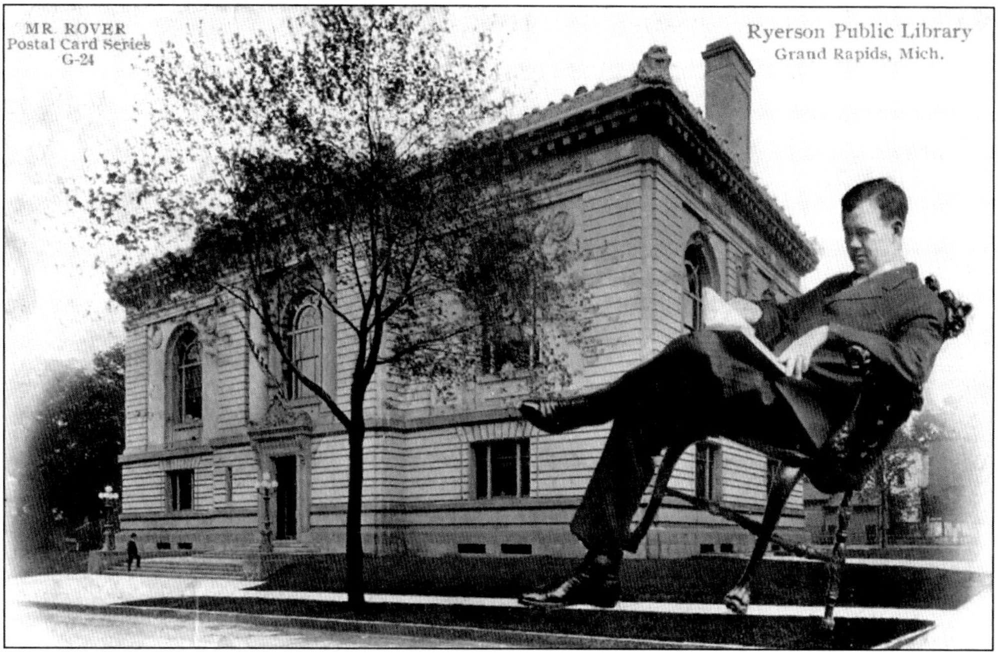

In card No. 24 of the series, Mr. Rover is seated, reading outside the Ryerson Public Library, which had opened in 1904, only three years prior to the publication of this card in 1907. (Collection of Justin Tieri.)

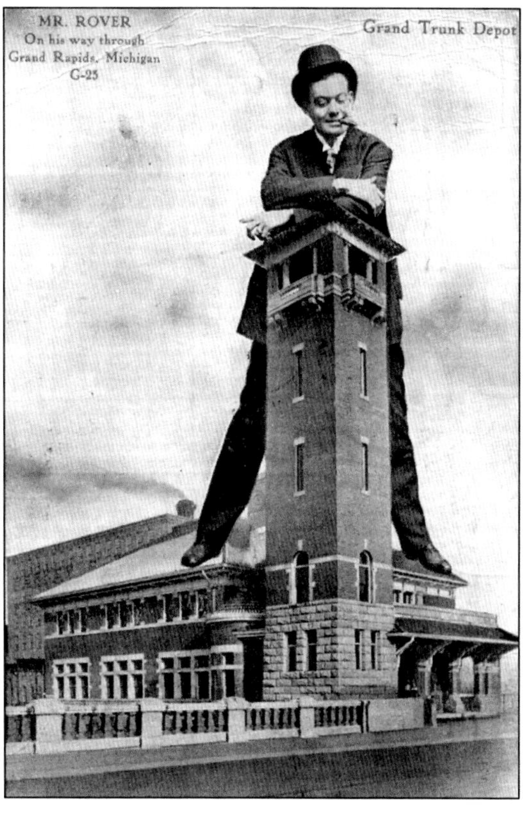

Here Mr. Rover leans comfortably on the newly constructed tower of the Grand Trunk Railroad depot, finished only the year before this card, No. 25 in the series, was published in 1907.

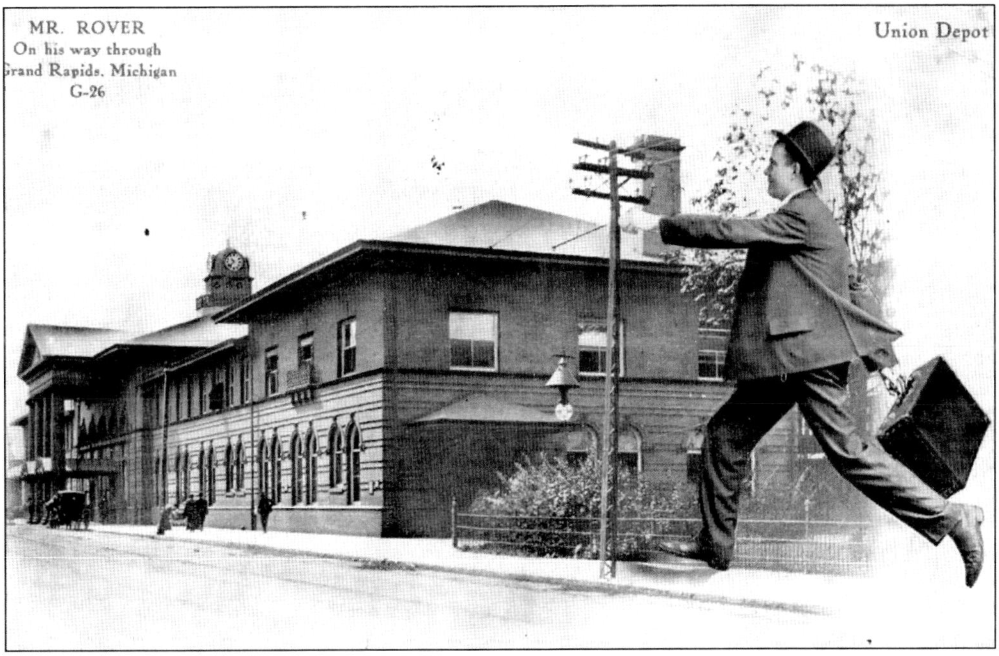

The 26th card in the series shows Mr. Rover running to catch a train at the Union Railroad depot on South Ionia Avenue.

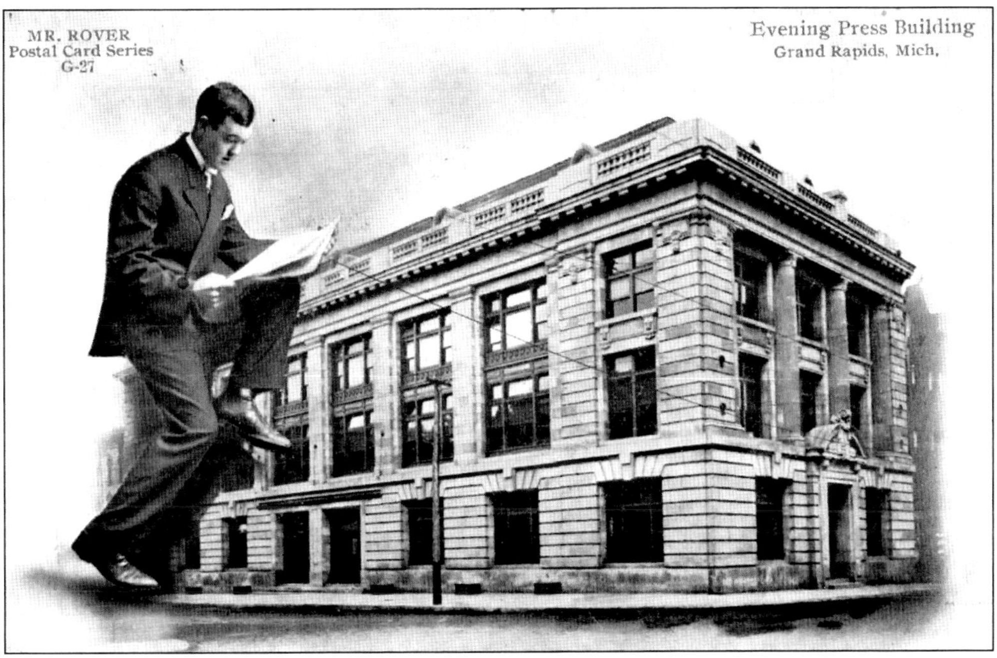

Mr. Rover, reading the newspaper, sits on the eaves of the Grand Rapids Evening Press Building, formerly located at the corner of Sheldon Avenue and Fulton Street, across from Veteran's Memorial Park. This is card No. 27. (Collection of Justin Tieri.)

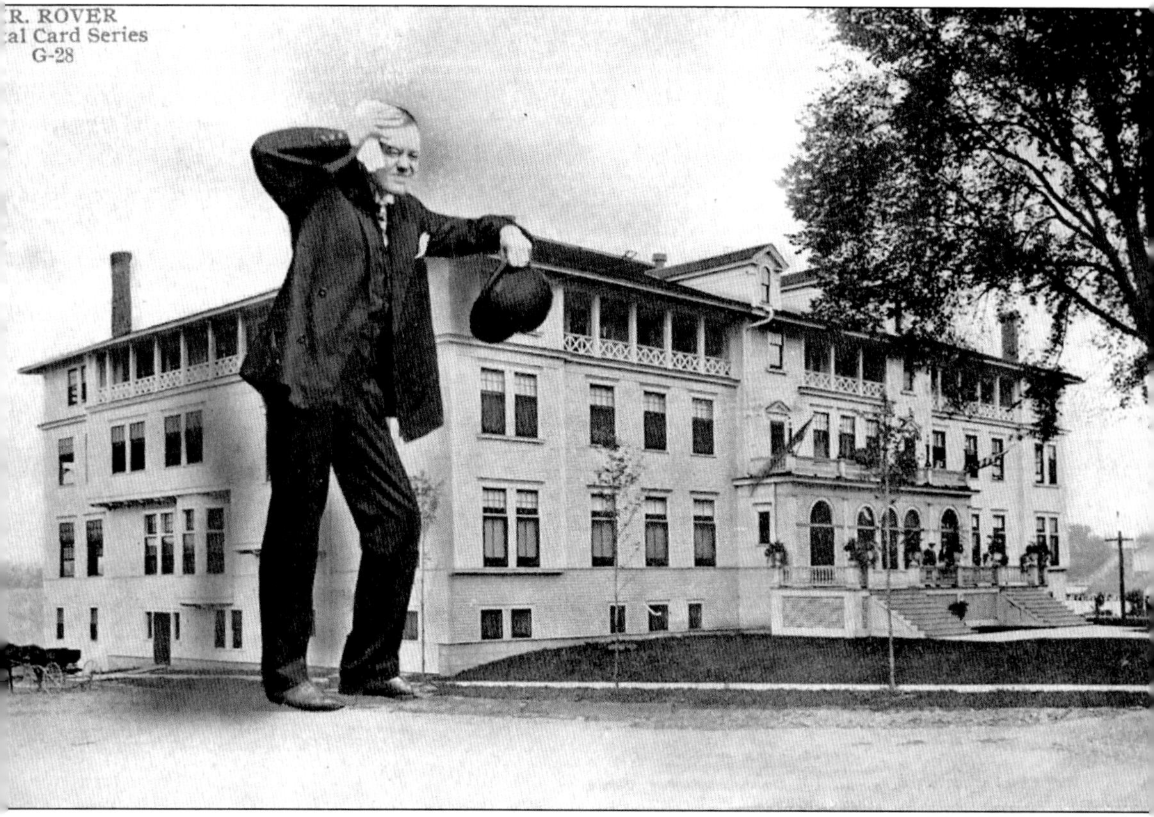

Back out at Reeds Lake, in East Grand Rapids, Mr. Rover is here leaning against the north side of the Lakeside Club building in card No. 28. The lake is visible in the background. (Collection of Justin Tieri.)

Six

The 1910 Homecoming

In the late 19th and opening decades of the 20th centuries, parades and public celebratory spectacles were wildly popular and very well attended by local citizens and visitors from near and far. A geographically smaller city, as well as the absence of movies and television, made such events very attractive and popular entertainment in Grand Rapids. Nearly every national holiday provided an excuse for a gala parade and celebration, which often included music and evening fireworks. Masonic and fraternal organizations often participated grandly in these occasions, with their members garbed in exotic uniforms, marching down Monroe Avenue before thousands of welcoming spectators.

In 1900, on the 50th anniversary of the incorporation of the city, an effort was made to organize a grand celebration of this milestone, but, inexplicably, the event, plagued by an apparent lack of organization and funding, fizzled before it ever took place.

Recognizing the opportunity to promote the city, which had been lost by this failure, a largely self-appointed committee of local businessmen decided that the 60th anniversary for the city would not pass unheralded. In the fall of 1909, it was announced that a grand homecoming would be staged in Grand Rapids in August of the following year, to which all past and present Grand Rapids residents were warmly invited. The event was chaired by local streetcar magnate Benjamin Hanchett, who along with a number of others, including future U.S. senator Arthur VandenBerg, planned an extensive, five-day schedule of commemorative and celebratory events.

Most businesses were closed during the five days of the celebration, from August 23 to August 27, 1910, and events were conducted at nearly every public and semi-public building in the city. Fireworks, music, circus performances, and balloon ascensions were all part of the schedule, but no event was more heavily attended, or more thoroughly documented by local postcard producers, than the grand parade on Monroe Avenue in the middle of the week.

The postcards that were produced of the homecoming consist of both printed, mass-produced cards, which were intended largely to be sent out of town in advance to urge attendance (and which sport the official seal and colors of the event, green, pink, and white), and several dozen printed and real-photo cards, which document the elaborate parade. All of these cards, along with an assortment of official souvenirs, were produced locally, the printed cards by the Cargill Company, and are much collected today.

The event as a whole was a huge success and set a standard that was never equaled by a number of similar commemorative events that occurred on later anniversaries, such as the Campau Centennial in 1926.

What follows is a series of ten colored, printed cards that were designed and used to send to out-of-town Grand Rapids natives, imploring them to return home for the homecoming celebration in August 1910. They clearly were intended to display buildings recently constructed, as well as nostalgic appeals for visitors to come and enjoy the festivities.

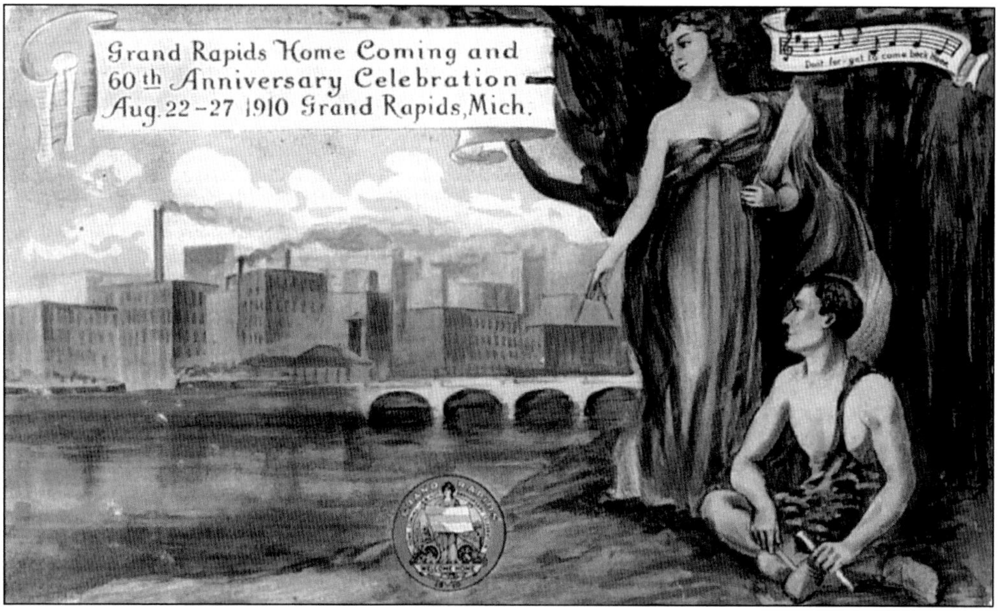

This, the first in the series of printed promotional cards created for the homecoming, depicts an idealized view of the city, including the Bridge Street Bridge. At the right are the heroic figures, Progress (left) and Labor, who appear on several of the cards in the series. At the center is the official seal of the homecoming event, and at the upper right, the first bar of a song especially written for the occasion.

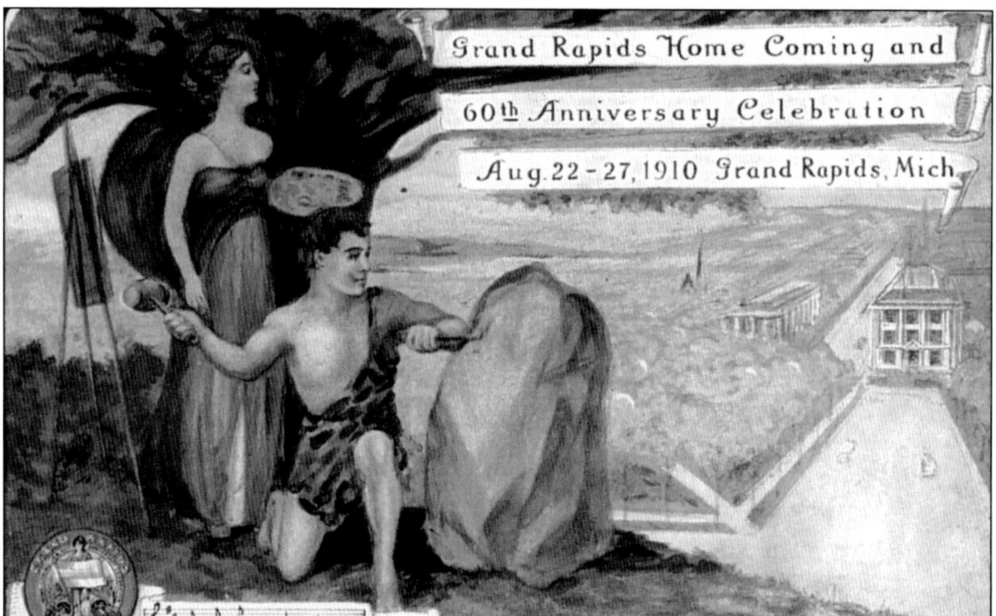

Here, Labor, directed by Progress, is depicted in the process of hewing the city of Grand Rapids from the wilderness during the previous 60 years of its life.

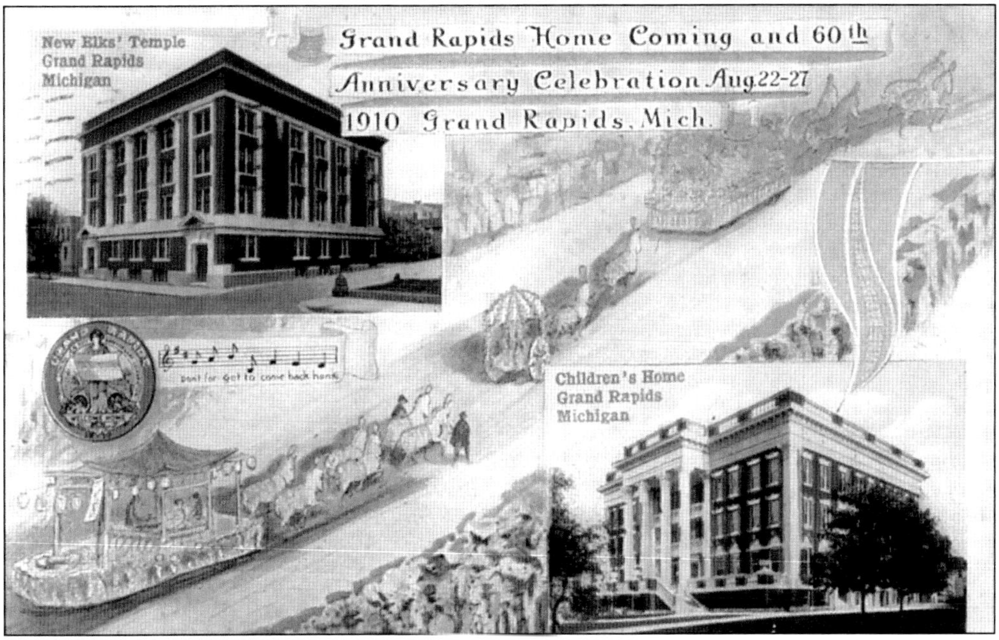

This card, the third in the series, depicts the look of the parade which had already been planned, along with the then-new Elks temple, located downtown, and the D. A. Blodgett Home for Children, located in the near southeast end of the city.

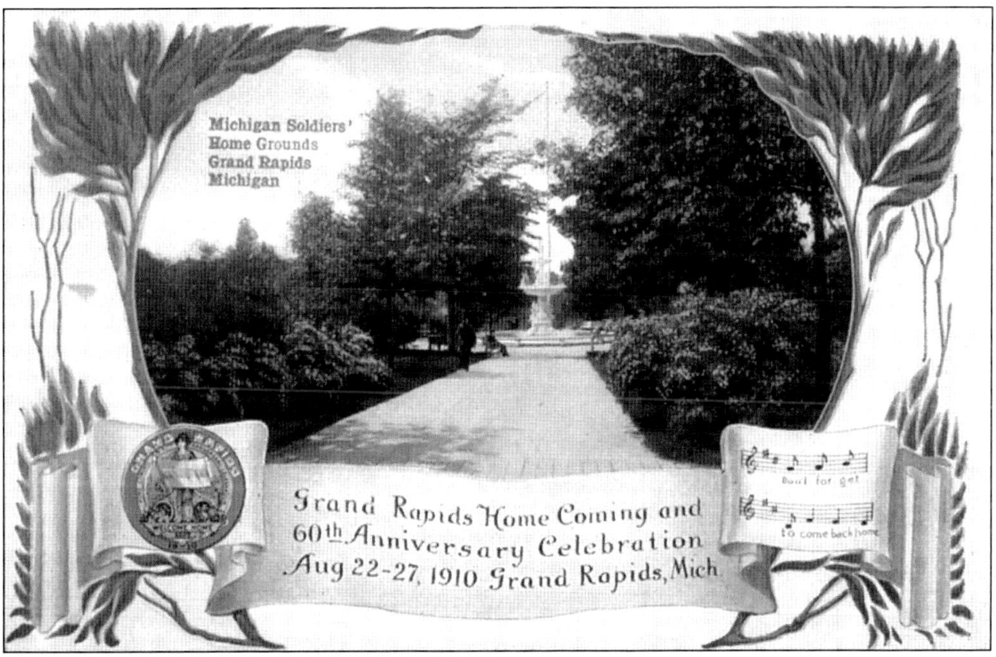

This card also depicts the seal and song of the homecoming celebration, showing the park at the Michigan Soldiers' Home, just north of downtown.

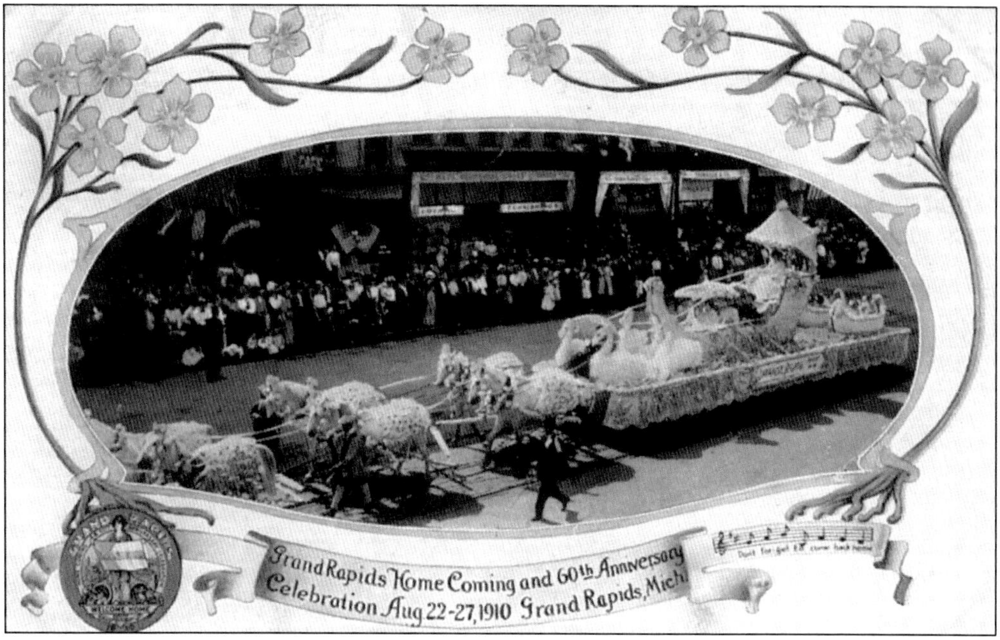

This image, the fifth in the series, makes use of a parade image from a preceding occasion to lure visitors to Grand Rapids for the Grand Homecoming Parade.

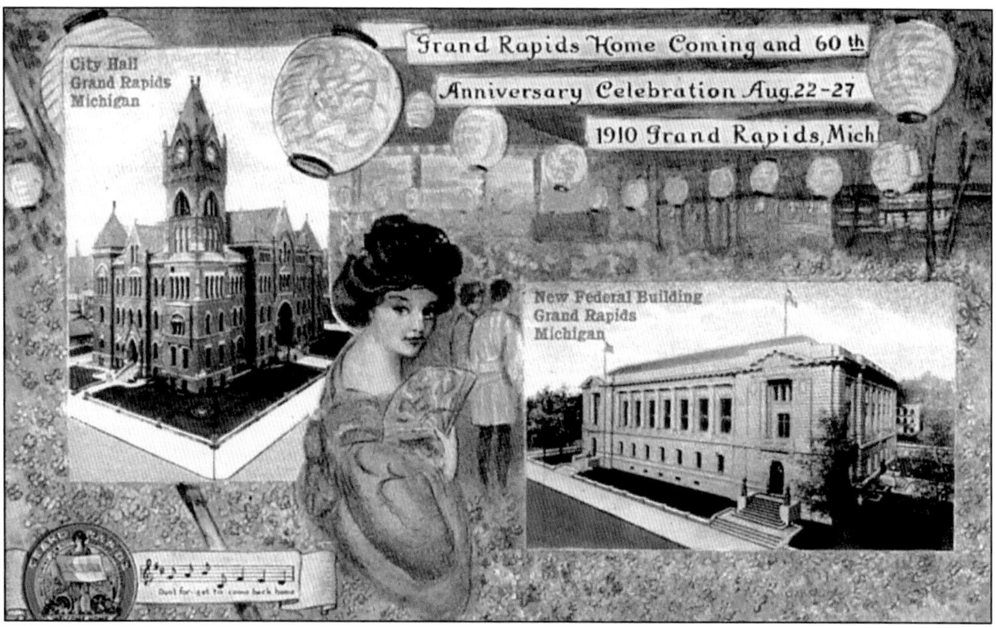

Here a young geisha beckons visitors to Grand Rapids, with views of the city hall, built in 1888, and the then newly constructed Federal Building, now the Grand Rapids Art Museum.

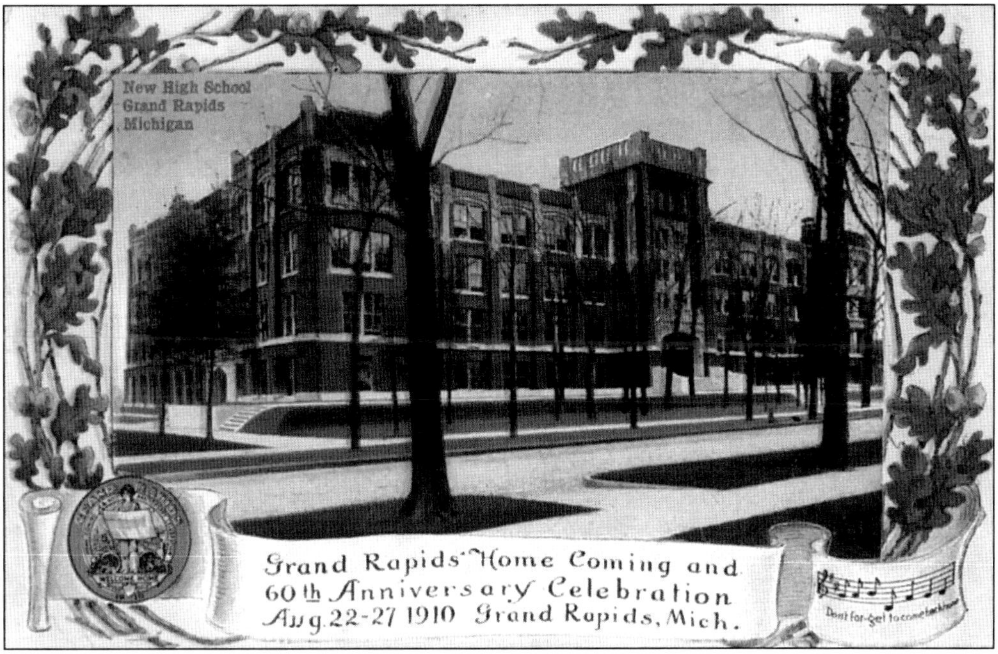

The pride of the organizers of the homecoming event is evident in this depiction of the "new" Grand Rapids (now Central) High School, in this, the seventh of the series of printed homecoming cards.

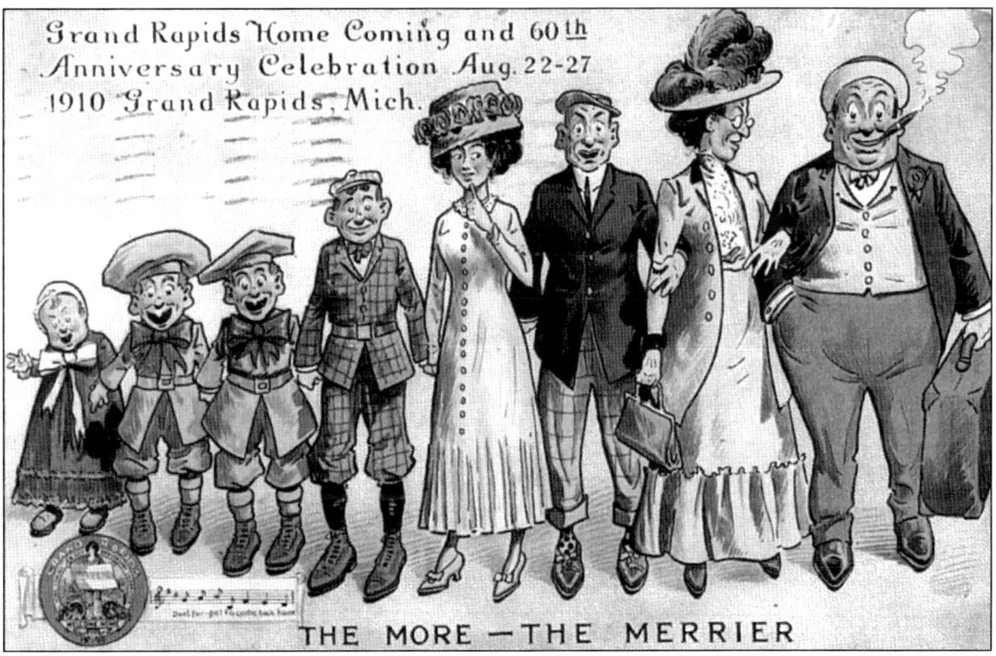

Here, the whole family has arrived for the festivities, all apparently living out of the same suitcase in Grandpa's hand (at right).

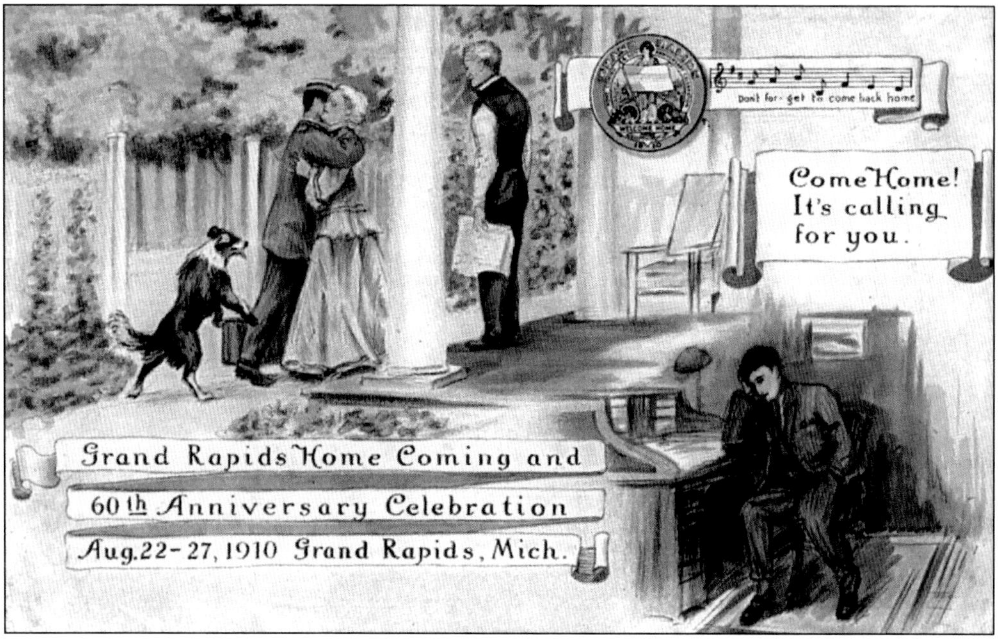

In the most sentimental card of the series, the recipient is urged to "Come Home! It's calling for you." And come home they did, by the thousands, to make the entire week of festivities a huge success.

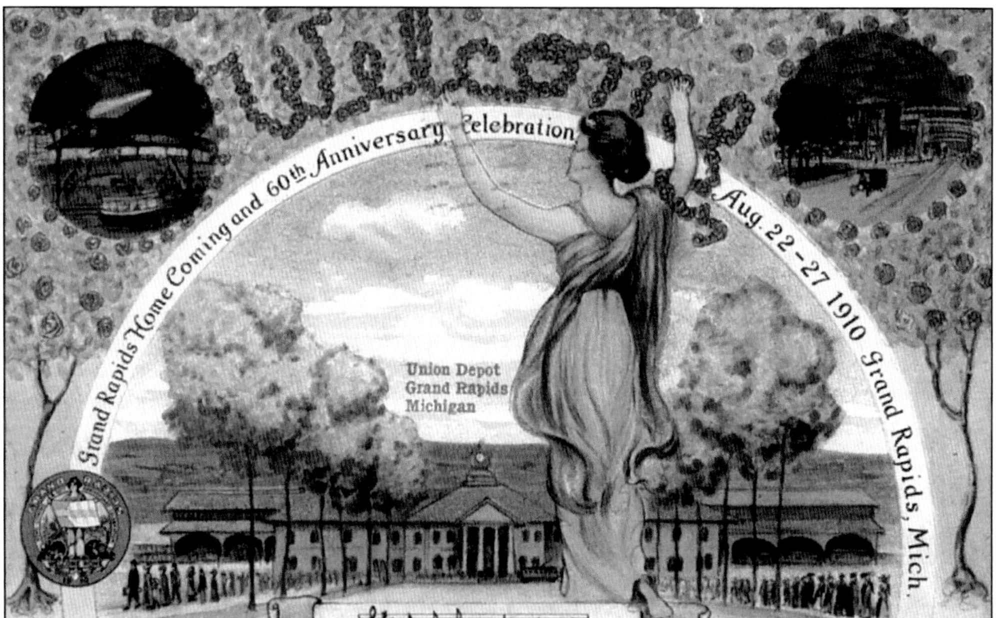

In the last card in the series, Progress is seen completing her floral welcome sign. In the background is the Union Station, located on South Ionia Avenue, and in the upper left corner, a view of the Ramona resort area on Reeds Lake.

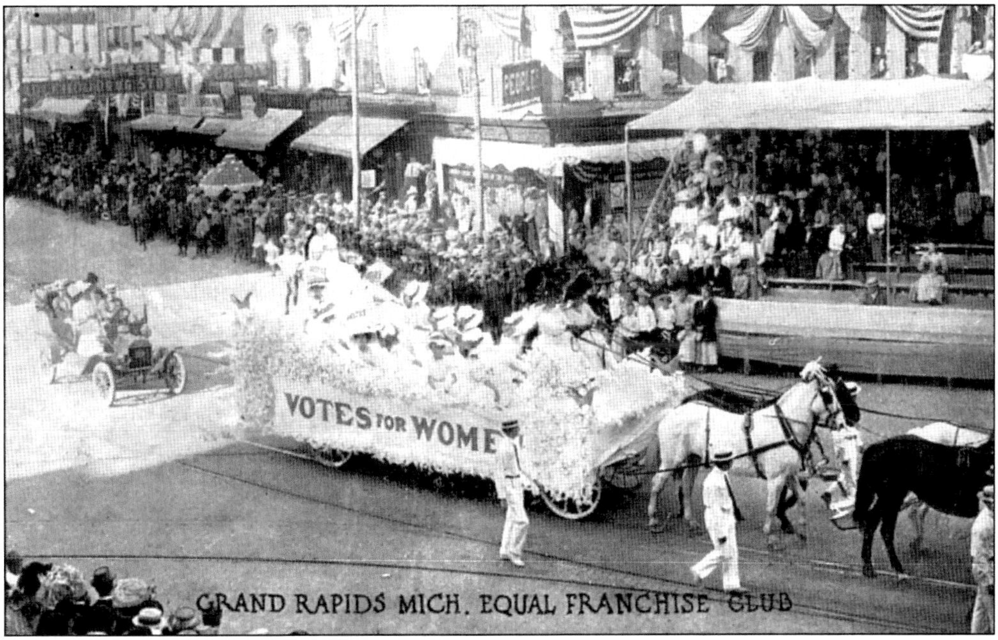

There were a few actual printed cards of the homecoming parade that were sold, including this one of a float sponsored by the Grand Rapids Equal Franchise Club, promoting the extension of suffrage rights to women.

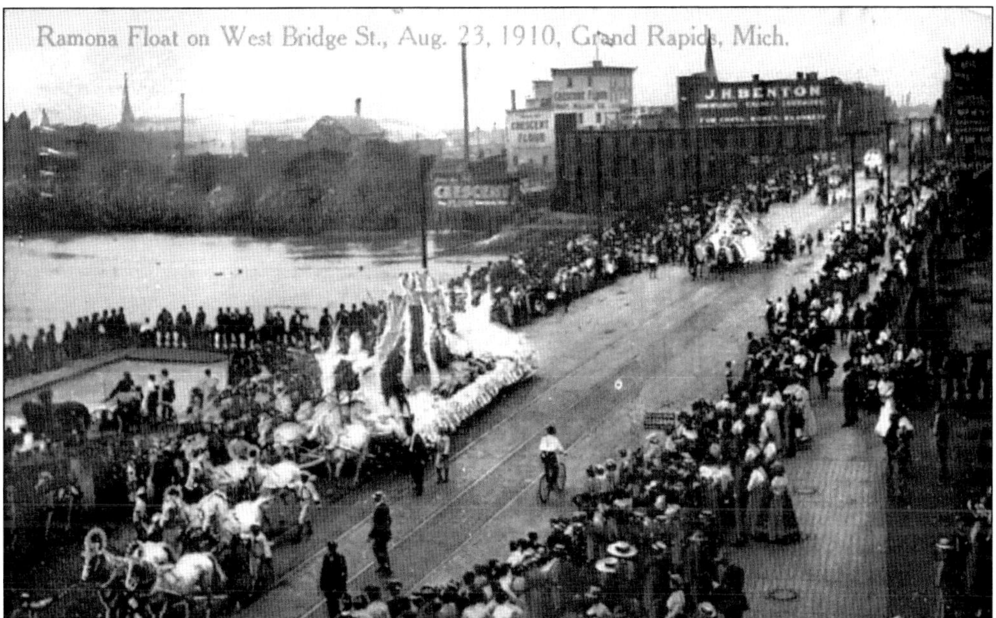

This is a view of the parade during homecoming week, as it worked its way from the west side of the city, across the Bridge Street Bridge, and into downtown. At the left is a float sponsored by the Ramona Amusement Park from East Grand Rapids.

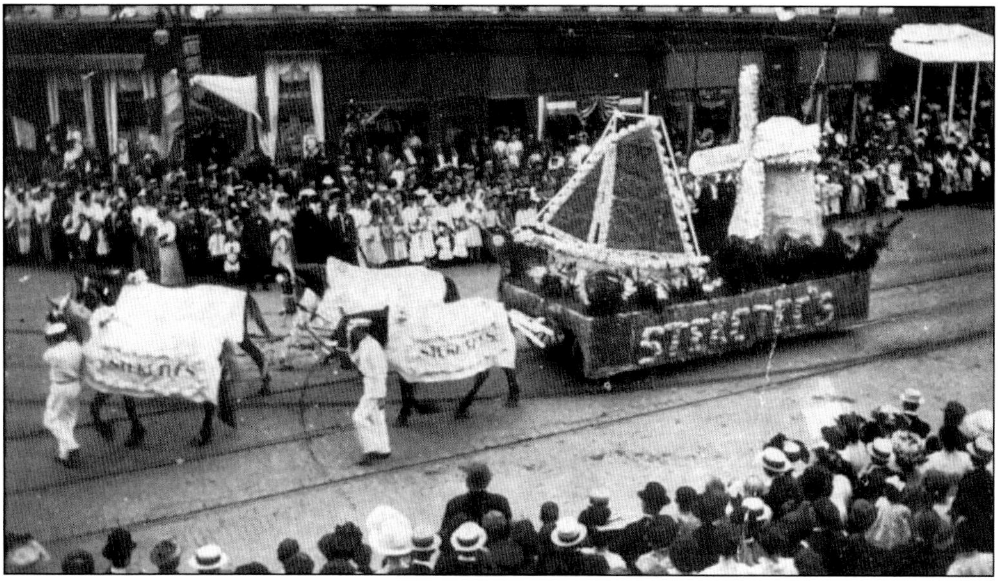

This is an unusual printed (as opposed to a real-photo) card of the parade on Monroe Avenue during homecoming week. Depicted at the corner of Monroe and Division Avenues is the float of the Steketee Department Store. Most of the postcards that actually depict the homecoming week events were real-photo cards such as those which follow, produced by unknown sellers in moderate quantities for sale to attendees, probably while the weeklong celebration was still in progress. Most of these cards appear to have been produced by one individual or company, based upon their labeling and format, but it is impossible to know if this is actually true.

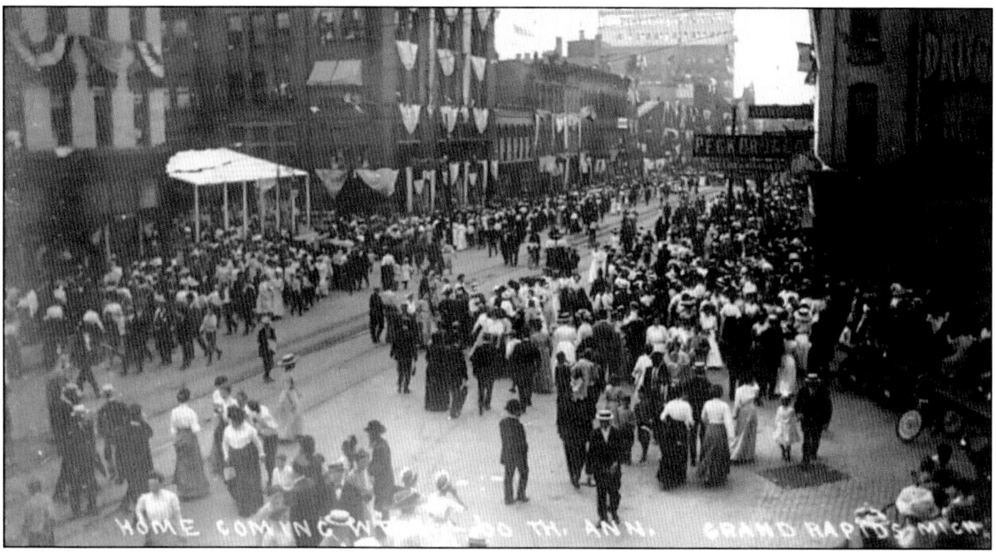

This is a view looking west, from the corner of Division Avenue, down Monroe Avenue on the day of the great parade at either the beginning or end of the festivities, as attendees either found or left their seats. At the right is the Peck Drug Store, a longtime presence at this location. At the center is the Gilbert Building on the corner of Commerce Avenue, decked out with patriotic bunting, as were most of the buildings downtown. The construction of the grandstand across Commerce Avenue at Monroe, at the center, presaged the closing of this street some 40 years later when the new Herpolsheimer Store was built on the site.

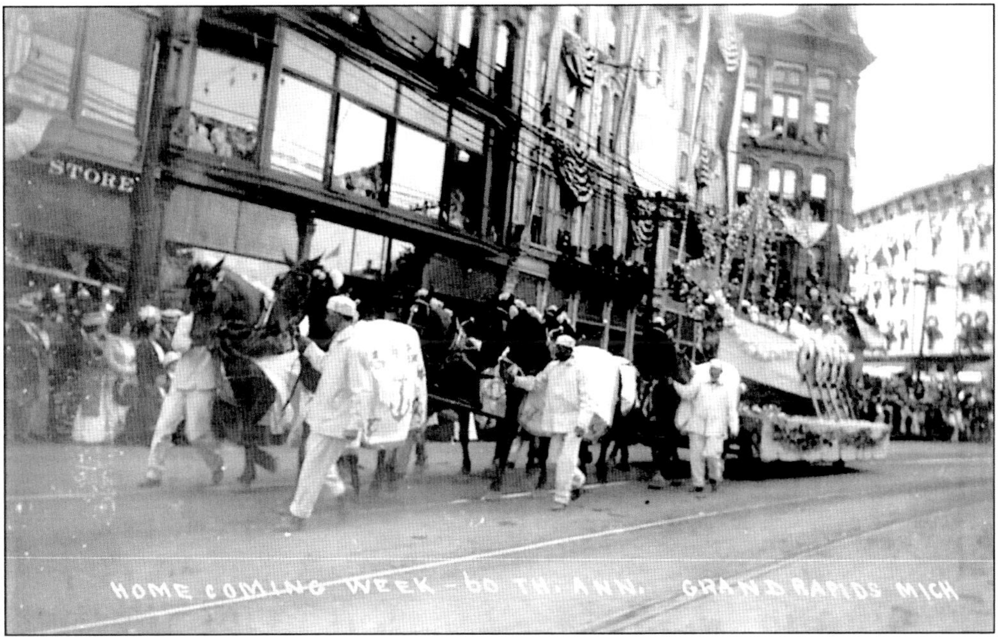

A view of the grand parade in progress on Monroe Avenue at Campau Square in seen here. At the right is the old Pantlind Hotel, to be replaced with the present structure some five years later. Note the people watching the parade from the upper-story windows.

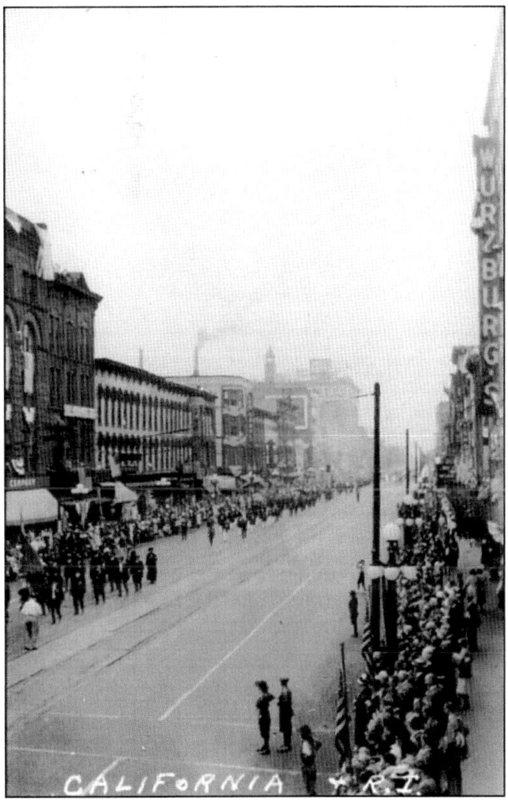

A view looking south on Canal Street (lower Monroe Avenue) during the parade features, at the extreme right, the original Wurzburg Store, which later moved farther up Monroe Avenue. At the center of the photograph, visible faintly in the mist, is the tower of the Berkey and Gay Furniture factory, located farther down Canal Street, on the river.

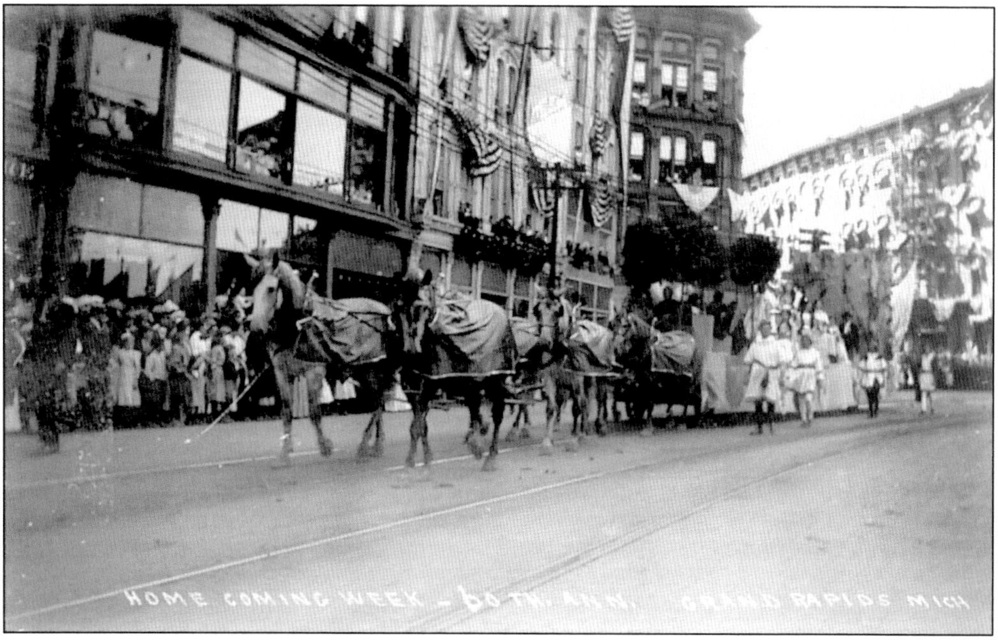

Another view of this parade on Monroe Avenue at Campau Square is pictured here.

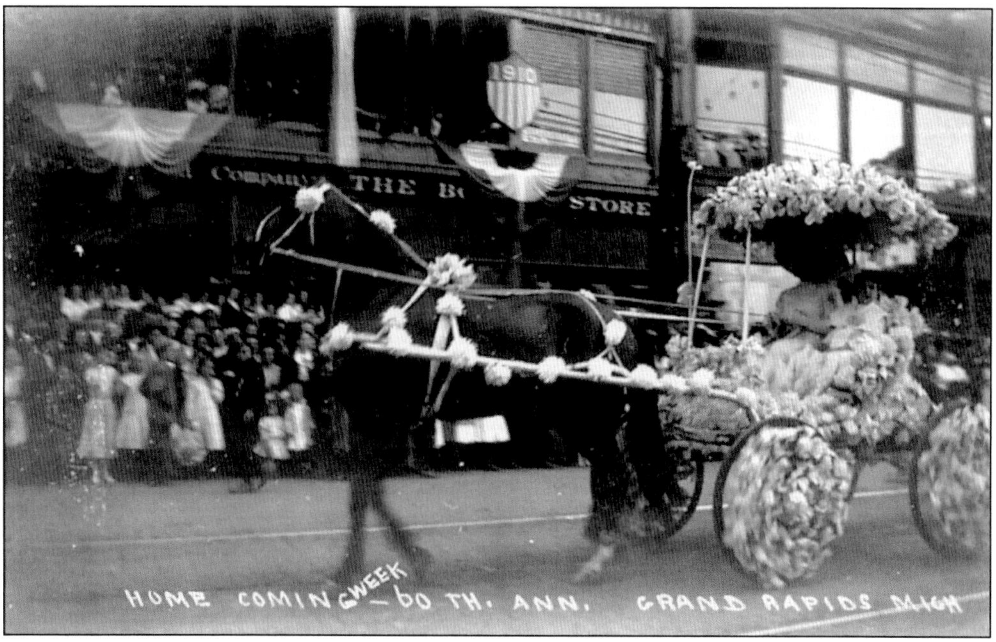

This is another view of one of the many floats, nearly all horse drawn, in the parade, on Monroe Avenue at Campau Square.

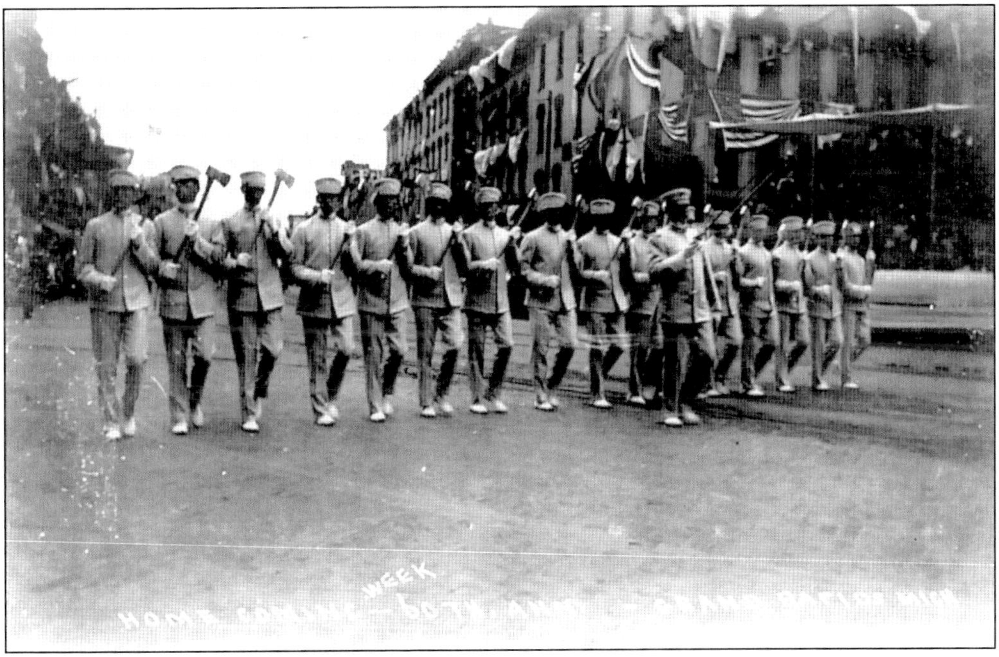

The drill team of the Modern Woodmen of the World, one of many fraternal participants in the festivities, makes the turn up Monroe Avenue from Canal Street (lower Monroe Avenue) at Campau Square.

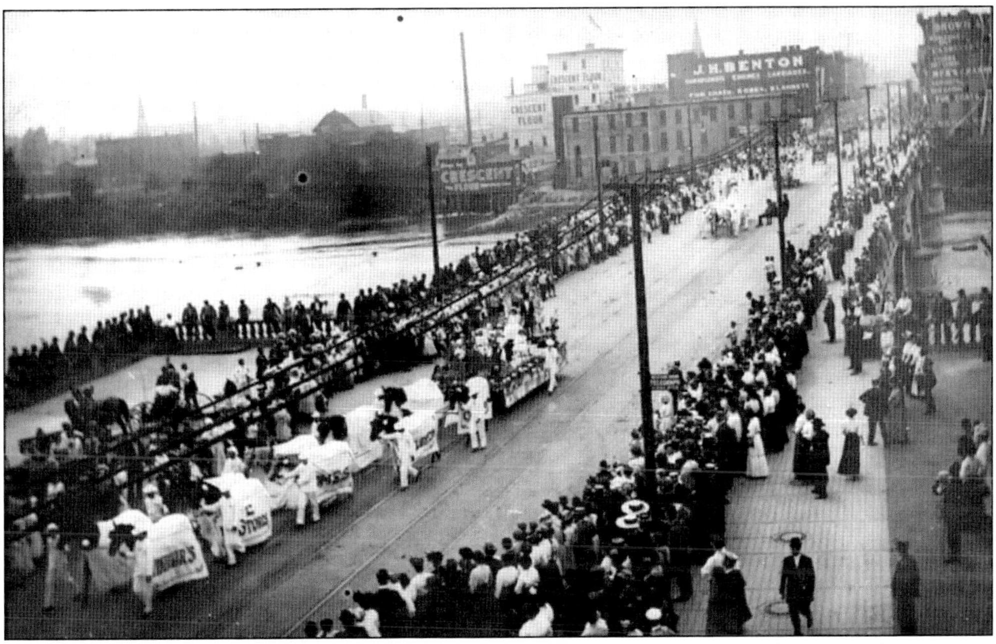

The homecoming week parade moves east, across the Bridge Street Bridge, into downtown. At the center of the photograph, on the west bank of the river, is the Voight Crescent Flour Mill. This photograph was probably taken from the tower of the Grand Trunk Railway Station, which was located at the lower right corner of the photograph on the present site of the United States post office.

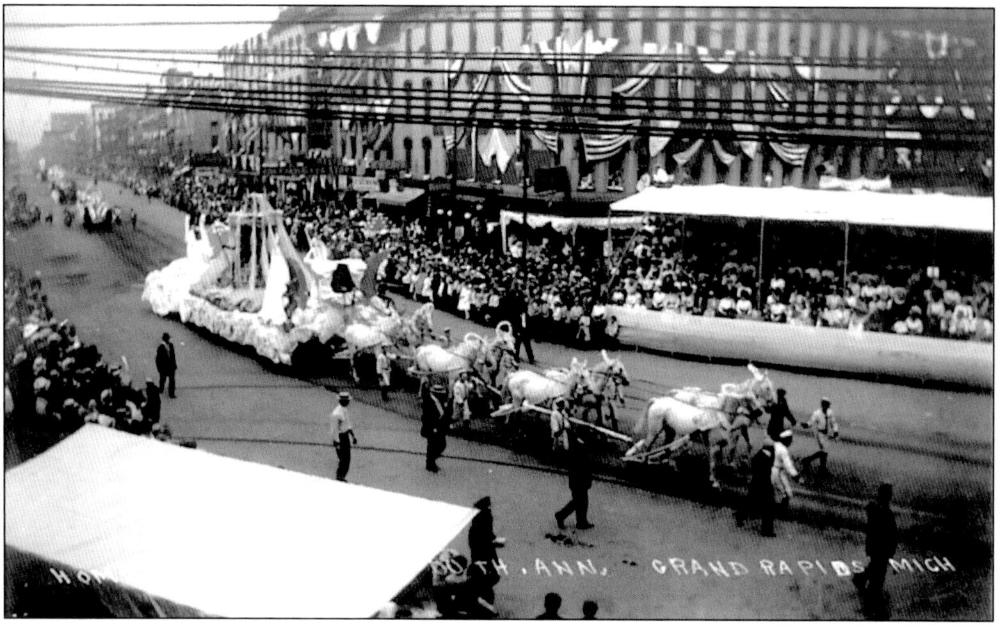

In a view from Campau Square, looking north down Canal Street (now lower Monroe Avenue), the large crowds and filled grandstands indicate that this event was very well attended.

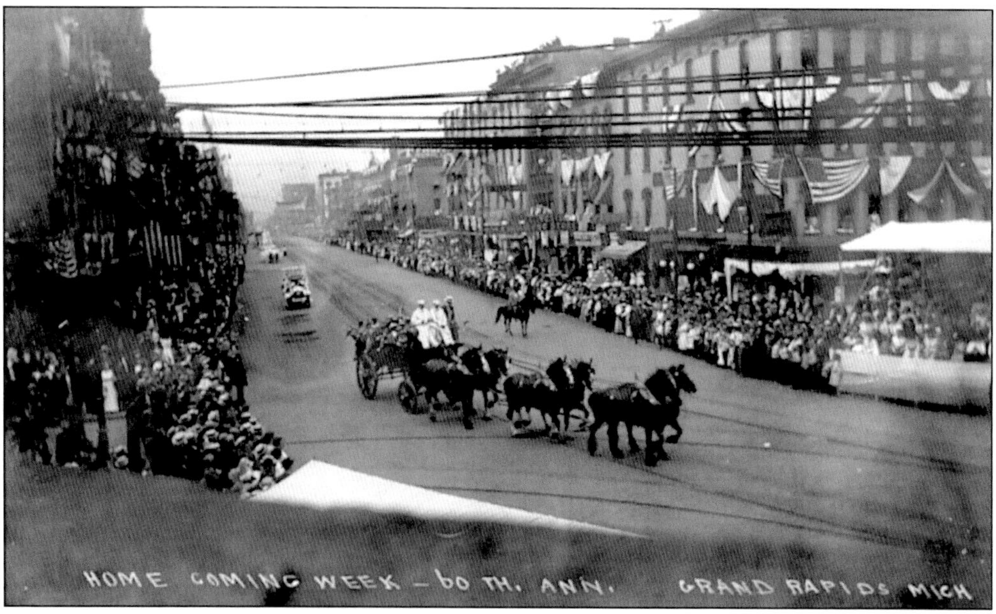

This is another view of the parade in progress, looking north on Canal Street. In the center of the picture is an automobile, one of the very few that appeared in the parade, probably included in the procession for the simple reason that it was, in 1910, unusual.

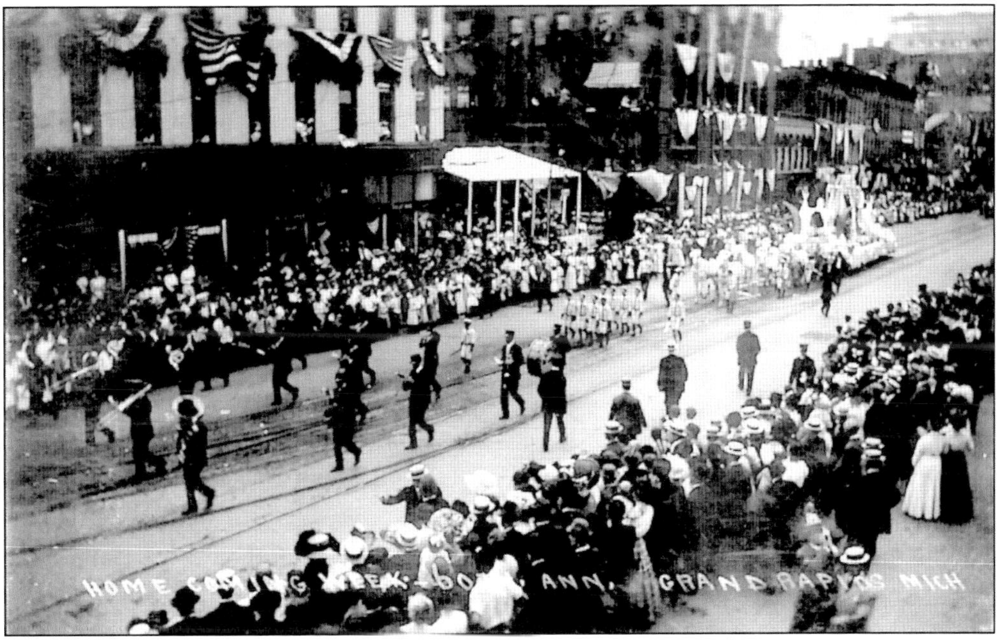

Another view of the parade, as it progressed up Monroe Avenue, just west of the intersection of Division Avenue, is seen here.

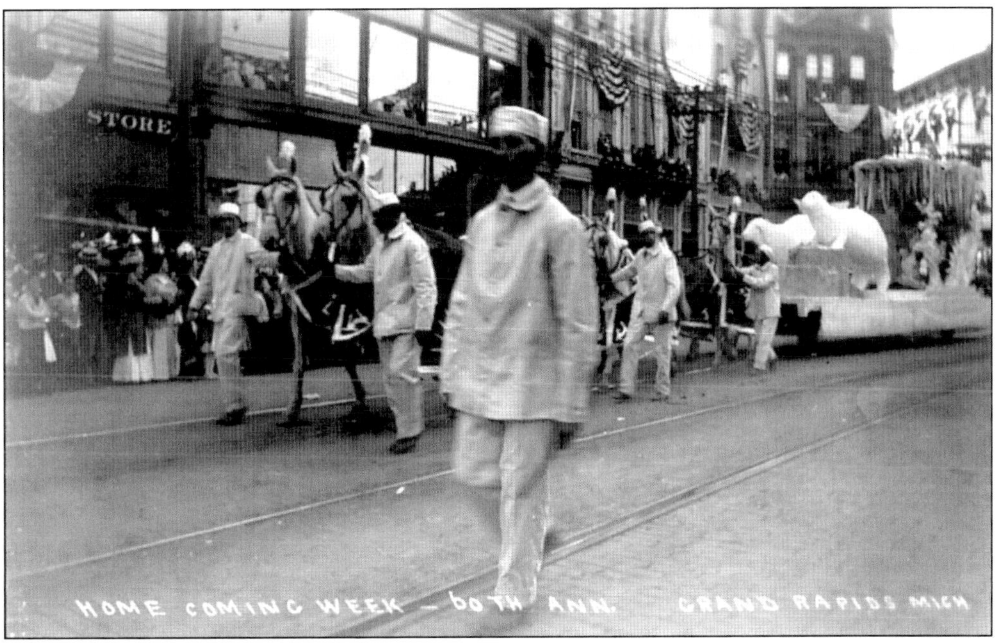

It is unknown who the sponsor was for this extravagant polar seal float in the parade, shown here at Campau Square.

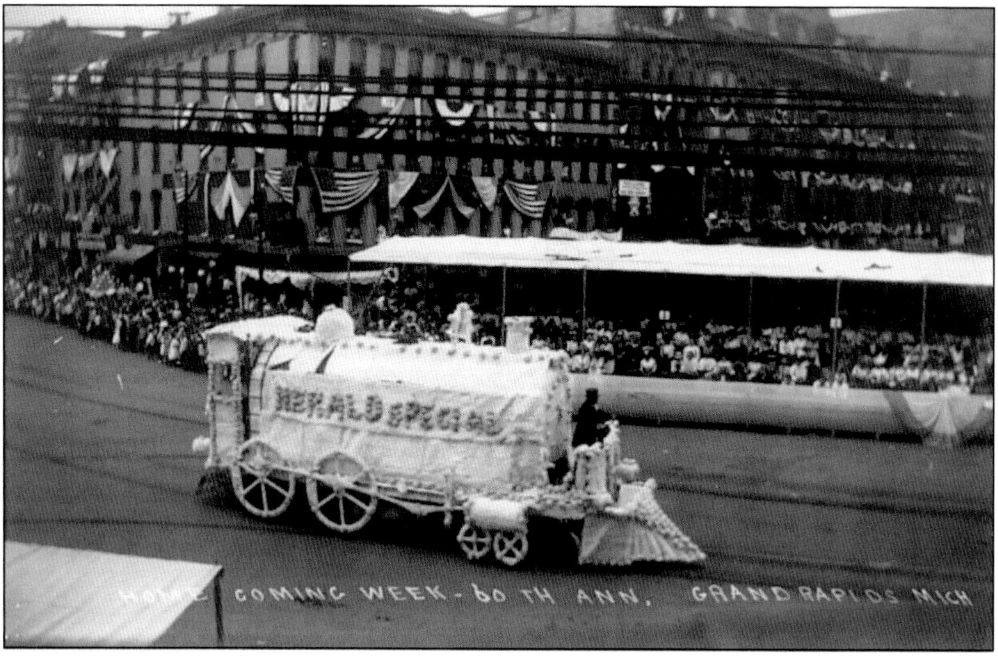

This is a real-photo postcard of the parade float sponsored by the *Grand Rapids Herald*, the local morning newspaper. Many of the floats and decorations in the parade were provided by local businesses, which heavily sponsored and promoted the entire homecoming event.

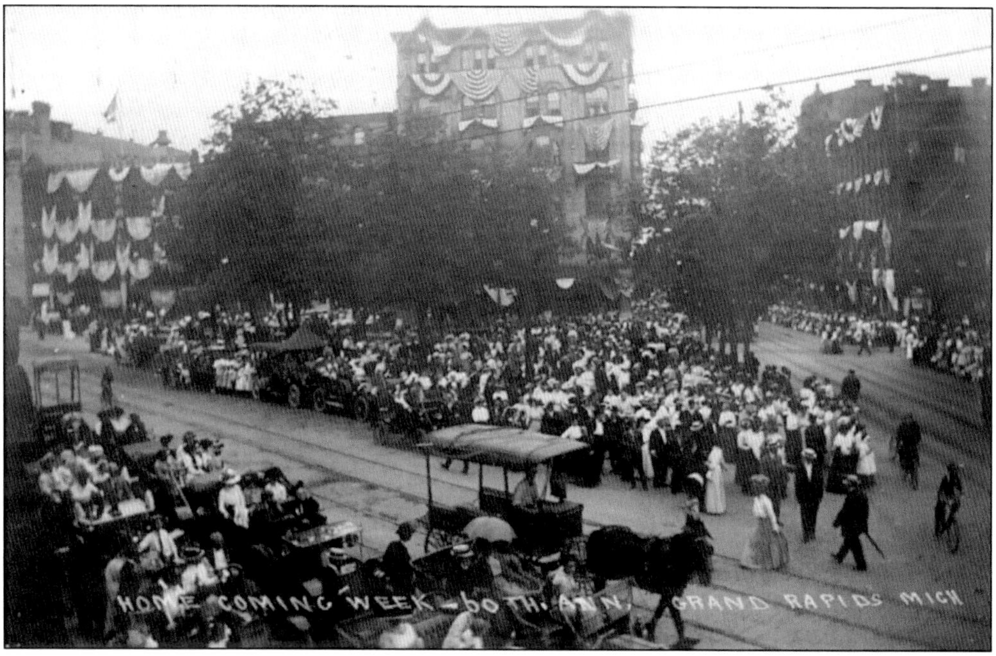

The parade eventually wound its way up Monroe Avenue to the corner of Division Avenue and Monument Park, seen at the center of this photograph. The large building at the center rear is the decorated Livingston Hotel, the first six-story building in Grand Rapids when it was built in 1887. The smaller, heavily decorated building to the left is the office of the *Grand Rapids Herald*, one of the principal sponsors of the event.

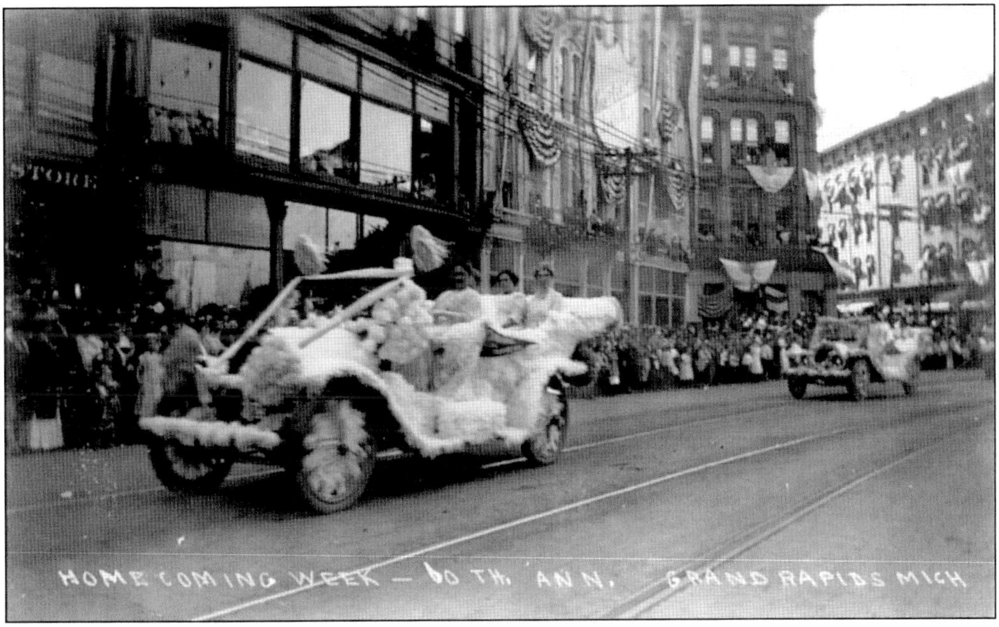

Two of the very few automobiles that appeared in the parade are seen here at Campau Square.

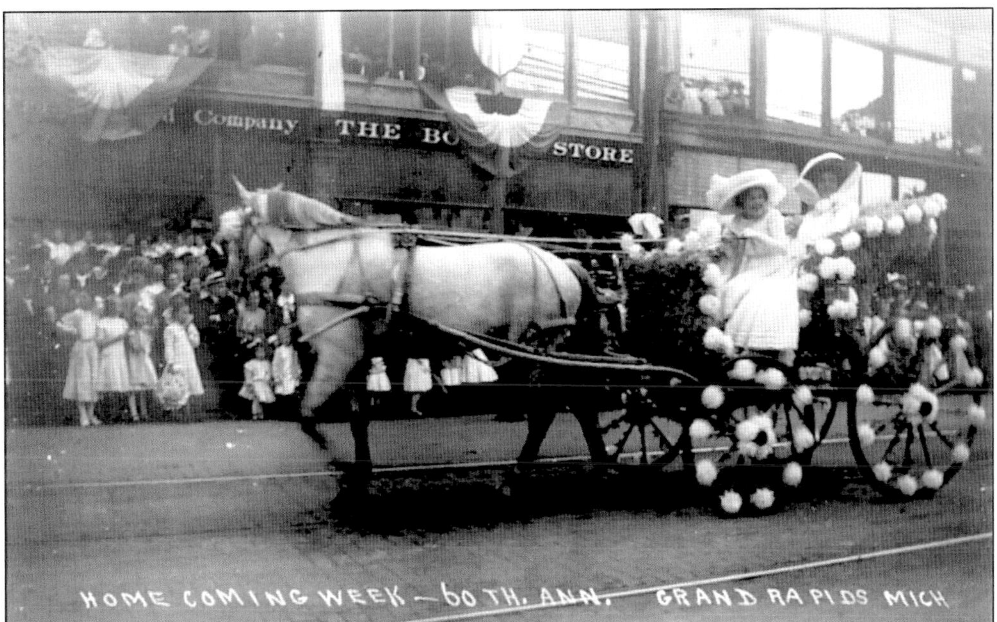

All manner of horse-drawn vehicles were used in the parade, including this small carriage with two happy occupants.

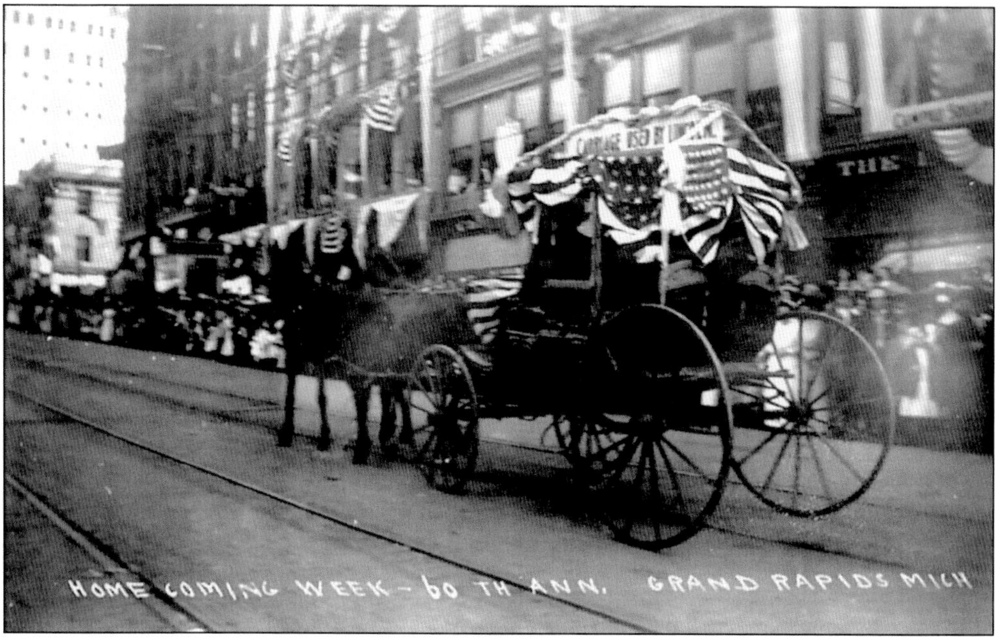

This carriage, purportedly once used by Pres. Abraham Lincoln, was imported to the city for use in the parade, shown here on Monroe Avenue at Campau Square.

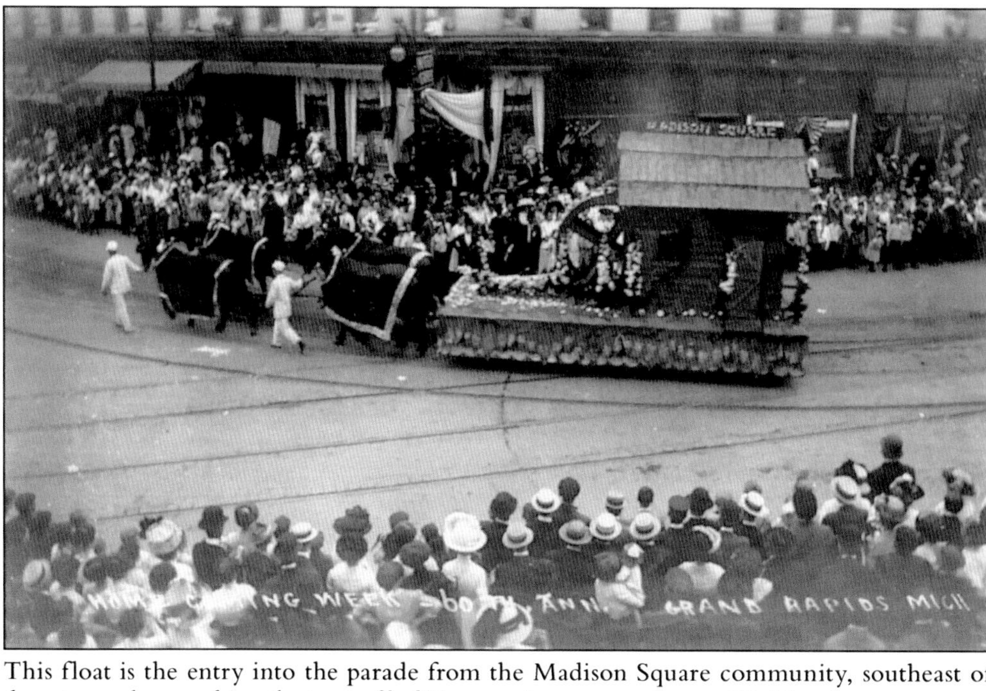

This float is the entry into the parade from the Madison Square community, southeast of downtown, here making the turn off of Monroe Avenue, south onto Division Avenue.

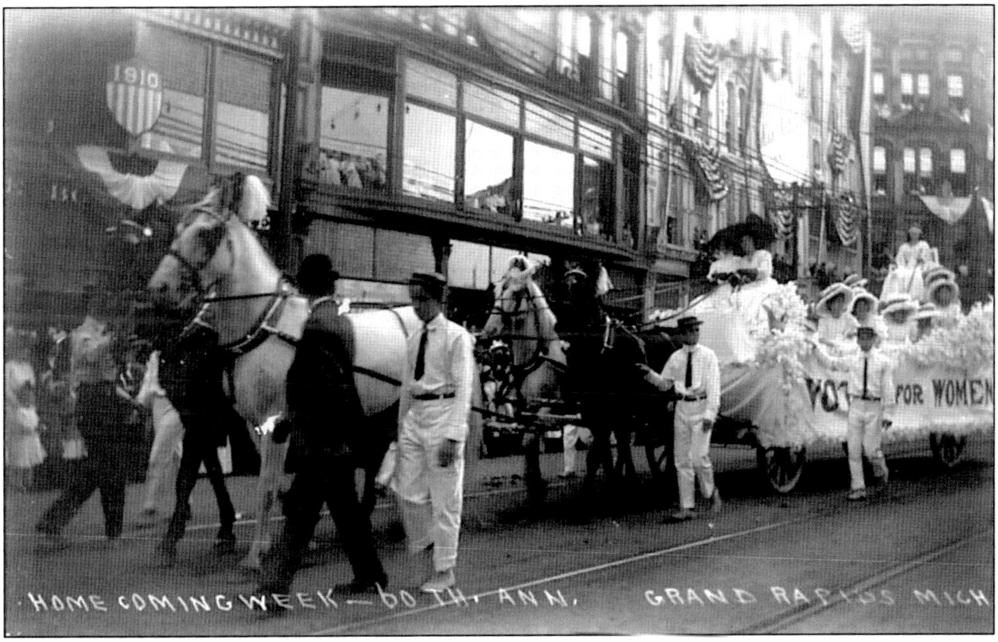

This is another view of the float of the Grand Rapids Equal Franchise Club, previously shown on page 113, as it comes through Campau Square and up Monroe Avenue.

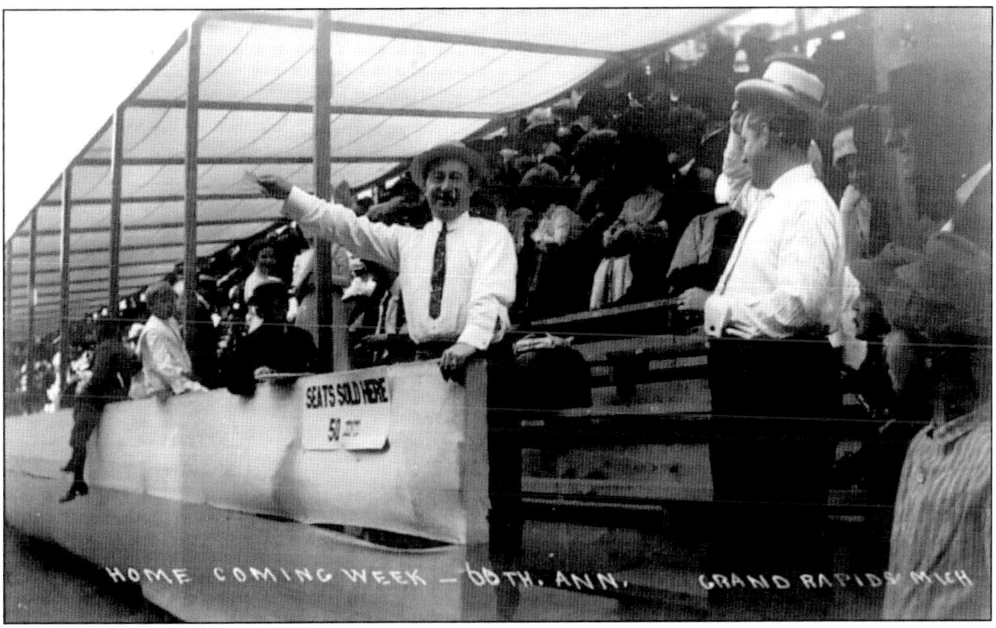

Seats in the grandstands were sold to view the parade, at the surprising expense, in 1910, of 50¢.

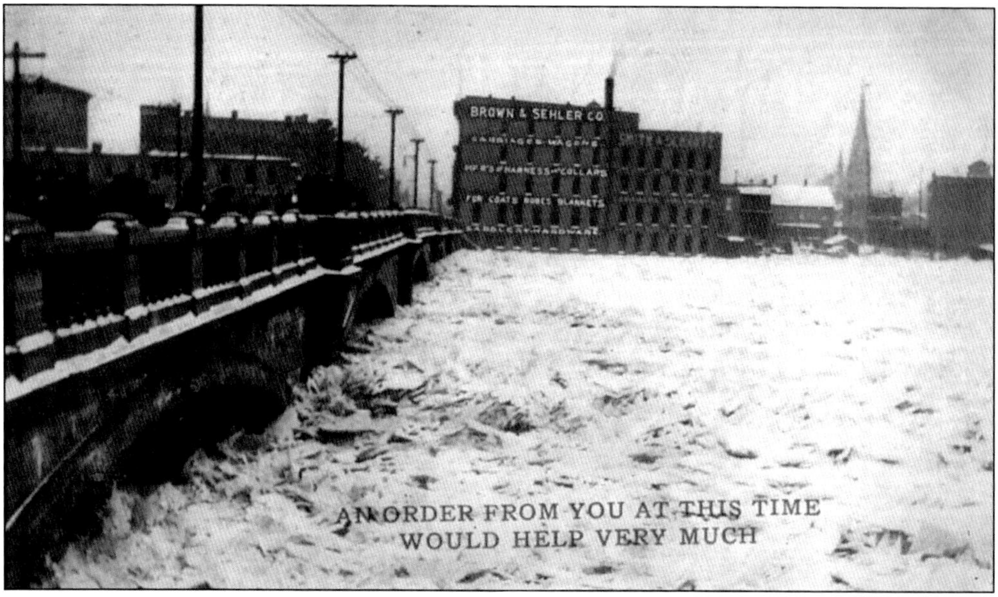

This is a view of the ice jam, dated January 24, 1907, looking west across the river on the northern edge of the Bridge Street (Michigan Street) Bridge. The factory building at the center of the photograph is the Brown and Sehler Company, manufacturers of harnesses and saddlery. An interior view of this company appears on page 35. The message printed (in red) on the photograph is an obvious appeal to customers of the company, to whom this card was sent, seeking orders at a time when business was suffering.

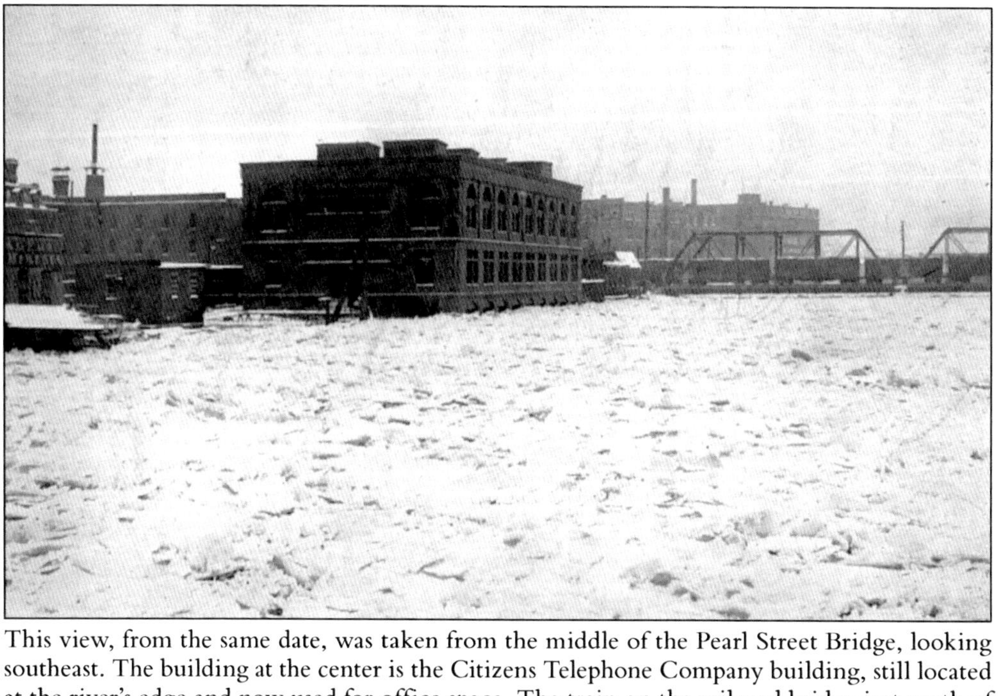

This view, from the same date, was taken from the middle of the Pearl Street Bridge, looking southeast. The building at the center is the Citizens Telephone Company building, still located at the river's edge and now used for office space. The train on the railroad bridge just south of the Citizens building was likely placed on the bridge to add weight, to stabilize the span against being swept away by the rising ice and water.

Seven

The Flood of 1907

In the 180-year history of the city of Grand Rapids, the Grand River has risen over its banks many times. The floods have been caused by unusually heavy rainfall, by logjams, and on many occasions by the accumulation and jamming of ice floes on the river, usually in the early spring of the year. Great floods occurred here in the spring of 1904, the summer of 1905, and, later, in the springs of 1947 and 1948, finally being brought under some level of control, at least in the city itself, by the construction of high walls on the banks of the restless river.

In January 1907, as an early thaw in the area allowed the temporary movement of the ice that had formed on the Grand River, a vast ice jam developed on the river in the downtown area. Soon the water flowing in the river, pressing the ice jam ever tighter, began to rise and ultimately flooded the near-west side of the city as well as other areas not protected by the higher riverbanks present on the east side of the river.

Desperate, though not very effective, efforts to break the ice jam on the river were made, including the use of ice-breaking boats and explosives, all to no avail. As typically happens, the pressure exerted on the ice jam by the rising waters increased, the ice ultimately gave way, and the floodwaters receded. The crisis dissipated after several weeks but not before this series of printed postcards of the flood were produced and marketed by the Will Canaan Company in 1907.

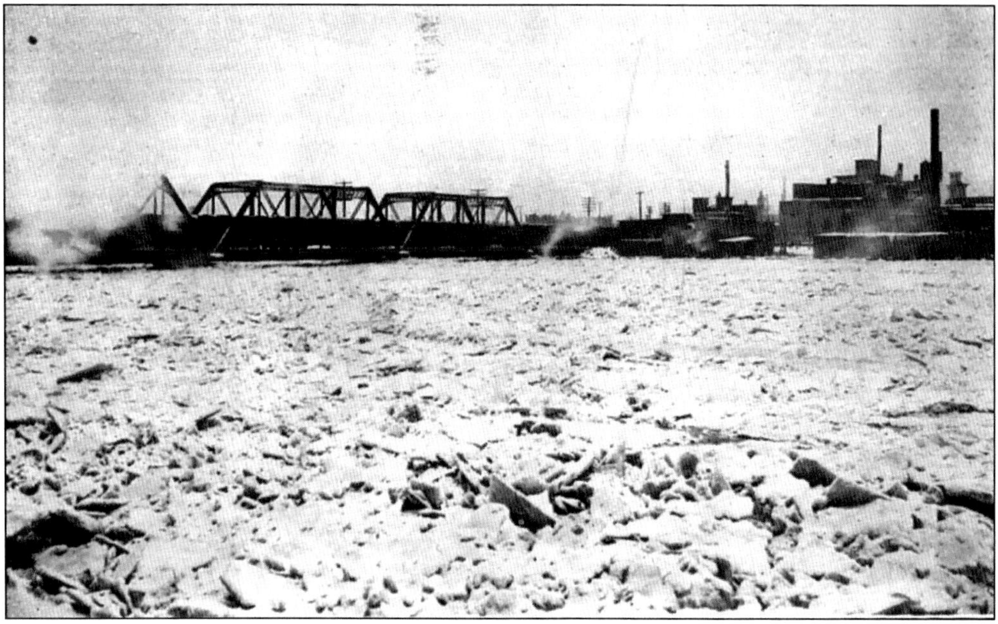

Pictured is another view of the Grand River and ice jam of January 1907, this time looking southwest across the river from the east bank. The Grand Rapids and Indiana Railroad Bridge, between Pearl and Fulton Streets, is visible at the center.

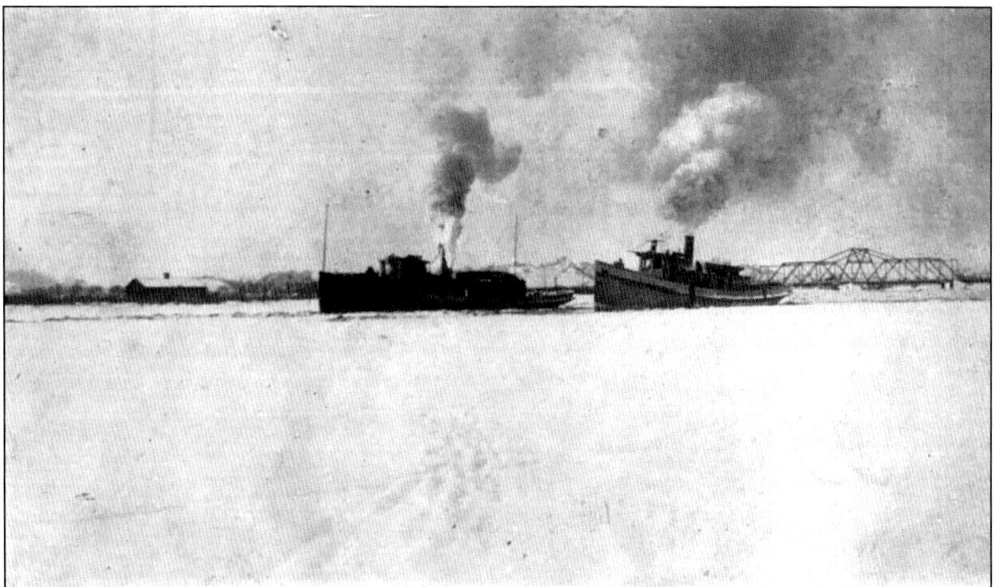

Tugs Dornbos and Gunderson Bucking Ice Jam in Grand River, Feb. 1, 1907.

As the jam continued and intensified, efforts were made to find a way to break the ice and send it moving downstream. On February 1, 1907, two tugboats, the *Dornbos* and the *Gunderson*, were brought in to attempt, unsuccessfully, to break up the ice.

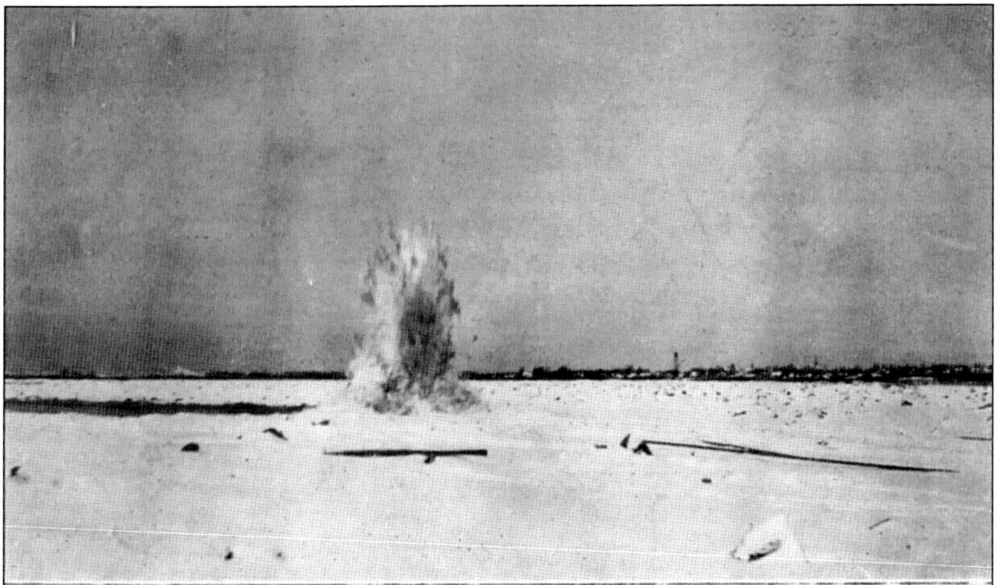

Dynamiting Six Feet of Ice in Grand River, Feb. 4, 1907.

On February 4, 1907, dynamite was used in another unsuccessful effort to move the ice and relieve the pressure of the rising waters.

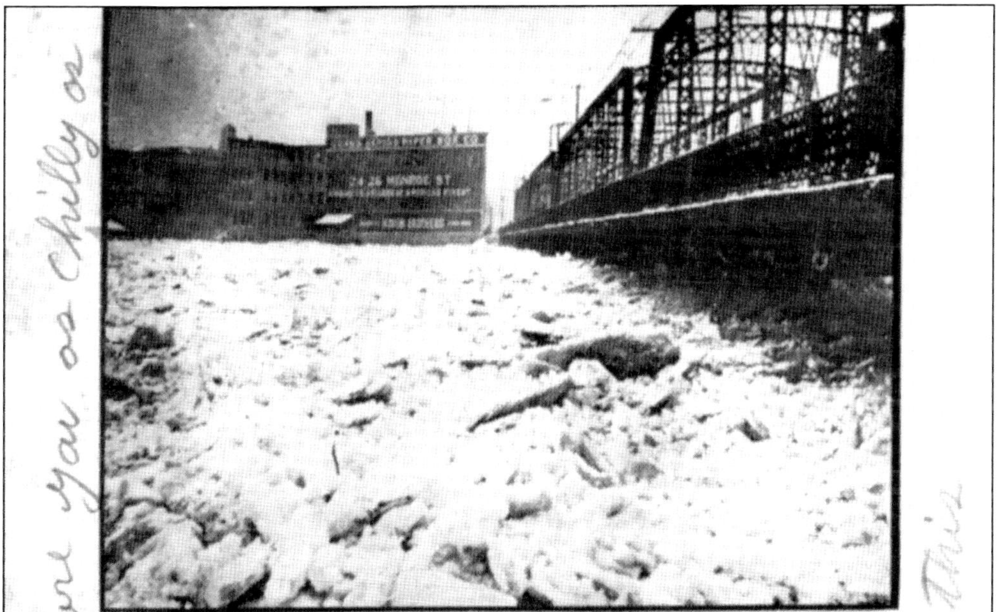

Ice Gorge at Fulton Street Bridge Jan. 24 1907

This is a view, taken from the east bank of the river, looking west along the southern edge of the Fulton Street Bridge, showing the ice accumulating by January 24, 1907.

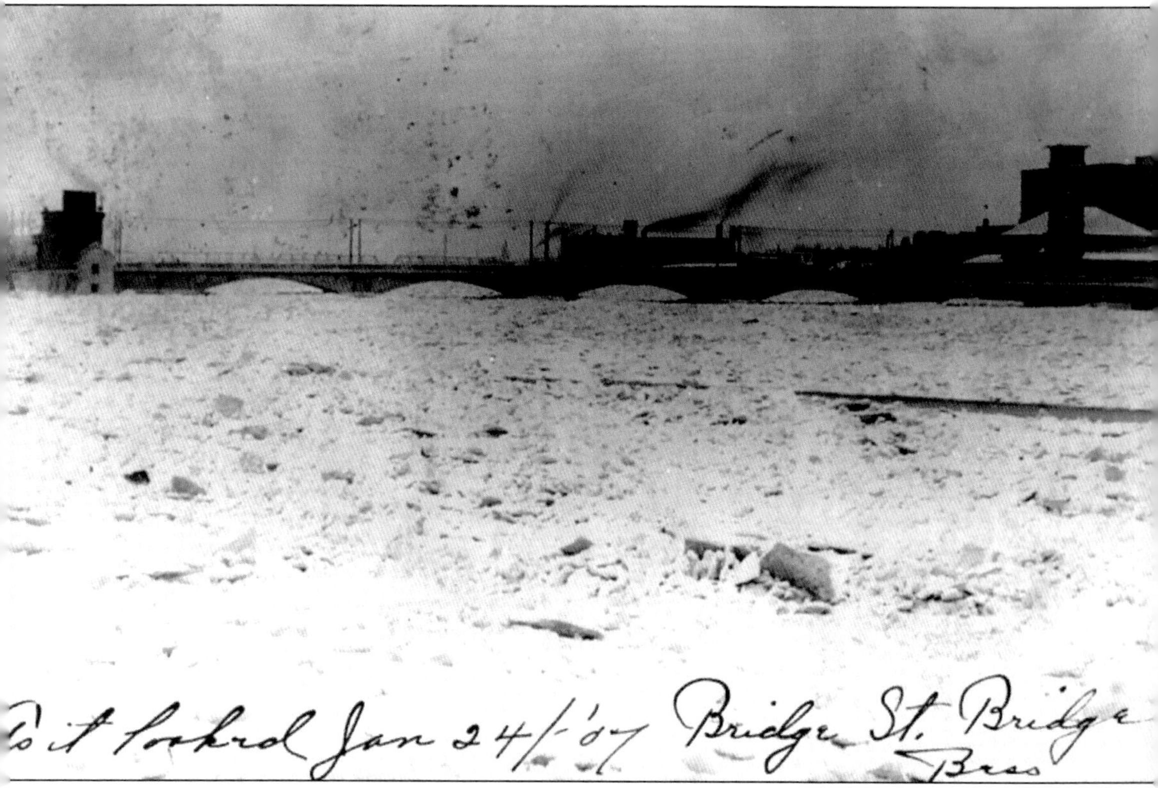

This real-photo card, a homemade postcard of the dramatic occasion, shows the river, looking north, again on January 24, 1907, from the Pearl Street Bridge. The Bridge Street Bridge is in the distance, and at the right edge of the photograph, the Grand Trunk Railroad Station is visible.